HOW COUPLE RELATIONSHIPS SHAPE OUR WORLD

The Library of Couple and Family Psychoanalysis

Series Editors: Susanna Abse, Christopher Clulow, Brett Kahr, David Scharff

Other title in the Series:

Sex, Attachment, and Couple Psychotherapy: Psychoanalytic Perspectives
edited by Christopher Clulow

HOW COUPLE RELATIONSHIPS SHAPE OUR WORLD

Clinical Practice, Research, and Policy Perspectives

Edited by

*Andrew Balfour, Mary Morgan,
and Christopher Vincent*

KARNAC

Figure 3.1 and Figure 3.2 originally from Hughes, L., and Pengelly, P. (1997). *Staff Supervision in a Turbulent Environment: Three into Two Won't Go*. London and Philadelphia: Jessica Kingsley Publishers. Reproduced with kind permission of Jessica Kingsley Publishers.

First published in 2012 by
Karnac Books Ltd
118 Finchley Road
London NW3 5HT

British Library Cataloguing in Publication Data

A C.I.P. for this book is available from the British Library

ISBN-13: 978-1-85575-837-7

Typeset by Vikatan Publishing Solutions (P) Ltd., Chennai, India

Printed in Great Britain

www.karnacbooks.com

CONTENTS

Susanna Abse is CEO of the Tavistock Centre for Couple Relationships. Before training as a psychotherapist she worked for many years with troubled adolescents. She is a full member of the British Society of Couple Psychotherapists and Counsellors and past vice chair. More recently she has co-developed a new intervention which aims to diminish destructive interparental conflict over parenting matters which is now undergoing an RCT. In 2010 she sat on the expert reference group developing the competencies for couple therapy for depression for the DoH. She has written practice and policy papers on work with couples and families, and lectures and teaches on a range of related subjects.

Eia Asen, FRCPsych, is a consultant child and adolescent psychiatrist as well as a consultant psychiatrist in psychotherapy. He grew up in Berlin where he also studied medicine. He came to the UK in the early 1970s and then started his psychiatric training at the Maudsley Hospital in London. He is now the clinical director of the Marlborough Family Service in London and also visiting professor at University College London. Until 2002 he also worked as a consultant psychiatrist at the Maudsley Hospital, as well as being a senior lecturer at the Institute of Psychiatry. He is the author and co-author of nine books in addition to many scientific papers and book chapters. He has been involved in a number of research projects, on depression, eating disorders, family violence, and educational failure.

Andrew Balfour is director of clinical services at the Tavistock Centre for Couple Relationships. He originally studied English Literature before going on to train as a clinical psychologist at University College London and then as an adult psychotherapist at the Tavistock and Portman NHS Trust, and as a couple psychotherapist at the Tavistock Centre for Couple Relationships. He worked for many years in the adult department of the Tavistock Clinic where he specialised in old age and he has also been a staff member at TCCR since 2001. He has published a number of papers and has taught and lectured widely both in Britain and abroad.

Samantha Callan is a social research and policy expert who advises politicians and policy-makers from across the political spectrum on family relationships, early years, mental health, and work–life integration. She is currently Chairman-in-Residence at the leading Westminster-based think tank, the Centre for Social Justice, for whom she has chaired four major social policy reviews. She is also an honorary research fellow at Edinburgh University's Centre for Research in Families and Relationships. A published academic, she has recently co-authored the latest introductory textbook for family studies, *Understanding Families: a Global Introduction* (Sage, 2012) with Linda McKie, professor of sociology at Durham University.

Christopher Clulow, is a senior fellow of the Tavistock Centre for Couple Relationships, London, where he works as a visiting lecturer and researcher. He has published extensively on marriage, partnerships, parenthood, and couple psychotherapy, most recently from an attachment perspective. He is vice chair of the British Society of Couple Psychotherapists and Counsellors, a fellow of the Centre for Social Policy, Dartington, and a member of the editorial boards of *Couple and Family Psychoanalysis* and of *Sexual and Relationship Therapy*.

Carolyn Pape Cowan, professor of psychology, emerita at the University of California, Berkeley, is co-director of three longitudinal preventive intervention studies, and has published widely in the literatures on couple relationships, family transitions, and preventive intervention. Dr Cowan is co-editor of *Fatherhood Today: Men's Changing Role in the Family*

(Wiley, 1988) and *The Family Context of Parenting in the Child's Adaptation to School* (Lawrence Erlbaum, 2005), and co-author of *When Partners Become Parents: The Big Life Change for Couples* (Lawrence Erlbaum, 2000).

Philip A. Cowan, professor of psychology, emeritus at the University of California, Berkeley, served as director of the Clinical Psychology Program and the Institute of Human Development. He has authored numerous scientific articles and *Piaget with Feeling* (Holt, Rinehart & Winston, 1978), co-authored *When Partners Become Parents: The Big Life Change for Couples* (Lawrence Erlbaum, 2000), and co-edited four books and monographs, including *Family Transitions* (Lawrence Erlbaum, 1991) and *The Family Context of Parenting in the Child's Adaptation to School* (Lawrence Erlbaum, 2005).

Lynne Cudmore is a consultant child and adolescent psychotherapist and senior couples psychotherapist at the Tavistock Clinic. She has a special interest in working with parental couples and is currently developing a service to support teenage parents as they make the transition to parenthood. Previously she worked for many years at the Tavistock Centre for Couple Relationships where for a time she was the organising tutor of the clinical training in couple psychoanalytic psychotherapy. She also took part in research projects on the impact of infertility and the death of a child on the couple relationship.

Gordon T. Harold is professor of behavioural genetics and developmental psychopathology at the University of Leicester. He has published more than seventy scientific articles, books, and book chapters examining family influences on children's emotional, behavioural, and academic development. Specific to the area of interparental conflict and child development, a paper published in the international journal *Child and Family Law Quarterly* (Harold & Murch, 2005) has been highlighted as "one of the most significant articles and papers of the past twenty years in key aspects of family law from an international perspective" (Family, Law and Society Series, 2008).

Leezah Hertzmann is both a couple and individual psychoanalytic psychotherapist based at the Tavistock Centre for Couple Relationships where she is head of the Parenting Together Service. Prior to this she was child mental health adviser to the Department of Children, Schools and Families in the UK, working on the development of policies and practice in the area of family mental health in educational settings. Her previous experience includes working as research psychotherapist at the Tavistock and Portman NHS Trust, on a number of published research studies, investigating and developing interventions for parents and children. She has a particular interest in the role of conflict in family life and the development of psychological interventions to address its consequences.

David Hewison is Head of Research at the Tavistock Centre for Couple Relationships. He is a couple psychoanalytic psychotherapist and a Jungian analyst, and has a long-standing interest in links between individual and couple therapy, and psychoanalytic and Jungian thinking. He developed Couple Therapy for Depression for use in improving access to psychological therapies (IAPT) services in the NHS and is co-principal investigator with Leezah Hertzmann of TCCR's first randomised controlled trial of its Parenting Together intervention.

Lynette Hughes works in North Wales as a psychoanalytic psychotherapist, seeing individuals and couples and providing clinical consultation to practitioners in a range of settings. She previously worked as principal social worker in the Children's Department of the Maudsley and Bethlem Royal Hospitals, as senior psychotherapist in the Tavistock Centre for Couple Relationships and as therapist in CAMHS in Manchester. With Paul Pengelly she co-wrote *Staff Supervision in a Turbulent Environment* (J. Kingsley, 1997).

David Lawlor is a staff member of the Tavistock and Portman NHS Foundation Trust. He is the head of the social work discipline and member of the Trust Clinics Committee. He is the organising tutor of a multi-professional PhD programme. He is a consultant to social care organisations. He specialises in the "fit" between people and structures in order to optimise the technical aspects of work and the relational aspects of the work group. He trained in organisational consultancy and psychoanalytic psychotherapy at the Tavistock Clinic.

Julian Leff began working with the families of patients with schizophrenia in 1976. With his colleagues he developed an intervention which was effective in ameliorating the family emotional environment and thereby greatly reducing the patients' relapse rate. Two subsequent studies showed that working with the relatives only was as effective as including the patient as well, and that training community psychiatric nurses to work with families was cost-effective. These studies contributed to the evidence leading to NICE guidelines on professional support for family carers of people with schizophrenia.

Leslie D. Leve is a senior scientist and the director of science at the Oregon Social Learning Center, USA. She specialises in the area of developmental psychopathology, with a focus on understanding the effects of families on child and adolescent development. This has included preventive intervention research with youth in foster care and with adolescents in the juvenile justice system, as well as genetically informed twin and adoption studies.

Mary Morgan is a couple psychoanalytic psychotherapist, psychoanalyst and member of the British Psychoanalytical Society. She has worked at the Tavistock Centre for Couple Relationships for over twenty years, where she currently holds the readership in couple psychoanalytic psychotherapy. She is head of the couple psychoanalytic psychotherapy training, MA and PD. She has a particular interest in the psychoanalytic understanding of couple relationships and the technique of couple psychoanalytic psychotherapy, about which she has published many papers.

Mervyn Murch, CBE, is an emeritus professor at Cardiff Law School, where he has been based since 1993. He read jurisprudence at the University of Oxford and obtained postgraduate qualifications in applied social studies at Bristol University where he previously taught and established a socio-legal centre for family studies. His forty-year research career has focused on the inter-disciplinary work of the family justice system and has contributed to policy and practice developments and to law reform in divorce, adoption, and child protection. He was appointed a CBE in the Queen's Birthday Honours in 2007 for services to the family justice system.

Felicia Olney had a background in social work before training in individual and couple psychotherapy. Whilst on the staff at TCCR she had a particular interest in staff supervision training and in consulting to individuals and staff groups about work related problems. She continues this work in private practice and is also a visiting clinician and lecturer at TCCR. She is a full member of the British Society of Couple Psychotherapists and Counsellors.

Honor Rhodes, OBE, director of strategic development at TCCR, has spent twenty-five years working with children and families. She is interested in chaotic, deeply troubled families and how to help them. She has written a series of short guides, *How to Help Families in Trouble* (FPI, 2007), *Supervising Family and Parenting Workers* (FPI, 2008), *Knowing What You Do Works: Measuring Your Own Effectiveness with Families, Parents and Children* (FPI, 2009) and, most recently, *A Short Guide to Working with Co-parents: What We Don't, why We Should and how We Could* (TCCR, 2011).

Michael Rustin is professor of sociology at the University of East London and a visiting professor at the Tavistock Clinic. He is author of *The Good Society and the Inner World* (1991) and *Reason and Unreason* (2001).

Felix A. Schwarzenbach is a psychiatrist and psychotherapist in private practice in Switzerland. He is married and has two daughters. He trained in group analysis, systemic therapy, cognitive and behavioural therapy, and pharmacological therapy. He was a research fellow for the Swiss National Foundation of Science at the Medical Research Council. He works as a medical expert in disability welfare and as a consultant for the pharmaceutical industry (www.scienceindustries.ch). For further information please refer to www.dr-schwarzenbach.ch.

Avi Shmueli, is a psychoanalyst and couple psychotherapist, having initially trained as a clinical psychologist. He has worked in the NHS, the Anna Freud Centre and was a staff member at the TCCR for many years. He now works in private practice and supervises the work of the TCCR's divorce and separation unit. Committed to psychoanalysis as a theory for understanding the mind and as a mode of clinical practice, he has pursued its different applications, including empirical research and its application to the fields of both family and criminal law.

Philip Stokoe is a consultant social worker in the adult department of the Tavistock and Portman NHS Foundation Trust, where he was the clinical director from 2007 to 2011; he is honorary visiting professor, mental health at City University; he is a psychoanalyst (fellow of the Institute of Psychoanalysis) in private practice working with adults and couples and an organisational consultant, providing consultation to a wide range of organisations. He has taught and written about the application of psychoanalysis in many contexts: supervision, leadership, groups, organisations, ethics, psychological services in the NHS and couple relationships.

Christopher Vincent is a couple psychoanalytic psychotherapist in private practice. He was formerly a senior staff member and is now a visiting lecturer at the Tavistock Centre for Couple Relationships where he developed a research and clinical interest in couples who are divorcing. His current clinical practice is combined with a research project looking at the impact of a diagnosis of early onset dementia on couple relationships.

Janet Walker, OBE, FRSA, AcSS, emeritus professor, studied social sciences before training and practising as a probation officer, family therapist and family mediator. In 1985 she established a successful research centre at Newcastle University, retiring as its director in 2006. She led over fifty multidisciplinary studies in the fields of marriage and divorce, parenting, policing, and youth justice. She is a long-standing board member of the Canadian Institute for Law and the Family, deputy chair of the Social Security Advisory Committee, and a trustee of Relate.

FOREWORD

Brett Kahr

This bold and timely book, *How Couple Relationships Shape Our World: Clinical Practice, Research, and Policy Perspectives*, appears as the second volume in our newly inaugurated Library of Couple and Family Psychoanalysis, a joint venture between the British Society of Couple Psychotherapists and Counsellors and the Tavistock Centre for Couple Relationships. We launched this monograph series in order to publish the most cutting-edge work in the field of couple mental health—work which will be of great relevance to psychological practitioners, to researchers, and to policy-makers alike. At a time in history when divorce rates have risen, and when the institution of marriage has lost much of its appeal to many, this comprehensive book offers many important insights into the causes of couple breakdown and into the ways in which such ruptures may be healed.

Nowadays, most Western couples enjoy infinitely more freedom than did our ancestors, and most will embark upon coupledom in states of high satisfaction. Yet over the first fifteen years of marriage, levels of marital satisfaction will deteriorate, and many relationships will end in divorce. Happily, however, specialist psychotherapists and counsellors can provide relief, support, and treatment for intimate couple relationships which have become problematic.

The editors have chosen an inspiring title for this book, namely, *How Couple Relationships Shape Our World*. With the wisdom that derives from decades of dedicated work in the mental health profession, the editors have stated with justifiable conviction that "the apparently nebulous world of our close attachments to our partners has the most material, measurable consequences for our lives". Our intimate partnership relationship (whether a legal marriage or a cohabitation arrangement) really does mould our lives. And, as the editors have highlighted in the very first paragraph of their introduction, the nature of our partnerships will have a documentable impact upon such vital medical considerations as the likelihood of hospitalisation from disease, the degree of progression in dementia, and even the rate of our mortality. The editors have surveyed the growing wealth of data, which now demonstrates that a good marriage or partnership can lengthen and even save our lives, while a depressed or violent relationship will contribute powerfully to illness and to reduced life expectancy.

In fact, mental health clinicians, psychological researchers, and family policy makers now have clear evidence that when intimate adult relationships flounder, they do so at great cost. Not only do partners endure an impaired quality of life, at least in the short-term, but also many will suffer from an increased risk for depression and even suicide, not to mention other mental health problems such as anxiety disorders and alcoholism. Unhappiness in couple relationships results not only in a higher incidence and prevalence of psychological difficulties, but also can affect physical health adversely. We now know, for instance, that unhappy couples will find themselves at a much greater risk for cardiovascular disease, obesity, diabetes, and other health concerns (cf. Meier, 2011).

In addition, the impact of marital or partnership dissatisfaction on children cannot be overestimated. The offspring of chronically conflicted couples will be much more likely to develop a plethora of psychological and physical problems, ranging from impaired school performance to greater likelihood of childhood obesity and clinical depression. As Professor Gordon Harold and Dr Leslie Leve have reported in this volume, inter-parental conflict and parental psychopathology will contribute to the development of far too many adverse consequences for children, such as heightened levels of anxiety as well as greater anti-social behaviour and even criminality.

Since its inception in 1948 (as the Family Discussion Bureau), the world-renowned Tavistock Centre for Couple Relationships has remained at the forefront of the couple and family mental health movement in Great Britain and beyond. Andrew Balfour, Mary Morgan, and Christopher Vincent, three distinguished mental health practitioners who specialise in couple psychotherapy, have worked at the Tavistock Centre for Couple Relationships for many years, and have drawn upon their rich network of colleagues from the fields of couple psychotherapy and counselling, from law, from academia, and from public policy to commission an inspiring volume of essays that chronicles the current state of cutting-edge research and clinical practice in the field of couple and family mental health care. Not only do the chapters contained within this book reflect the state-of-the-art, but also they set the agenda for the future of good practice within this arena.

These essays, written by leading figures from the worlds of mental health, academia, and social policy, provide the reader with a wealth of knowledge and insight about:

i. What causes disharmony and disaffection in partnerships;
ii. What adverse consequences result from partner distress;
iii. What the cost of marital rupture will be for our society—medically, psychologically, and financially;
iv. What can be done in terms of short-term and long-term interventions to ameliorate the situation.

In short, the editors and the authors have sculpted a veritable blueprint for how we might achieve a relationally healthy society—a blueprint that will save unnecessary expenditure, prevent unnecessary suffering, and that will lengthen and deepen the quality of our lives and the lives of our children.

As the pioneering reformer of the family justice system Professor Mervyn Murch has reported, many couples who experience difficulties in their relationship will often be met with indifference or with unhelpfulness. In his study of female divorce petitioners, described herein, Professor Murch found that some professionals often responded unsympathetically to those women experiencing marital violence. Other women, who had turned to friends and family for assistance, soon realised that their loved ones "did not want to get involved in the couple's domestic problems". Clearly, couples deserve and demand specialist professional help from those trained to the very highest level in the art and science of couple mental health, as we cannot always rely upon our family physicians or our friends to help us with highly difficult, challenging relationship breakdowns.

Many of the contributors to this volume have, in fact, trained or worked at the Tavistock Centre for Couple Relationships, and, therefore, possess a unique lens with which to understand the hidden, unconscious sources of malcontent and misery that tarnish close relationships. Similarly, the contributors have amassed plentiful clinical experience as counsellors and psychotherapists, helping couples to overcome their deep-seated hostilities, abuses, sadnesses, losses, misattunements, and misunderstandings. The clinicians recognise that one cannot repair a damaged marriage in only one or two sessions of psychotherapy; but with creativity, the contributors have chronicled the successes that derive from both long-term, intensive couple psychoanalysis and psychotherapy, and from short-term psychoanalytically informed couple counselling or mentalization-based therapy, as well as targeted psychosocial interventions offered at critical moments in the family life cycle (e.g., the birth of a child, the onset of adolescence, children leaving home, the death of an ageing parent, etc.). As co-editor, Mary Morgan has observed, based on her extensive work as a couple psychotherapist and psychoanalyst, many parents struggle to care for their own children because of their *own* longstanding, deep-seated need to be parented properly. Tavistock-style couple psychotherapy can provide couples with a profound experience of being thought about, of being cared for, and of being looked after *psychologically*, which enhances their subsequent capacity to nurture themselves and their own offspring. Psychotherapy might allow a couple to move from a mental state of narcissistic preoccupation to a state of concern for one another; to develop from fused and merged people into two separate people who can work creatively as a couple and as parents.

When I entered the field of couple mental health many years ago, as a trainee at the Tavistock Marital Studies Institute, my fellow students and I learned how to work psychotherapeutically with predominantly heterosexual, married couples. We met very few gay or lesbian couples, and very few single parents. The organisation then changed its name to the Tavistock Centre for Couple Relationships to better reflect the shifting demography of British coupledom, providing, as ever, high-level psychological services for all who struggle with couple relationships, irrespective of marital status, parenting status, or sexual orientation. But we still have far to go. As child psychotherapist and couple psycho-therapist Lynne Cudmore has reminded us, at present, Great Britain's Child and Adolescent Mental Health Services do not employ couple psychotherapists, and this lacuna must be addressed.

Many experts continue to treat marital distress with psychotropic medication, or by "prescribing" parenting classes and parenting skills training without attending to the underlying relationship problems. Although such interventions may prove to be useful, the original research outlined in this volume indicates that *psychotherapy works more effectively* than medication, and that parenting skills do not improve couple relationships per se; but rather, improvements in the couple relationship *through psychotherapy* and *counselling* will enhance parent-ing skills. By offering psychological treatments for couple distress, one not only helps the parents to function more effectively as a couple, but one will also help to repair dented or ruptured marital relationships, and, hopefully, to reduce the likelihood of violent, high-conflict divorce proceedings, which often traumatise the children (as well as the adults) in the process.

I salute this book as a magnificent achievement, one of which the editors and contributors should be most proud. While many tomes in the field of mental health advance the discipline by tiny increments, this volume—*How Couple Relationships Shape Our World: Clinical Practice, Research and Policy Perspectives*—has the potential to make giant strides, offering us so many of the tools and insights that will help us to facilitate a brighter future for our intimate partnerships, for the well-being of our children, for our nation's finances, and for our nation's health.

Professor Brett Kahr
Chair, British Society of Couple
Psychotherapists and Counsellors

REFERENCE

Meier, Richard (2011). *Briefing Paper 1*. London: Tavistock Centre for Couple Relationships, Tavistock Institute of Medical Psychology. [www.tccr.org.uk].

FOREWORD

Samantha Callan

In considering the importance of the couple relationship in the broadest terms, this book ranges over the social, psychological and legal contexts that national and local government policy has to address in a robust and coherent way in order to alleviate the adverse consequences of family breakdown. The policy implications in every chapter make this book profoundly relevant to politicians, policy makers, and advisers. The aim of this foreword is to make these explicit in six major and interrelated areas, revealing the necessary centrality both of family policy and support for the couple relationship within it.

To set the scene a little, in comparison with many of its European neighbours, the United Kingdom has been slow to accept the need for a comprehensive body of family policy; an Englishman's home is, after all, his castle. The profound ambivalence very many feel about any kind of state effort to bring order into the messiness of family relations is, however, being challenged by the welcome emphasis on well-being, particularly of children. There is also a growing sense that child poverty should more accurately be framed as family poverty, and that simple income measures insufficiently capture the range of resources that children need to flourish, and which, ideally, families provide. Welfare states will always struggle to "redistribute" relationships and care, regardless of their philosophical underpinnings and however financially generous they are. The very real and current concern in many welfare regimes is the fiscal stringency undermining their ability even to make money available.

The first and overarching policy implication to draw from this book is that good quality relationships, of mutual trust and regard, are themselves a resource. TCCR has argued from the introduction of the last government's "Think Family" practice that fully supporting families requires us to "Think Family—Think Couple" because the relationship between parents acts as the fulcrum of the whole family system. If couples have a sense that relationships are sources of help and places where learning can take place in creative exchange, this can transform their ability to take advantage of support from extended family, community members, and from professionals such as health visitors and midwives.

The key to unlocking many problems is for couples to think and work together and this has to be recognised and exploited in the "building on strengths" approach to many social policy initiatives such as family nurse partnerships and programmes to help "troubled" or "complex" families. When an intergenerational cycle of relationship dysfunction and breakdown has been established, breaking the pattern can be achieved by the co-creation of a couple's strengthened developmental partnership.

When every penny in public services has to be spent effectively we have to ensure resilience factors like this are built in from the outset of these intensive interventions, so that autonomy is fostered and dependence on professionals is reduced over time. Helping couples to develop their capacity to work together not only protects their own relationship but also establishes a more functional blueprint for deriving any necessary assistance from trusted professionals and others. Therefore, couple relationship support should be included in a greater range of family interventions than is the case at present.

To sum up, couples do not only need financial assistance or professional (and therefore costly) solutions; their own capacity to develop the potential resources inherent in their relationship has to be harnessed and augmented where necessary. This will maximise the effectiveness of other sources of help.

The second area where the couple relationship impinges on government priorities is in the interconnectedness of healthy parental functioning and the welfare of children, particularly in their early years. For example, working with couples on their relationship as they seek to adjust to the demands of parenting can prevent severe problems from emerging later on. Antenatal and postnatal services are being eroded by spending cuts but this government is piloting a range of relationship education services for the perinatal period. This suggests it has already taken some note of the clear messages this book sends about the importance of timely couple support for reducing future distress, but piloting is the means not the end, and the mid-term priority lies in ensuring effective interventions are made universally available.

Arguably the current government has been more comfortable than its predecessors about recognising the importance of couple relationships to family and child well-being, but the public purse has never been more constrained to make good on that receptivity. The emphasis on localism also requires that, to some extent, an awareness of the couple relationship's importance has to be fostered in every local authority, primary care trust, and clinical commissioning group, given that these are where even more spending decisions are now made. Health and well-being boards will be vital in ensuring joint commissioning takes place between all these bodies given the health and social service savings to be made if this preventive work is funded.

Sorely needed in this area are models of early intervention which clearly demonstrate social returns on their costs to the public purse. For these group work models to be adopted there needs to be an acknowledgment that their benefits, including a reduction in social isolation, result from their being introduced at a stage when problems are emerging but are not entrenched. Strengthening couple relationships at other challenging points in the family life cycle would augment social capital in the broadest sense and help support efforts to build community cohesion.

Third, the imperative in education policy to raise standards in schools and increase attainment of children from less-advantaged backgrounds has to take on board the theme running through much of this book that children's outcomes tend to be better when their parents' relationship works well. Understanding that their psychological development is influenced by how the couple relationship plays out, as a salient feature of the "complex ecology" children inhabit, goes beyond recognising that parenting is affected by partnering.

Children's ability to handle conflict around them without self blame and succumbing to pathological levels of distress is profoundly affected by how their parents manage that same conflict. This might sound like common sense, but the implications for policy are still largely under-recognised; billions are being invested, quite rightly, in making the school environment as conducive as possible for learning, while funding to enable the couple dimension of the home environment to support achievement remains in the very low millions.

Similarly, in a fourth area, how couples relate after separation has great relevance in family law, which has a high profile for the current government. This is due in part to contractions in the Ministry of Justice budget and draconian reductions in legal aid for private family law matters. Without expert representation, those bitterly contested disputes that go all the way to final and repeated hearings will increasingly require judges to accommodate litigants in person with the delay and, thus, higher costs this entails. The salience of such family law issues is also due to sustained lobbying from fathers' rights groups who combat what they see as the pro-female bias in the family law system. At the level of the individual couple, perceived injustices make settlements concerning contact and residence very difficult to achieve or maintain. Disputes rumble on and frequently become issues of public law when accusations and counter-accusations of domestic abuse and neglect are made.

Related to these concerns is this government's determination to reduce the costs of child maintenance and its enforcement following divorce and separation; the view of the current minister responsible is that we cannot expect couples who are still battling after parting to find it easy to make and keep to child support arrangements. She correctly perceives that far more is required than a system that efficiently administers financial transactions. Services that go beyond mandated mediation to help couples achieve a new and better emotional equilibrium and, perhaps most importantly, better enable them to keep their child(ren)'s interests paramount, have a heightened importance in the evolving family law environment.

The implications of unresolved post-separation conflict spread beyond family law and into a fifth policy arena which is that of children's and adults' mental health. Emotional dimensions of family change are often underestimated, yet coming to terms with loss, a sense of betrayal, feelings of almost overwhelming disappointment and failure, and the often unrequited need for vindication can take an enormous toll on the well-being and mental health of family members. Working therapeutically with parents and children (and grandparents) requires understanding unconscious assumptions that are not accessible as rational thought processes.

Making such therapy available on the kind of scale required, given the quasi-normative status of divorce and separation in current society, is a significant policy challenge. There are also many other "intact" couples in which one or both has depressive or other symptoms and who are likely to benefit more from couple therapy than from individual counselling. Within-couple resources can and should be developed where possible when women are suffering from post-natal depression (PND). Couple relationship counselling and group work for women with PND and their partners in children's centres in low income London boroughs have shown improvements not only in mental health but also in the way couples relate and in their very young children's well-being.

The government is currently working on guidelines for local health commissioners to assist them in buying therapeutic services on a payment by results basis. Ensuring effectiveness will require that the role of couple therapy is not neglected but it will also require all providers to submit themselves to a much greater level of research scrutiny, not least by collecting outcomes data far more assiduously than many do at present.

It will also require recognition that practice-based evidence can provide a substantial "bottom up" flow of information to justify commissioning therapies that have not (yet) received approval from the National Institute for Health and Clinical Excellence (NICE) because of the lack of relevant "gold standard" evidence (typically obtained through a number of randomised control trials).

Ensuring effective couple therapies are more widely available can make a vital contribution in a number of areas—preventing or mitigating family breakdown, boosting the success of programmes designed to promote early child development and educational achievement, and reducing symptoms of adult mental distress with consequential benefits for children. There are also wider mental health implications that go beyond the natural territory of family policy and into employment policy, the sixth and final field of policy identified here.

Getting people work-ready after long periods on incapacity benefits or preventing them from dropping out of the labour market is a very high cross-government priority; mental illness plays a role that is under-recognised by society but well within the sights of ministers in the Department for Work and Pensions. While it is likely that they will need some help to think beyond the bounds of individual counselling to see how couple therapy can also play a vital role in addressing underlying determinants of poor mental health, the current government's acknowledgement that family breakdown is both a key driver and outcome of unemployment, disadvantage, and poverty suggests they will be responsive.

The cross-governmental importance of family policy is becoming solidly established and although there is much progress still to be made, support for couple relationships is increasingly being seen as a vital area within it. This book is timely and thorough in its consideration of the ways these intimate partnerships impinge on a very broad range of issues and policy: couple relationships do indeed, as the title suggests, shape our world.

How couple relationships shape our world: clinical practice, research, and policy perspectives

If you have picked this book off a shelf, with some curiosity perhaps about the claim in its title: that couple relationships *shape* our world, you may be wondering, "What can they mean by such an extravagant assertion?" Persist a little longer. This is an exciting time for those of us interested in the importance of the couple relationship. We are not speaking here in crude terms about nuclear families, or making a case for a particular model of heterosexual adult coupling. We are concerned, instead, with the importance of our most intimate relationships in shaping our worlds: whether our couplings are same or opposite sex, whether we are married or not, whether we have children or not. The evidence now is clear: the qualities of our relationships have profound implications from our earliest years, for the emotional, cognitive, and physical development of our children, to our latest years—in old age, affecting the likelihood of hospitalisation, the rate of progression of disease in dementia, and even mortality rates. In these materialistic times we can say with some certainty that the apparently nebulous world of our close attachments to our partners has the most material, measurable consequences for our lives. Two generations ago, our professional forebears at TCCR were publishing radical books—researching, for example, how people with learning disabilities who made lasting relationships became better able to function and achieve an independent life away from the institutional setting; or capturing the underlying picture of disturbed relationships hidden behind the individual referrals to social workers in front line settings. They based their thinking on detailed case studies and painstaking clinical work. But now, for the first time, there is a convergence of evidence: from the qualitative data of the clinical experience of the therapist, to the empirical data of the developmental researcher: each tells the same, or at least a similar, story. These different disciplines, of research, therapy, and social policy at last are moving together, allowing us to be surer of the ground we are on than at any other time before. This book marks the point we have reached, aiming to put alongside each other clinical, research, and social perspectives, each with its own language and point of view, in order to give the reader a composite lens through which to view the convergent picture that is emerging of how couple relationships do indeed shape and form our world.

So this book is about the importance of the couple relationship in the broadest terms. It draws on clinical research into the inner lived world of adult couples, empirical developmental research into children and parenting, as well as the legal setting when relationships break down. It aims to bridge the inner and outer worlds, showing how our most intimate relationships have vital importance at all levels, from the individual and the family, to the social setting—and explores the implications for practice and policy. Above all, it is a book about applications of clinical thinking linked with research knowledge, as tools for front line workers and policy makers alike. It draws on the tradition of applied clinical thinking and research of the TCCR, linking current thinking with the history of ideas in each area it covers, as well as considering implications for the future.

To this end, the book is structured in a very particular way. Each substantive chapter has its own commentary—commissioned from an expert, which contextualises the chapter, and draws out its implications for the field more broadly. Our very particular approach, of using alternating commentaries with substantive chapters will, we hope, allow us to combine a "depth" of analysis with a broad discussion of more applied, contextual issues.

Where principal chapters are written by TCCR staff we have invited commentaries by colleagues outside the institute and vice versa. Our intention in adopting this format is to assist the reader to pursue a critical and constructive appraisal of each chapter, an intention that has spared the editors from taking on such a weighty task!

While we rely on the commentaries to provide a detailed response to each chapter, it is our responsibility, however, to provide the reader with a series of signposts to help gain the most from a book which is very wide in scope and application. Although we have decided against dividing the chapters and commentaries into broad sections (we believe this would create a mistaken expectation of discrete categories and would understate the extent to which important themes recur through-out the whole book), we have chosen to sequence the chapters in a way that reflects their aims and emphases.

The first three chapters meet the needs of the reader wanting to know about the research evidence that justifies couple-focused inter-ventions in families and how couple interventions have been thought about and developed within TCCR in recent years. The first chapter by Carolyn Pape Cowan and Philip A. Cowan makes the case for pre-ventive interventions focusing on the couple relationship at a variety of family transition points. They make the point that programmes that aim to improve couple functioning lead to improved child outcomes, as well as couple relationship satisfaction, while the reverse does not hold: parenting interventions improve parenting behaviour, but not the qual-ity of the couple relationship. In her commentary, Leezah Hertzmann draws on her experience of working with parents in groups. She argues that practitioners do not need to have a partner in the room for a couple to be held in mind, to be thought about and talked about (a point Avi Shmueli repeats later in the book). Her experience also reminds us to think beyond the conventional image of mother and father as the only configuration of a co-parenting partnership. In modern families there are many variations on what a parenting couple might look like involv-ing wider kin and intergenerational mixes.

Gordon Harold and Leslie Leve then consider how investment in families is best targeted to maximise the benefits to children. They show that, while parental conflict adversely affects the way children are parented, this is only a part of the problem. Their research provides convincing evidence that children are also adversely affected by the direct impact of witnessing parental conflict itself. Hence their work underlines the crucial importance of interventions at the level of the adult couple relationship for improving the developmental outcomes of children. In addition, they discuss how certain risks predispose some children to adverse outcomes and emphasise the need to identify those factors that encourage resilience in children. In her commentary Susanna Abse describes the work of the TCCR Parenting Together Programme which utilises mentalisation based therapy to help reduce levels of conflict within the parental couple relationship. She describes the essential features of a mentalisation based approach which seeks to develop the reflective capacities of parents such that they are better able to identify with, rather than oppose and negate, the thoughts and feelings of their partner and, thereby, to reduce conflict.

By contrast, Mary Morgan's chapter explores the experiential dimensions of what it is like to be in a healthily functioning adult partnership. This is one that becomes a resource parents can draw upon when the challenges of parenting young children threaten their equilibrium. She describes this well-functioning relationship as a "creative couple" and as one where each partner is able to develop the mental space to reflect on the experience of self and partner and, as a result, to form an image in the mind of them both of operating as a couple. In her commentary on this concept, Lynne Cudmore, a child and adolescent psychotherapist, talks about her experience of working in a front line child and adolescent service where there tends to be a split between a focus on the child and a focus on the parents' relationship, such that the latter gets disregarded even though it may be of crucial importance in contributing to the difficulties presented by the child or young person.

The focus of the book now switches in the two chapters that follow on the work within and adjacent to the family courts system. The first of these is by Mervyn Murch who provides a comprehensive overview of the system, key research findings as they relate to families and children, and important policy dilemmas facing its future. He makes recommendations for a new unified system whose design will reflect important research findings. He argues for a court system that utilises ritual and symbols to facilitate participant justice. In response to Mervyn Murch, Christopher Clulow draws on his clinical and research experience to argue that within a judicial framework court processes must enable divorcing partners to adjust to the emotional dimensions of the significant changes they are experiencing. He stresses that this is not easy to achieve in a system that is seeking to balance a range of conflicting values and priorities.

While Murch and Clulow take a broad overview of the court system and its functioning, Avi Shmueli offers a chapter on working with high conflict couples. Arising from his work in the TCCR divorce and separation unit, he proposes a way of conceptualising high conflict divorce and a way of addressing this behaviour in therapeutic terms. His thesis is that high conflict arises from a resistance of both partners to come to terms with the failure of their marriage to fulfil the unconscious hopes that underpinned their initial attraction to one another. Rather than being able to mourn these losses appropriately and move on in their lives, the couple remain stuck in an angry deadlock. In responding to Avi Shmueli, Christopher Vincent describes the characteristics of those high conflict couples who for a variety of reasons are more likely to be seen by agencies such as CAFCASS and social services departments rather than a therapeutic service. He also suggests that attachment theory can offer insights into the psychodynamics of high conflict couples and that this understanding has implications for ways of intervening.

Both Shmueli and Vincent describe ways in which angry and conflicted interaction can be understood as defences against mourning when the latter is a needed and healthy reaction to the loss of a partnership. But the reverse can also apply and depressed states of mind can severely interfere with a couple's capacity to engage with stress and painful feelings. Exploring the ways depression can be helped by using couple therapy is the theme of the next chapter by Julian Leff, Eia Asen, and Felix Schwarzenbach. They describe how, using a random controlled trial (RCT), they evaluated the effectiveness of couple therapy, anti-depressant medication and CBT in treating depression and preventing relapse. As it turned out, their study had to drop the CBT arm because of the high drop-out rate from this, and the authors speculate that perhaps CBT is designed more for depressed patients with a recent onset of depression who could be expected to recover quickly. This was not the case for the participants in their study, who had long-standing histories of depression. Their results provide evidence for the superiority of couple therapy over antidepressant therapy in reducing symptoms and maintaining improvement, and an economic analysis indicates that the cost of the couple therapy was no greater than the cost of the antidepressant treatment. It was also found that there was a high satisfaction rate for couple therapy as evidenced by the low drop-out rate and this finding echoed other studies by showing that, when given a choice, service users prefer talking therapies to other treatment modalities. In his commentary on this chapter Christopher Clulow raises some fundamental questions about the nature of depression—whether it is a medicalised construct or one which needs to be understood in an interactional context with the implications that such a broader view would hold for the design of future studies.

In the chapter that follows, David Hewison takes up the baton from Christopher Clulow in discussing research methods. He looks at the pre-eminent position that RCTs hold in the research hierarchy and points to the many technical and practical problems that arise when attempting to accommodate the transient and fluid nature of mental functioning within their tight structure. Moreover, many symptoms derive their specific significance and meaning from their interconnectedness with other aspects of a patient's life, including the experiences of their partners and family. These crucial links and connections may be overlooked by a reductive RCT approach with the consequence that some of the richness and complexity of experience may be lost. Hewison, therefore, makes the case for a pluralistic evidence base which draws on different forms of evidence generated by different research methodologies. He gives an account of the different research methods and measures used by TCCR staff in past studies, and offers an agenda for future research projects which builds on these different approaches. In his response to this agenda Michael Rustin makes a radical plea that, in the face of pressures to adopt a pluralistic approach to research, sight is not lost of the unique contribution a psychoanalytic research orientation makes to our understanding of the interior life of couples and families.

Throughout its history, TCCR's clinical, training, and research interest in the workings of adult partnerships has demanded a capacity in its staff to think in an open systems fashion. An open system is one that survives and prospers by interaction with its environment, and to do this it utilises a permeable boundary through which it interacts with the outside world. Adult partnerships can be thought of as open systems in that they both influence and are influenced by their current social environment. The study of this two way process—of how partnerships affect and are themselves affected by outside forces—emerges as a dominant theme in the next three chapters of the book.

In the first of these chapters Andrew Balfour traces how public and political concern about couple problems has been linked historically to moral panics. He suggests that the political debate reflects the conflict in all of us as to whether we think that families are a good or a bad thing and that, in adopting extreme positions we are in danger of losing sight of the hard evidence that links healthy child development with stable parental relationships. In his commentary Philip Stokoe picks up on Balfour's argument about the difficulty of recognising what is frequently in front of our eyes if only we can bear to see it. He discusses the phenomenon he encounters repeatedly in his work as consultant to child protection teams where so-called "incompetent practice" arises from an emotional disconnection between practitioner and client that results in warning signs being overlooked. He argues that our ability to apprehend reality can be facilitated by strong consultation/supervision that addresses psychodynamic aspects of interaction.

Honor Rhodes in the penultimate chapter continues the exploration of couple work and the body politic. As a way of crystallising the absurdity of radical social engineering she considers whether the establishment of a Ministry of Love along the lines envisaged by Orwell in his novel, *Nineteen Eighty-Four*, would be feasible and helpful in contemporary Britain. In doing so she identifies some of the recent policy initiatives that have adopted a coercive philosophy and approach to families. In response Janet Walker grounds our thinking in evidence to date that shows a balance has to be struck between state requirements and citizen aspiration and consent. Her summary provides clear signposts for how social policy and practices can be developed.

In whatever ways social policies towards couples and families are developed they have to be translated into operational forms that enable staff in agencies of different kinds to deliver them. Front line managers will turn to their supervisors to ensure that performance outcomes are met by their staff. Lynette Hughes and Felicia Olney conclude the book by describing a generic model of supervision where the top-down requirements of the organisation intersect with the two other major aspects of the supervisory task. These are to attend to the face-to-face work of the supervisee and to facilitate the supervisee's professional development. These three aspects of the supervisor's role are always in an uneasy tension and have become even more so in recent years when the intrusive impact of organisational pressures and dynamics are threatening the survival of professional competence. David Lawlor's commentary endorses this picture and suggests that the "audit culture", with its prioritisation of the evaluation of performance outcomes at the expense of considering the processes by which these outcomes are achieved, can provide psychological escape mechanisms for staff at all levels to avoid the pain and difficulty of face-to-face front line social work with disturbed families.

We would like to thank Oliver Rathbone, Director of Karnac Books, for his enthusiastic support for the project from its inception, and Kate Pearce, Project Manager at Karnac, who has guided us through the process of production with great efficiency, charm—and tolerance! Psychoanalysis teaches us, as Lynette Hughes and Felicia Olney remind us so clearly, to be wary of the pitfalls of three-person working groups, as the tendency to form pairings runs the risk of one of the three being left out or scapegoated. We want to record that our editorial triad has proved to have been a thoroughly enjoyable, creative, and stimulating working experience, helped in large part by the emotional grounding that comes from being closely linked to our colleagues in the Tavistock Centre for Couple Relationships. To each other and to our colleagues we say "Thank you".

Finally, we would like to say how grateful we are to the contributors to this book. From diverse fields, they give us a convergence of view of the crucial importance of the couple relationship across the different facets of our social world. We hope that the reader too is convinced, by these assembled voices, of the need to move beyond the historic tendency to ignore the couple relationship in favour of an individual focus, in research, in social and mental health care, and in the formulation of social policy. In all these domains, as the contributions to this book highlight, the evidence shows us that the couple relationship needs to be at the heart of our thinking.

Andrew Balfour
Mary Morgan
Christopher Vincent

CHAPTER ONE

Prevention: intervening with couples at challenging family transition points

Carolyn Pape Cowan and Philip A. Cowan

Couples come to TCCR, to other clinics, and to private therapists when aspects of their relationship have broken down so that one or both partners are unhappy and at a loss for how to make things better. In recent decades, theories about how to help troubled couples have become more complex and detailed as they have attempted to match the complexity and specificity of problems that therapists and clients confront. As the field of couple therapy made significant gains over the past six decades, an alternative pathway for troubled couples emerged. This path, involving preventive strategies for helping couples, was guided by the strong belief that it is both possible and desirable to intervene early as relationship processes are unfolding, to prevent severe relationship distress from taking hold, or to reduce the severity and aftermath of couple dysfunction when it occurs. The preventive intervention pathway is the main focus of this chapter.

From the current high incidence of couple dissatisfaction and divorce and the increasing tendency of couples not to marry (Cherlin, 2009; ONS, 2009), it is clear that couples face a daunting challenge in their attempts to maintain an intimate romantic relationship over a lifetime. While clinicians and marital researchers know that peaks and valleys in distress levels are to be expected, most partners who begin relationships in a rosy glow are caught off guard when their satisfaction drops and their relationship feels tenuous. We argue here that it makes sense to help couples to deal with troubling relationship issues before a cumulative downward spiral leads to even more serious problems that feel intractable and impossible to resolve.

We begin by describing what we mean by preventive intervention. Next, we define the concept of family transitions in an attempt to rescue the term from its vague current usage in which any change in an individual is described in transitional terms. To provide empirical weight to our argument, we present evidence from studies of preventive interventions designed to help partners who are approaching marriage, making the transition to parenthood, shepherding a first child into primary school, or sorting out their decision to divorce. We use these accounts of empirically validated interventions as a basis for speculation about other family transitions in which interventions with couples might produce beneficial results for parents, children, and the relationships between them. Finally, we present several examples of ways in which our perspective on preventive interventions for couples might have implications for the way governments and foundations allocate funds to support and strengthen couples and families.

Defining prevention

The concept of prevention emerged first in the field of public health and then in the fields of community psychology and community psychiatry. The public health example that provides a core definition of prevention harks back to the time when attempts to treat widespread outbreaks of yellow fever were based on two discoveries—(1) the elimination of polluted wells and marshlands after it was established that they were breeding grounds for mosquitoes (i.e., reducing risk), and (2) the development and distribution of a vaccine that substantially reduced the likelihood of an individual contracting yellow fever (i.e., enhancing personal resources to ward off risk). In the field of public health, prevention was initially defined in absolute terms—whether or not the actions taken resulted in the occurrence or elimination of the disease. In the fields of community psychiatry and community psychology, the criteria for whether a preventive intervention could be deemed successful were, and still are, less clear cut. A preventive intervention does not necessarily eliminate individual or relationship distress, but it does reduce the probability that the distress will occur in a specified population and/or reduces the severity of the problem when it does occur.

Based on the fact that interventions can occur at various points in the unfolding of a problem, theorists have identified three levels of prevention.

Primary prevention refers to interventions that inhibit the development of a problem, disorder, or disease before it occurs. This level draws heavily on the medical metaphor of vaccinations in which one injection may be adequate to ward off a specific disease. In reality, we are unlikely to find such a potent substance in the field of couples work. It is probable that "booster shots" will be needed along the life course, and that new interventions will be required as family members face the new challenges associated with expectable and unexpected life changes.

Secondary prevention involves detection and treatment of a problem early in its occurrence. Couples who have a solid relationship but experience a stormy period while their children are young might enrol in a course or workshop, hoping to learn some strategies to help resolve their current disequilibrium or lower their level of distress.

Tertiary preventions such as psychotherapy or couples counselling by mental health professionals or religious leaders are designed to reduce the debilitating outcomes of already existing problems and restore adequate functioning to the individual partners or the relationship—for the health and well-being of the parents, the children, and the family.

The definition of what constitutes primary, secondary, and tertiary prevention depends on how wide a lens we apply to the desired outcomes. For example, we would have no trouble describing the process of therapy with a couple on the brink of divorce as tertiary prevention. The therapist and the couple are working together to mitigate the severity of the marital problems and to restore some degree of positive couple interaction, if only to work collaboratively on parenting their children. But from the vantage point of children's well-being (not often considered in the couple therapy literature), the couples therapist may be engaging in primary prevention by helping the parents establish a collaborative co-parenting relationship, regardless of whether their marital relationship remains intact. The distinctions among primary, secondary, and tertiary prevention become relevant when planners are considering how wide a net to cast for a new programme or how narrowly defined and targeted the intervention should be.

Why, when so many couples are already in distress, should we be thinking about devoting scarce resources to prevention? We propose that the need for an approach that offers help to couples at times of major family transitions can be justified by a set of well-established research findings. More than thirty studies in a number of Western industrialised countries reveal that, on average, couples begin their marital or cohabiting relationships high in marital satisfaction, but their satisfaction declines over the next fifteen years (Hirschberger, Srivastava, Marsh, Cowan & Cowan, 2009). By that time almost half of the couples' descriptions of their relationship are comparable to those of partners enrolled in couple therapy—they feel disappointed, unhappy, angry, misunderstood, and so on. The point here is that studies in the US, Canada, the UK, Germany, and Israel indicate that it is normative for couples to fight more or be silent more and to evaluate their relationship more negatively after being together for some years. We think of preventive intervention because almost half of the couples with these kinds of relationship difficulties ultimately dissolve their marriages.

The normative slide in couple relationship satisfaction is debilitating for the partners, of course, but it also poses a risk for the couples' children. In the last three decades, a growing body of research indicates that dysregulated conflict between the parents (arguments out of control or long-standing patterns of not expressing emotion) is likely to have negative effects on the quality of each parent's relationship with the children and on children's social skills, academic competence, and emotional well-being (e.g., Shelton & Harold, 2008). That is, whether partners stay together or separate, failure to resolve their difficulties increases the probability that their children will also suffer the consequences.

In sum, given the prevalence of couple conflict and distress, the negative effects on both partners and their children, and resulting costs for the family and society, it makes sense to provide services earlier in the life of a couple (primary prevention) or earlier in the course of relationship breakdown (secondary prevention).

Defining family transitions

Some of the early work on transitions emerged in England. Rhona and Robert Rapaport (1977), pioneers of community psychiatry, attempted to apply Erik Erikson's theory of normative intrapsychic crisis as *necessary* for growth to non-normative catastrophic events (natural disasters, personal losses). Like Gerald Caplan in the United States

(1964), the Rapaports argued that the disequilibrium associated with these events produced crises, but that crisis embodies both danger and opportunity for growth, as in the Chinese ideograph. In his explorations of grief and mourning, Colin Murray Parkes (1971) argued that transitions are not so much defined by events as by changes in one's "assumptive world". Previously held premises about how the world works no longer apply. Expectations about how roles should be defined and relationships operate are questioned. Not every aspect of one's view of the world is reorganised during what Parkes called "psycho-social transitions", but rather, seeing the world through new eyes can result in both positive and negative short-term and long-term outcomes. Others' work on transitions in the United States looked to stress and coping models to examine how individuals reacted to stressful life events (Lazarus & Folkman, 1984) and whether these reactions were adequate to meet the external challenges.

Elsewhere, one of us (P. A. Cowan, 1991) attempted to provide an integrative definition of individual and family life transitions as long-term processes that result in a qualitative reorganisation of both inner life and external behaviour. Passing a life marker (entering school), or completing a life milestone (getting married) does not in itself signify that a transition has been completed. The inner view refers to changes in one's sense of self or identity, one's assumptive world and affect regulation system. The complementary view from outside focuses on a reorganisation of life roles, a restructuring of coping systems to meet new challenges, and a reorganisation of central relationships. For example, a man who takes some time off during the week his son is born and then returns to his office as planned to continue his life as before, has become a father but not necessarily made the transition to parenthood. Another new father recognises changes in his sense of himself, develops new views about his responsibilities to family and community, and initially feels somewhat out of control. He shifts his arrangement of family and work responsibilities, learns new skills, and attempts to deal with the fact that his relationship with his partner is now on the back burner. With qualitative changes in both his inner and outer life, this man is in the process of making a major life transition.

Theories about the developmental crises associated with life changes generally describe two kinds of life transitions—normative and non-normative. Normative transitions are expectable life changes experienced by many or most within a culture. Almost all children experience developmental stage transitions (as defined by Freud, Erikson, or Piaget) and entrance to major social institutions (child care, primary school, secondary school). Transitions to adolescence, leaving home, and becoming an adult are major normative post-childhood life changes. Entering the world of higher education is normative for many, as is becoming employed, establishing an intimate relationship with a partner, moving in together, getting married, becoming a parent, and having more children (in either order). Other mid-to late-life transitions include changing jobs or careers, moving house, becoming a grandparent, caring for elderly parents, and the death of a parent or spouse. Non-normative transitions for children include moving far from friends, accidents that result in serious injuries, and the sudden illness or loss of a parent. For adults, unemployment or job loss, chronic ill health of a family member, and being the victim of violent crime or a natural disaster are non-normative transitions. In contemporary society, divorce is on the border between normative and non-normative—frequent enough to be considered expectable, yet not expected by most couples when they marry. A central factor associated with labelling a transition as normative or non-normative—expected or not—is whether it occurs on time or out of time. Women having babies in their late teens through to early thirties are entering a normative transition. A woman becoming a mother for the first time in her late forties is entering a non-normative transition.

Although most empirical studies focus on only one life transition at a time, the definition of transitions implies that there is a generic set of processes involved in both normative and non-normative transitions. For example, having a first child (normative) and being a victim of an earthquake (non-normative) are not similar on the surface but, except for the suddenness of the latter, they can both lead to reorganisations of one's internal and external worlds. This is the prime contribution that transition theory has made over the past decade—the idea that expectable and desired transitions may create a kind of disorder and displacement in one's personal life and relationships, just as unexpected and unwanted transitions do.

So far we have focused on the individual in transition. Yet, individual life transitions almost always occur in a family context. In becoming parents, both partners are involved in the "same" life event, but may make the transition to parenthood in different ways at different times, with each partner's reorganisation of self, roles, and relationships influencing the other's. A child entering adolescence is not only making a developmental transition of his/her own but also causing waves of change in the other adult and child family members. The systemic view of transitions leads us to see that the issue is not simply that one person's life changes have ripple effects throughout the family; there are usually also simultaneous but different transitions in the generations of the family. Parents who are getting divorced may have a child entering adolescence or heading for college. An adolescent entering the world of sexual relationships may have a parent changing careers or entering menopause and grandparents who are retiring or facing problems of ill health. No matter where in the generations transitions occur, they are likely to have effects on the relationships between adults and children, with important implications for the children's well-being or distress.

What implications does this formulation of transitions have for thinking about preventive interventions for couples? Our definition of major life transitions indicates that whatever the life change event, individuals and couples will be attempting to cope with shifts in both their inner life (identity, emotions, worldview) and social world (roles, competencies, relationships). Although such profound qualitative changes mean that both normative and non-normative transitions have the potential to place individuals and couples at risk for mild to serious levels of distress, they also have the potential to lead to developmental growth and a sense of competence if the individuals and couples find effective ways to meet new challenges successfully. Because developmental challenges bring family coping strategies into sharp relief, the choice to study or intervene with families as they face major life transitions is an excellent strategy for identifying family processes that facilitate or impede the healthy development of children and their parents.

We are not suggesting that it is desirable or practical for couples to receive psychological help from couples therapists or counsellors as they go through every normative and non-normative transition they face in a lifetime together. Rather, taking advantage of help when a major life transition creates more disequilibrium than a couple can manage can strengthen their relationship so that they are better prepared to handle the next ones they face.

Preventive intervention for couples at five family transition points: the evidence base

The transition to marriage. There has been considerable effort since the mid-twentieth century by university-based programmes, couples counselling organisations, and religious institutions to provide pre-marital counselling/education to partners about to marry. The programmes enrol couples in small groups, classes, or weekend workshops, with a curriculum that typically focuses on teaching communication skills. The best known, most well-validated programme—Premarital Relationship Education Program (PREP) (Markman, Stanley & Blumberg, 2001)—has shown long-term positive effects on couples' marital stability and quality. A small significant proportion of these couples do not go through with the marriage—an outcome the investigators view as a positive consequence of considering their relationship in some depth before committing to a lifetime together.

Three early childrearing transitions. Over the past three decades, the authors of this chapter have been devising and evaluating preventive interventions that involve weekly meetings of four to six couples in groups led by clinically trained mental health professionals. The leaders' roles were not conceptualised as teachers or skills trainers but as guides who help couples or fathers discover challenges or barriers to reaching their personal and relationship goals and work with them to make progress in that direction.

All three intervention studies showed statistically significant differences between intervention and control participants. In the Becoming a Family project (C. P. Cowan & Cowan, 2000), professionally led couples groups for partners becoming parents kept men's and women's marital quality and satisfaction from declining over the next six years until their children had begun their elementary school careers, whereas satisfaction declined for new parents without any intervention. In the Schoolchildren and their Families project (P. A. Cowan, Cowan, Ablow, Johnson & Measelle, 2005), compared to parents in a brief consultation condition, professionally led groups for couples as their first child made the transition to primary school kept men's and women's marital quality and satisfaction from declining, and their parenting style more responsive, appropriately structured, and less harsh. Furthermore, their children showed fewer academic, social, and emotional behaviour problems over the next ten years than those whose parents were in the control group. Being assigned to a couples group with an emphasis on couple relationship issues (compared to parenting issues) not only increased parenting effectiveness but also reduced conflict between the parents in a problem solving discussion.

In the Supporting Father involvement project (P. A. Cowan, Cowan, Pruett, Pruett & Wong, 2009), compared to low-income parents randomly offered a one-time meeting, those offered professionally led couples or fathers' groups reported greater involvement of fathers in caring for their children and fewer problematic behaviours in the children. Compared to parents in the control group and the fathers-only groups, those from a couples group *also* reported reduced parenting stress and no decline in relationship quality and satisfaction over eighteen months.

The divorce transition. The interventions described above focused on normative life transitions. Three evidence-based interventions targeted husbands (Cookston, Braver, Griffin, De Luse & Jonathan, 2007), wives (Wolchik et al., 2002), or both partners (Pruett & Barker, 2009) in the process of or shortly after divorce. All three formats used a combination of group meetings and individual sessions, which resulted in decreased conflict between the parents and salutary effects on the children. These outcomes are extremely important because the ability of divorced parents to collaborate in their communication about their children is the strongest predictor of children's and adolescents' adaptation and well-being after parents divorce (Johnston, Kline & Tschann, 1989).

Successful interventions at these family transition points support the argument we have been making for devoting time and resources to preventive interventions for couples during both normative and non-normative family transitions. Although the pre-marital interventions have not documented outcomes for children, the other interventions we described have all gone beyond establishing that couple conflict is correlated with negative child outcomes by demonstrating that working with both parents early in their relationship or during the divorce process has positive outcomes for the couple and for their offspring.

Some suggestions for couples group interventions at other family transition points

We are aware that in both public and private sectors, some communities do offer services for families in specific family transitions (e.g., parents of adolescents, parents of a child newly diagnosed with schizophrenia). It is our strong impression that very few of these services address the relationship *between* the parents, and even fewer capitalise on the power of groups for providing support, reducing isolation, and conveying the message that "We are not alone". All these group functions reduce the tendency for either partner to blame the other for what can more usefully be interpreted as normative distress.

The ideas that follow are not original to us, and some may already exist in some communities. We present them as speculations because as far as we know such specialised programmes have not been systematically evaluated. In the interests of conserving space, we describe each set of transition issues, but do not repeat our suggestion of couples groups as a potentially effective intervention modality.

Foster or adoptive families. We have been puzzled by the fact that with all the research attention to the transition to parenthood over the last four decades, there has been little systematic research and no systematic attention to offering help to couples about to adopt a child or become foster parents. The circumstances under which children come to be adopted or placed in foster homes are often traumatic for the child (death of parents, child abuse or neglect, domestic violence between parents), with an increased likelihood of, at least, temporary increases in problematic behaviour. Often the fostering parents are ill-equipped to handle their new roles, and the resulting tensions may exacerbate existing differences between them. While some agencies offer guidance around parenting issues, we know of no parallel help for the couple to address challenges to their relationship.

Parents of adolescents. From our own experience and from the research literature, we know that although adolescence is not always a period of *Sturm und Drang* for each teenager, it does represent a period of increased risk for acting out and depressive behaviour disorders and for schizophrenia, among other serious problems. What is not often recognised is the fact that adolescent changes can raise intrapsychic issues for parents, especially as their children become sexually active. Men and women who became parents in their late twenties are now entering their forties, when a host of personal and relationship issues can place them on a collision course with each other and with their autonomy-seeking teenagers. As parents struggle with feeling less in control while being responsible for adolescents who can get themselves into serious trouble, differences in when and how to set limits can raise the temperature in the family relationships.

Unemployment. An obvious candidate for preventive intervention, especially in stressful economic times, is help for couples when one or both partners lose their jobs. The evidence is clear that this non-normative (unexpected, undesirable) life change for one partner represents a critical stressor for that partner and the whole family.

Serious consequences for the couple can occur when each partner's worldview runs into the reality of a layoff, an identity no longer as "worker" or "professional", and abrupt role shifts (Howe, Levy & Caplan, 2004; Mattinson,1988). Not only can the relationship with one's partner feel under siege, but relationships with friends can become problematic as well.

Parents who have lost a child to suicide. Bill and Beverly Feigelman (2008) describe support groups for couples whose child committed suicide. The couples in these groups discuss how to deal with personal grief and loss, how to relate to surviving children, and how to preserve the couple relationship when inner losses and external life stresses feel daunting. Here too, the company of others facing similar tragedies and the guidance of mental health professionals can stave off more serious depression and hopelessness that can take an additional toll on the couple relationship.

Couples reuniting after long absences. What little aftercare is available when a person leaves prison is focused on the former inmate and rarely on the issues involved in reuniting with a partner and children. This is a very delicate time for couples who must resolve issues from before, during, and after the prison experience. Although the context is very different, similar issues confront military couples in which one partner has been away on duty and returns to civilian status. While both of these transitions are times of stress, with high risk for ending couple relationships, they also constitute opportunities to use the transition as a time for relationship growth and adaptation.

Couples caring for aging or ailing parents. Finally, we move to a transition late in life that is statistically normative—facing the vulnerability of one's aging parents—but non-normative in the sense that we never know when active involvement in the care of ill or aging parents will be required. The need for help by the older generation comes sometimes after slow physical or mental decline, sometimes suddenly after a heart attack, stroke, or diagnosis of a life-threatening illness. As the lifespan increases, most mid-life adults will be faced with tasks associated with looking after or making arrangements for the care of aging or ill parents. The burden of caregiving usually falls to women, even when the husband's parents are in need, but at these times, too, the couple relationship of the younger adult generation can be vulnerable to serious challenges. As each partner takes on the unfamiliar and challenging role of becoming a parent to his/her parent, fissures in the fault line of both relationships are likely to become visible.

Conclusions

We have argued that there are a number of family transition points that present opportunities for preventive intervention. In the ideal world, these interventions might begin early in the formation of couple relationships and function as primary prevention. More realistically, the interventions we have described and those we have suggested are focused on periods when families have already begun to struggle with stressful challenges and to feel signs of what may be mounting distress (secondary prevention).

While there are many family transitions that could benefit from preventive interventions, we have attempted to provide some examples that highlight the idea of targeting interventions to *couples* rather than to mothers or individual partners. Our preference is to use a group format so that partners can discover that they are not alone, and begin to work together while establishing a network of support at times when families tend to be isolated and disconnected, but couples therapists who prefer to work with the dyad could incorporate this approach into work with individual couples in the consulting room.

Policy implications

This chapter has focused on the need for couples-based preventive interventions. In the United Kingdom, the previous Labour government's policy emphasis on services for families for the past decade has led to reduced support for couples programmes and increased support for parenting programmes. Elsewhere (P. A. Cowan & Cowan, 2008), we offered evidence for reconsidering these policy priorities. Enhanced parenting skills are not necessarily followed by improved couple relationships, whereas enhanced couple relationship satisfaction seems to bolster the quality of both parent–child and couple relationships.

Some researchers, clinicians, and policy makers worry that an emphasis on couple relationships ignores the reality of many lone parents who could also use help. We and others have found that although many lone or single mothers are not connected with the biological fathers of their children, they are in relationships with someone who plays an active and ongoing co-parenting role (their own parent, grandparent, friend, or partner). What has yet to be tested is the idea that these interventions can be helpful to other combinations of parenting figures who are actively involved in caring for children.

We have talked with civil servants in a number of countries about the idea of preventive interventions for couples that we have advocated here. Their first predictable set of questions has to do with cost. "If we can't fund the programmes we have now for families in serious distress, how can we find resources to support programmes for families in less obvious need?" Our response is both ideological and empirical. It is always possible to ask "How much will it cost eventually *not* to fund preventive programmes?" The challenge in answering this question is that there are few cost-benefit analyses of existing programmes to establish whether they will save money in the long run.

Finally, to return to where we began, let us re-emphasise that couple therapy, as it is practised today at TCCR and in other public and private settings, is already engaged in preventive intervention with respect to the children of couples who are treated. If therapists in these settings would document the benefits for the couples they see—and note, even informally, what happens to the children of these couples—they could provide stronger justification for their arguments that public and private financial support for couples work are necessary and worthwhile candidates for strengthening couple and family relationships, with ultimate benefits for all.

References

Caplan, G. (1964). *Principles of Preventive Psychiatry*. New York: Basic.

Cherlin, A. J. (2009). *The Marriage-Go-Round: The State of Marriage and the Family in America Today* (1st edn.). New York: Alfred A. Knopf.

Cookston, J. T., Braver, S. L., Griffin, W. A., De Luse, S. R. & Jonathan, M. (2007). Effects of the Dads for Life intervention on interparental conflict and coparenting in the two years after divorce. *Family Process*, 46(1): 123–137.

Cowan, C. P. & Cowan, P. A. (2000). *When Partners Become Parents: The Big Life Change for Couples*. Mahwah, NJ: Lawrence Erlbaum.

Cowan, P. A. (1991). Individual and family life transitions: A proposal for a new definition. In: P. A. Cowan & E. M. Hetherington (Eds.), *Family Transitions* (pp. 3–30). Hillsdale, NJ: Lawrence Erlbaum.

Cowan, P. A. & Cowan, C. P. (2008). Diverging family policies to promote children's well-being in the UK and US: some relevant data from family research and intervention studies. *Journal of Children's Services*, 3(4): 4–16.

Cowan, P. A., Cowan, C. P., Ablow, J., Johnson, V. K. & Measelle, J. (2005). *The Family Context of Parenting in Children's Adaptation to Elementary School*. Mahwah, NJ: Lawrence Erlbaum.

Cowan, P. A., Cowan, C. P., Pruett, M. K., Pruett, K. D. & Wong, J. (2009). Promoting fathers engagement with children: Preventive interventions for low-income families. *Journal of Marriage and the Family, 71*: 663–679.

Feigelman, B. & Feigelman, W. (2008). Surviving after suicide loss: The healing potential of suicide survivor support groups. *Illness, Crisis & Loss, 16*: 285–304.

Hirschberger, G., Srivastava, S., Marsh, P., Cowan, P. A. & Cowan, C. P. (2009). Married with children: Attachment, marital satisfaction, and divorce in the first fifteen years of parenthood. *Personal Relationships, 16*: 401–420.

Howe, G. W., Levy, M. L. & Caplan, R. D. (2004). Job loss and depressive symptoms in couples, common stressors, stress transmission, or relationship disruption? *Journal of Family Psychology, 18*: 639–650.

Johnston, J. R., Kline, M. & Tschann, J. M. (1989). Ongoing postdivorce conflict: Effects on children of joint custody and frequent access. *American Journal of Orthopsychiatry, 59*(4): 576–592.

Lazarus, R. S. & Folkman, S. (1984). *Stress, appraisal and coping*. New York: Springer.

Markman, H. J., Stanley, S. M. & Blumberg, S. L. (2001). *Fighting for Your Marriage: Positive Steps toward Preventing Divorce and Preserving a Lasting Love* (new and revised). New York: Wiley.

Mattinson, J. (1988). *Work, Love and Marriage*. London: Duckworth.

Office for National Statistics. (2009). *Marriage Rates Fall to Lowest on Record*. Office for National Statistics: London. Available at http://www.statistics.gov.uk/pdfdir/marr0209.pdf (accessed 1 January 2011).

Parkes, C. M. (1971). Psycho-social transitions: A field for study. *Social Science & Medicine, Vol. 5*(2): 101–115.

Pruett, M. K. & Barker, R. K. (2009). Effectively intervening with divorcing parents and children: What works and how it works. In: M. Schulz, M. Pruett & R. D. Parke (Eds.), *Strengthening Couple Relationships for Optimal Child Development*. Washington, DC: APA Books.

Rapaport, R., Rapoport, R. & Streilitz, Z. (1977). *Mothers, Fathers, and Society: Towards New Alliances*. New York: Basic.

Shelton, K. H. & Harold, G. T. (2008). Interparental conflict, negative parenting, and children's adjustment: Bridging links between parents' depression and children's psychological distress. *Journal of Family Psychology, 22*(5): 712–724.

Wolchik, S. A., Sandler, I. N., Millsap, R. E., Plummer, B. A., Greene, S. M., Anderson, E. R., Dawson-McClure, S. R., Hipke, K. & Haine, R. A. (2002). Six-year follow-up of preventive interventions for children of divorce. A randomized controlled trial. *JAMA: Journal of the American Medical Association, 288*(15): 1874–1881.

COMMENTARY ON CHAPTER ONE

Leezah Hertzmann

Introduction

For many years now, clinicians at the Tavistock Centre for Couple Relationships (TCCR) have worked closely with the Cowans in the area of preventive interventions for couples and parents. TCCR shares the Cowans' conviction that there is a need to focus on the relationship *between* both parents rather than just looking through the lens of parenting. This conviction has informed and shaped much of our fruitful collaboration. It has also contributed to the development of TCCR's range of interventions for couples and parents, as well as the development of highly regarded models of training and consultation to front line practitioners in this area.

Drawing on these areas of work, I begin my response to their chapter by describing the current situation in the UK regarding prevention and early intervention with couples at challenging family transition points. I then describe some work which TCCR clinicians have been developing for parents experiencing high levels of interparental conflict. Next, I draw on two theoretical concepts from the body of psychoanalytic ideas and theories developed within TCCR, which front line practitioners have found to be particularly useful in their interventions with couples and parents. Finally, in keeping with the spirit of the Cowans' chapter, I present some further thoughts about other populations who might usefully benefit from the kinds of preventive interventions described here.

Prevention and early intervention—the current situation

Family transitions present different challenges for each individual within the family and for couple relationships specifically. The Cowans have long understood the need to map the course traversed by individuals and families as they encounter life challenges, in order to understand more about the range of adaptive and maladaptive responses (Cowan, 1991). Here in this chapter, they describe the need for a preventive intervention pathway, with clear definitions of family transitions supported by empirically validated interventions, accurately targeting particular domains of functioning, most specifically with couples. (For further reading, see Cowan, Cowan, Pruett, Pruett & Wong, 2009; Cowan, Cowan & Mehta, 2009.)

Many countries now provide preventive interventions in the form of parenting support programmes to help families manage the challenges of bringing up children, and it is widely understood that making these programmes available early in the child's life will result in better outcomes for families. In 2009, the Department for Children Schools and Families (now called the Department for Education) conducted a review of parenting support across twelve European and non-European countries (Boddy et al., 2009). The research identified and distinguished between four levels of accessibility in parenting support—from support embedded within universal services, delivered by workers *in* that setting (for example in schools), to targeted specialist support, whereby parents and families identified as meeting certain criteria access specialist services. However, despite the reported effectiveness of many of the parenting support programmes in this review, very few offered support for the relationship *between* the parents at times of challenging transition points. So it would seem the area of support for the couple's relationship, whether as partners and/or co-parents, both in the UK and in other European countries, is largely overlooked. This concurs with the Cowans' findings in the USA—that more attention is generally paid to the relationship parents have with their children, rather than the relationship between themselves, and the bearing this may have on the quality of parenting offered.

"Think Family—Think Couple"

From April 2009, local authorities in the UK received increased funding to support the introduction of "Think Family" practice. This was designed to ensure that children, adult, and family services work together in order to fully take account of how individual problems affect the whole family. The aim is to provide targeted and timely evidence-based support for parents and families that is well integrated and coordinated. However, what appears to be lacking in this model is any recognition of the importance of support for the couple relationship, despite it now being widely acknowledged that the quality of the relationship between parents can affect the whole family (Davies & Cummings, 1994; Grych & Fincham, 1990; Harold & Conger, 1997). "Think Family" as a model of integrated support for families appears to overlook the important fact that interventions may need to be directed to the couple relationship or the relationship between both parents as co-parents, in order to fully support families. "Think Family" as an attempt to join up services is a beginning, but in TCCR this idea has been expanded. In order to fully support families, we need to "Think Family—Think Couple".

TCCR has been using this idea of "Think Family—Think Couple" in the training of and consultation to front line practitioners supporting couple and parenting relationships. TCCR has a long and well-established history of work in this area as well as in developing a range of interventions which can be flexibly used in a variety of settings (for further reading see Hughes & Pengelly, 1997). A central focus of the training, consultation, and intervention with families involves enabling practitioners to "Think Couple" whichever family members they are in contact with. Thus it is important to keep in mind a broader definition of who might be understood as a parenting couple beyond the conventional image of mother and father living together. Some parents will have separated yet need to actively co-parent together. Equally, the idea of couple can also be applied to a co-parenting pair such as a mother and grandparent, or a same gender couple, or any other of sort of pairing where two people come together to parent a child.

A group intervention to reduce inter-parental conflict

At TCCR, clinicians regularly deliver training and consultation using the idea of "Think Family—Think Couple". Using this idea, we have recently undertaken to replicate some of the Cowans' work in a group intervention project for parents who are experiencing high levels of interparental conflict. Many of the children of these parents have attended child and adolescent mental health services, presenting with emotional and behavioural difficulties. The aim of the group intervention is to reduce the levels of interparental conflict and to strengthen the parental alliance so that children can be better supported. A robust parental alliance has been shown not only to be of benefit to children, but is also associated with lower levels of parenting stress and improved parental functioning for both parents (Abidin & Brunner, 1995; Floyd, Gilliom & Costigan, 1998).

All clients referred to the groups have acknowledged problems in co-parenting their children who have a range of emotional and behavioural difficulties. While the focus of the intervention is to help address the child's difficulties, attention is necessarily given to strengthening the parental alliance and the relationship between both parents. Parents attend the group either alone or with their co-parent but whereas the Cowans' research involved delivering the intervention to both parents, in the intervention I am describing, although it is offered to both parents together, in fact most of the parents attend alone, for which various explanations are given. For example, some parents are divorced or separated and do not wish to attend with the child's other parent present, whereas others are together but only one parent chooses to attend the group. Our clinical experience is that the couple relationship—whether both parents are together or not—can still be treated and improved even with one parent attending the group.

In the group discussion, parents are offered the opportunity to think about interparental conflict and their part in it. They are also encouraged to think about their child's experience of the conflict and thereby helped to notice and attend to the effects on their child. Our experience has been that even when only one parent, rather than both partners, has attended the group the opportunity to reflect on their own and their child's experience has resulted in less parental conflict overall and benefits to their child. Parents reported the lessening of arguments with their co-parent and the growing ability of children to express their feelings appropriately rather than act them out in a negative and destructive manner. Consequently, they were able to help their child develop better coping strategies which were less disruptive to family life.

In projects such as these, TCCR clinicians liaise closely with practitioners in local services to identify participants for the group. Once parents are identified and recruited, TCCR clinicians then deliver the short-term group intervention alongside one of the practitioners acting as co-facilitator. Running in parallel with this group, practitioners are also trained in the relevant skills required to deliver the group intervention to parents. Once trained, practitioners then meet regularly for consultation with the TCCR clinicians where the progress of the group and the model of intervention can be monitored. This cascade model of training and consultation which uses an apprenticeship stance has many advantages. It enables the group to be widely available to a range of parents in a variety of settings, as well as ensuring that front line practitioners are better equipped to work with interparental conflict. This in turn means that practitioners are better placed to think about the relationship between parents, whether they are together or apart.

In the process of identifying participants for the group, many practitioners describe a parent as single or lone, which generally reflects the way that parents define themselves. It is striking how little appears to be known about the quality of relationships between parents. In the group work intervention project described here, it was interesting to discover that parents are often not single or lone in an informal sense despite the fact that they might describe themselves in these terms. This means that not only is there another adult in the child's life, but there is also a couple relationship and, at least, a potential co-parenting relationship, although one that may not necessarily involve both birth parents. We suspect that many parents describe themselves as single or lone because they feel alone without the day to day support of a co-parent or partner who, if more actively involved, might reduce the burdens of lone parenting.

Another recurring issue which parents report is how, at challenging transition points in family life, their couple relationship broke down and, in the absence of help, became irrevocably damaged. This damage then became enacted in their co-parenting which, by the time they separated, was highly conflictual and adversely affecting the child. (For further reading on how interparental conflict adversely affects children's development see Chapters Two and Four.) Parents frequently remark that although they were offered good parenting support by various professionals, they were never offered support for their couple relationship, particularly in making the adjustment at key times of transition such as becoming parents, parenting adolescents, or indeed how to co-parent after separating.

Two user-friendly theoretical concepts about couple relationships

In order to help practitioners acquire the knowledge, skills, and abilities necessary to provide preventive interventions to couples and co-parents, a significant investment of resources is required. Sadly, this is not always available especially in the current economic climate. When resources are strained and training opportunities limited, it becomes especially important to garner support and learning from all quarters. The overarching idea of "Think Family—Think Couple" is one approach that will help practitioners keep alive the importance of attending to couple and co-parenting relationships in the course of their work. In addition there are two key concepts developed within TCCR over the past sixty years which practitioners tell us have been found helpful in the course of their work with families.

The first concept found useful is the "couple state of mind" (Morgan, 2001) which has evolved from the rich and wide-ranging clinical experience of staff at TCCR. The "couple state of mind" refers to the capacity of practitioners to keep in mind and reflect upon the significance of current relationships with which their clients are involved. This capacity is demonstrated when a practitioner is able to think in this way when also relating individually to each partner in the relationship. It will also be present when, working with an individual parent, it is possible to think of the wider couple relationships with which that person is involved. This can take the form of, firstly, having the idea of another partner in mind, and then enquiring about the relationship and its quality, thereby, communicating its importance.

As previously stated, more attention is paid in the training of front line workers to the relationships parents have with their children rather than the relationship *between* parents. This avoidance can be further compounded by the reluctance of practitioners to ask about couple relationships. This personal reluctance may be overcome if practitioners are helped to understand the reasons for it. For some, couple functioning, with its links to intimacy and sexuality, may feel like a very private area which they feel nervous venturing into, and in which they do not feel skilled to intervene. For others, a professional interest in couple relationships may reverberate uncomfortably with difficulties in their own relationships or with difficulties in the relationships of friends and relatives close to them. It is important that workers are helped to see that their own ability to have a "couple state of mind" may sometimes be compromised by their personal experiences in the past and present.

A second concept which practitioners report finding very useful is that of the relationship as a "psychological container" (Colman, 1993). When a couple's relationship is functioning well, the relationship itself becomes a resource for the couple to draw upon and to augment. The idea of a relationship being a benign receptacle or container allows for the idea that both partners can place their good experiences within it as an asset on which they can depend in a helpful way. These experiences may relate to the external world of shared reality as well as their own subjective experiences in their inner world. In the crucible of the relationship, both inner life and external behaviour coalesce to strengthen and support each partner's adjustment to the challenges they face both as a couple and individually, including the challenge of parenting together.

When practitioners are helped to understand more about the couple relationship acting as a container, they are also able to understand what happens when the container develops stress fractures and can no longer contain both partners' experiences. Under these circumstances the notion of a benign container may transform into that of a malign receptacle or claustrum in which bad experiences overwhelm the good. Practitioners have described to us that when they understand these ideas, they feel more skilled to venture into the area of supporting the relationship between both parents in the course of their work with families.

Final thoughts …

The Cowans' idea of a preventive intervention pathway which is empirically validated highlights the need to think more widely about the populations likely to benefit. In keeping with the spirit of their chapter, I, too, would like to end by making two further additions to the Cowans' already comprehensive list. These are populations where support for couple and co-parenting relationships urgently needs to be made available.

Firstly, teenage parents, where the relationship with the child's other parent may have a fragile or tentative formation and where the focus of the intervention is often largely on the teenage mother. Teenage parents are a particularly vulnerable group and the children of these young parents face high risks of poverty, of externalising and internalising problems, and are more likely to become teen parents themselves (Pogarsky, Thornberry & Lizotte, 2006). Secondly, support for gay, lesbian, and transgender couples who may face particular challenges which heterosexual couples do not have to traverse. These include having to contend with homophobia in social contacts and also within themselves, presenting as "internalized homophobia" (Malyon, 1982). Dealing with homophobia can have an adverse impact on both the quality of life and the mental health of gay, lesbian, and transgender people (King et al., 2003). In turn, the quality of partnerships and parenting is likely to be compromised. The populations I have listed here and those identified by the Cowans are by no means an exhaustive list and there are many other groups who could benefit from preventive interventions to support couple and parenting relationships.

Carolyn and Philip Cowan's substantial contribution in the area of understanding couples and parenthood has provided important empirical evidence to strengthen the case for preventive work with couples at key moments of transition. At TCCR it has long been our impression from clinical experience that outcomes for children and their parents are significantly better when interventions target the relationship between the parents and not just parenting on its own. Now the Cowans have provided empirical evidence to support these clinical impressions (Cowan & Cowan, 2008; Cowan, Cowan, Ablow, Johnson & Measelle, 2005; Cowan, Cowan, Pruett, Pruett & Wong, 2009). Although much has been done, there is more to do in a number of ways. Firstly, to establish whether the interventions which have been shown to be effective with birth parents could also be helpful when other figures such as another family relative, a new partner, or network of friends co-parent. Secondly, to convince governments that priority must be given to preventive and early intervention programmes for couples at challenging family transition points. As the Cowans have demonstrated and as Professor Gordon Harold's chapter in this book further elaborates, parenting interventions alone are not enough to support children's well-being.

References

Abidin, R. R. & Brunner, J. F. (1995). Development of a parenting alliance inventory. *Journal of Clinical Child Psychology, 24*: 31–40.

Boddy, J., Statham, J., Smith, M., Ghate, D., Wigfall, V. & Hauari, H. (2009). International perspectives on parenting support: non-English language sources. Report, DCSF-RB114. London: Thomas Coram Research Unit and Department for Children Schools and Families website.

Colman, W. (1993). Marriage as a psychological container. In: S. Ruszczynski (Ed.), *Psychotherapy with Couples*. London: Karnac.

Cowan, P. A. (1991). Individual and family life transitions: A proposal for a new definition. In: P. A. Cowan & E. M. Hetherington (Eds.), *Family Transitions* (pp. 3–30). Hillsdale, NJ: Lawrence Erlbaum.

Cowan, P. A. & Cowan, C. P. (2008). Diverging family policies to promote Children's well-being in the UK and US: some relevant data from family research and intervention studies. *Journal of Children's Services, 3*(4): 4–16.

Cowan, P. A., Cowan, C. P., Ablow, J., Johnson, V. K. & Measelle, J. (2005). *The Family Context of Parenting in Children's Adaptation to Elementary School*. Mahwah, NJ: Lawrence Erlbaum.

Cowan, P. A., Cowan, C. P. & Mehta, N. (2009). Adult attachment, couple attachment and children's adaptation to school: an integrated attachment template and family risk model. *Attachment and Human Development, 11*(1): 29–46.

Cowan, P. A., Cowan, C. P., Pruett, M. K., Pruett, K. D. & Wong, J. (2009). Promoting fathers' engagement with children: Preventive interventions for low-income families. *Journal of Marriage and the Family, 71*: 663–679.

Davies, P. T. & Cummings, E. M. (1994). Marital conflict and child adjustment: An emotional security hypothesis. *Psychological Bulletin, 116*: 387–411.

Floyd, F. J., Gilliom, L. A. & Costigan, C. L. (1998). Marriage and the parenting alliance: Longitudinal prediction of change in parenting perceptions and behaviors. *Child Development, 69*: 1461–1479.

Grych, J. H. & Fincham, F. D. (1990). Marital conflict and children's adjustment: A cognitive-contextual framework. *Psychological Bulletin, 108*: 267–290.

Harold, G. T. & Conger, R. D. (1997). Marital conflict and adolescent distress: The role of adolescent awareness. *Child Development*, 68(2): 333–350.

Hughes, L. & Pengelly, P. (1997). *Staff Supervision in a Turbulent Environment: Managing Process and Task in Front-line Services*. London: Jessica Kingsley.

King, M., McKeown, E., Warner, J., Ramsay, A., Johnson, K., Cort, C., Wright, L., Blizard, R. & Davidson, O. (2003). Mental health and quality of life of gay men and lesbians in England and Wales: a controlled, cross-sectional study. *British Journal of Psychiatry*, 183: 552–558.

Malyon, A. K. (1982). Psychotherapeutic implications of internalized homophobia in gay men. *Journal of Homosexuality*, 7: 59–69.

Morgan, M. (2001). First contacts: the therapist's "couple state of mind" as a factor in the containment of couples seen for consultation. In: F. Grier (Ed.), *Brief Encounters with Couples*. London: Karnac.

Pogarsky, G., Thornberry, T. P. & Lizotte, A. J. (2006). Developmental outcomes for children of young mothers. *Journal of Marriage and Family*, 68: 332–344.

CHAPTER TWO

Parents as partners: how the parental relationship affects children's psychological development

Gordon T. Harold and Leslie D. Leve

Setting the scene: the role of the parental relationship for child development

"If you wish for a happy life, you should choose your parents carefully"— this is the opening to a noteworthy recent report titled *Social Science and Family Policy* published by the British Academy (Rutter et al., 2010). This report examines changes in the landscape of family life in the UK and internationally and asks the question, how might scientific research inform family policy so as to benefit modern families and the individuals who comprise them?

As the opening to the report suggests, the parent–child relationship serves as a central feature of contemporary family policy in the UK. This focus is both a product of internationally derived scientific research highlighting the significance of the parent–child relationship for children's healthy emotional and behavioural development (Kagan, 1999), and a response to the rapidly shifting structural landscape of family life in the UK and internationally, which has seen the proportion of children who experience parental relationship breakdown exponentially increase over the past fifty years (Pryor & Rogers, 2001).

In response to what are recognised as the negative consequences for children of parental relationship breakdown, governments across the globe (OECD nations in particular) have committed substantial funds to welfare programmes aimed at strengthening families, with the objective of both reducing rising divorce rates and promoting support for children across different family types (single parent, cohabiting, married, remarried).

Historically, the primary focus of intervention within families has been on promoting positive parenting practices in alleviating disrupted family relationship influences on children. More recently, researchers have begun to ask the question whether a more holistic, wider family intervention that incorporates a focus on the interparental relationship might be of more sustainable benefit to children and parents within the context of general family stress and parental relationship breakdown (Cowan & Cowan, 2008). This proposal raises an important question from a contemporary policy and practice standpoint: as more and more children experience parental relationship breakdown, are programmes that focus exclusively on the parent–child relationship even more relevant, owing to the increasing proportion of children experiencing life in single-parent homes? Or, are programmes that promote couple focused relationship skills and that facilitate more adaptive relationships *between* parents a more effective approach to facilitating positive developmental outcomes for children in the context of general family stress and parental relationship breakdown? This chapter aims to review scientific evidence highlighting the adverse effects of acrimonious family relationships, specifically interparental and parent–child relationships, on children's psychological development, and to inform the debate as to where investment might best be targeted to both promote positive developmental outcomes for children in the short term and to rectify the intergenerational transmission of factors that lead to disrupted family relationships and family breakdown in the long term.

Contextualising the role of the parental relationship

Prior to the 2010 UK general election, the Department for Children Schools and Families (DCSF) produced a report titled *Support for All: The Families and Relationships Green Paper* (January 2010). The opening of this report states that "strong stable families are the bedrock of our society". The report goes on to build the basis of strong, stable families as a derivative of "strong, stable *relationships* within families":

> The evidence is clear that it is strong, stable relationships between adults in the home—parent, grandparents and other caring adults— and among all these adults and the children in a family, that have the biggest impact on children's happiness and healthy development. (p. 4)
>
> [Additionally] marriage is recognised as an important and well-established institution that plays a fundamental role in family life in our society. (p. 3)

The question remains however, is it marriage that matters more for children, or is it the quality of relations between parents, couples, and married partners when it comes to understanding how the parental relationship affects children? According to a recent report by the Institute of Fiscal Studies (Goodman & Greaves, 2010), young children's cognitive or social and emotional development does not appear to be significantly affected by the formal marital status of their parents. This report goes on to conclude:

> The Conservative Party has announced its decision to recognise marriage in the tax system through a partially transferable personal allowance, which will benefit married couples where one pays tax at the basic rate, and the other is not a taxpayer. Our work shows that, even if more couples did decide to get married in response to the small monetary incentive, such a policy would have a limited effect on young children's development. (Goodman & Greaves, 2010)

This conclusion is in line with an increasing volume of international research suggesting that it is not marriage *per se* that accords children positive parental relationship benefits; rather, healthy, well-functioning parental relationships more likely facilitate healthy psychological outcomes for children and promote more functional and sustainable marriages among couples who choose to marry.

This chapter will review evidence underpinning this thesis, making the case that investment at the couple relationship level will pay substantial dividends in promoting positive outcomes for children within a family context. It is also proposed that such investment would lower the likelihood of relationship breakdown as well as the correlates of breakdown for families and children, including decreased adult mental health, poor parenting, heightened levels of interparental conflict and violence, and the intergenerational transmission of factors that lead to future family breakdown.

Policy and practice contexts of parental relationship influences on children

Several noteworthy reports have been produced in the UK over the past few years signalling the significance of family policy as a prominent issue on the political agenda, with a core interest in the domain of family and parental relationship breakdown and associated outcomes for children (DCSF, 2008; DCSF, 2010; DfES, 2007a; DfES, 2007b). A common theme among these reports is the role of the parental relationship both as a location within the family meritorious of direct support and as a facilitator of transferable influences to the welfare and well-being of children (sees *Every Parent Matters*, DfES, 2007b). These reports and their substantive policy focus are primarily borne out of evidence accumulated over the past fifty years pertaining to rising rates of parental relationship breakdown and associated negative outcomes for children (see Harold & Murch, 2005). While recent statistics suggest that the divorce rate is dropping for the first time in several decades in the UK and other OECD countries, so too is the proportion of couples choosing to marry (Office for National Statistics, 2009). Among those who do marry, the divorce rate in the UK is approaching a rate of one in two (45% likelihood of new marriages ending in divorce, ONS, 2008a). Interestingly, among couples who choose to divorce, 66% of women and 75% of men remarry (Pryor & Rogers, 2001), evidencing a trend towards rejection of a marital partner rather than a rejection of marriage per se. Among those couples who are also parents, children too experience the break-up of their parents' relationship. The number of children exposed to parental relationship breakdown in England and Wales has climbed steeply in recent years with approximately 71,000 children under the age of sixteen years experiencing the divorce of their parents in 1970 (ONS, 2006) compared to 117,000 in 2007 (ONS, 2008b). Over half (51%) of couples divorcing in 2007 had at least one child under the age of sixteen years, with 20% of these children under the age of five years and 63% under the age of eleven years (ONS, 2008b).

Several critical questions emerge from this brief synopsis of divorce statistics. First, what factors are associated with couple and parental relationship breakdown? Second, how are children affected by parental relationship breakdown? Third, where children are adversely affected by parental relationship breakdown, what supports can be offered to improve developmental outcomes in the short term and reduce the intergenerational transmission of family breakdown in the long term? Addressing these questions gets at the heart of promoting sustainable family relationships, both from a policy and practice standpoint and in terms of promoting bottom line benefit for couples and children. Furthermore, targeted investment in promoting sustainable family relationships should facilitate a reduction in the overall costs across family welfare, family justice, and family policy domains directed towards reducing the social, clinical, and financial costs of family breakdown in the UK.

Organising the orchestra of family influences on children: theory as a starting point

Family relationship breakdown is recognised as a risk factor for negative psychological outcomes among children of all ages (Hetherington, Bridges & Insabella, 1998). However, an important starting point in examining the impact of family breakdown on children is to recognise that not all children experience the breakdown of their parents' relationship in the same way. Some children exposed to risks such as parental relationship breakdown experience serious emotional and behavioural problems, while other children experience little or no such difficulties. What explains this difference in adaptation?

The essence of adaptation in the context of adversity is captured by the scientific field of resiliency research (Rutter, 2000). Resilience is recognised as a developmental feature that captures *individual differences* in adaptation to specific risk contexts or developmental hazards, as they are referred to in the scientific literature (e.g., parental relationship breakdown). The topic of individual resilience is one of considerable social, scientific, clinical, and policy concern, particularly in relation to policies that focus on the early identification, prevention, and treatment of mental health disorders and developmental impairment in young people. In planning prevention policies, it is incumbent to ask whether it is more useful to focus on the risks that render children vulnerable to developmental disorder or on the protective factors and associated processes that provide for resilience in the face of adversity (Rutter, 2000). Resilience research differs from traditional concepts of risk and protection in its focus on individual variations in response to comparable experiences. Accordingly, the research focus and translation to policy application need to be on highlighting factors that promote/ explain individual differences in adaptation to adversity and the causal processes that they reflect, rather than on resilience as a general quality (Rutter, 2000, 2006). Resiliency research, as a theoretical framework, guides the orientation of the evidence-based review presented throughout this chapter.

Moving from an outcome-oriented to a process-oriented perspective in capturing parental relationship influences on children

Historically, research examining family influences on children has employed an outcome-oriented perspective. That is, "What are the outcomes for children exposed to specific family risk factors, such as parental divorce, maltreatment, negative economic conditions, parent psychopathology (e.g., depression, anti-social behaviour problems)?" While research of this type has advanced our understanding of the types of problems children experience as a consequence or product of exposure to specific family risk factors, it has also highlighted the important research finding that individual differences exist in children's adaptation to these risks. In other words, children do not respond in the same way or with the same degree of severity to specific risk influences (e.g., parental separation-divorce). A more contemporary approach to examining family influences on children is to employ a process-oriented perspective to illuminate specific mechanisms (mediating and moderating factors) that underlie individual differences in children's adaptation to specific risk factors. In so doing, we are better able to explain "why, when, and how" a factor such as parental relationship breakdown influences negative outcomes in some children, but not all. By better identifying the mechanisms that operate to explain this important distinction in risk-related adaptation, we will be better equipped to develop more efficacious intervention programmes aimed at reducing the negative effects of parental relationship breakdown (and other related family risk factors) on children, parents, and future families.

Family influences on children: a process-oriented framework

Multiple family influences have been identified in past research as serving as risk factors for children's negative psychological development. Children raised in households exposed to acute or chronic economic strain (Conger, Ge, Elder, Lorenz & Simons, 1994), heightened levels of parental psychopathology (Downey & Coyne, 1990), interparental conflict and violence (Grych & Fincham, 1990; Rivett, Howarth & Harold, 2006), negative parent–child relations (Erel & Burman, 1995), and parental separation, divorce, and remarriage (Hetherington, Bridges & Insabella, 1998) have been shown to experience a variety of negative psychological outcomes, including increased anxiety, depression, aggression, hostility, anti-social behaviour, and criminality. Conger and colleagues point out however, that rather than operating as single influences on specific psychological outcomes for children, these factors may work in concert with each other such that harsh economic conditions affect parents' psychopathology (specifically their symptoms of depression), which adversely affect levels of couple relationship quality, which in turn affect couples' efficacy as parents (promoting negative parenting practices) and children's symptoms of psychological distress (Conger, Ge, Elder, Lorenz & Simons, 1994). When parents struggle to meet basic economic needs as a result of direct economic hardship, or as a result of increased time commitments at work, their ability to provide the type of home environment necessary for children's long-term well-being is at risk. Therefore, according to this perspective, children are adversely affected through the impact that such pressure has on the couple relationship, parent–child relations and, in turn, children's psychological functioning. Importantly, this model identifies the parent–child relationship as a primary transfer mechanism (mediator) of family level influences (economic stress, parent mental health, poor couple relationship quality) on child behaviour and associated psychological symptoms. What is the evidence that parenting practices serve as a primary mechanism through which family factors affect children?

The parent–child relationship and associated psychological outcomes for children

As declared by Serot and Teevan (1961), one of the basic tenets of developmental psychology is the proposal that a child's early family environment, especially the pervading parental attitude or emotional tone of the parent–child relationship, is a fundamental factor in predicting children's long-term emotional and behavioural development. Research conducted across attachment and parenting traditions in the decades that have followed strongly supports this hypothesis (Patterson, Reid & Dishion, 1992; Waters & Cummings, 2000). Although it is widely recognised that parenting behaviours operate within a larger family system and social context, there is little dispute that parenting practices and parental disciplinary strategies (e.g., maltreatment, harsh parenting, parental supervision and monitoring, sensitive parenting, parental warmth) are associated with variation in children's psychological outcomes. It is also well documented that associations between parenting and child behaviour are bidirectional and reciprocal in nature (Scaramella & Leve, 2004), with heritable child characteristics also influencing parental behaviour towards their child (Dunn, Plomin & Daniels, 1986; Ge et al., 1996; Reiss, Neiderhiser, Hetherington & Plomin, 2000). Two theoretical perspectives stand out in articulating the salience of parenting practices in promoting adaptive and maladaptive developmental outcomes for children—attachment theory and social learning based coercion theory.

The attachment paradigm is a widely used theoretical approach for studying individual differences in child adjustment and factors affecting the quality of family interactions in childhood. According to Bowlby (1969), from the very beginning of life, infant behaviours, such as crying or fussing to keep attachment figures nearby, evidence the salience of the caregiver–infant relationship. Over the first twelve to eighteen months of life, infants learn which of their own behaviours elicit desired responses from their caregiver. Infants then adapt their behaviours to fit those of their caregiver, resulting in parent–child attachments of varying quality. An internal working model of relationships is formed based on young children's early interactions with their caregivers, which guides children's future interpersonal relationships with others (Bowlby, 1982; Bretherton & Waters, 1985).

A central assumption of attachment theory is that attachment behaviours are based on the interplay between parental sensitivity and the child's emotional response to the parent. Thus, maternal behaviour varies with the child's attachment category (Ainsworth, Blehar, Waters & Wall, 1978; Crittenden, 1995). Mothers of secure children tend to be responsive to their infant's need and willing to negotiate with their young child, helping them learn to handle their emotions on their own. Mothers of insecure-avoidant children tend to be less responsive to their children's needs, often rebuffing their child's attachment-seeking behaviours. This accounts for the children's later inability to use their caregivers to soothe them or help them manage their emotions. Finally, mothers of insecure-ambivalent children tend to be inconsistent in their responses to their children. These children may be unsure whether to approach or avoid their caregiver and may not be able to control their emotional responses because they have received inconsistent feedback. Associations between positive, sensitive parenting and children's attachment behaviours are well established. Maternal support, responsivity, and affection are linked to children's attachment security; lack of parental engagement, lack of support, and maltreatment are linked to insecure attachment (Bakermans-Kranenburg, van IJzendoorn & Juffer, 2003; Cyr, Euer, Bakermans-Kranenburg & Van IJzendoorn, 2010; Fagot & Pears, 1996; National Institute of Child Health and Human Development, Early Child Care Research Network, 2001). In turn, securely attached children tend to have higher social competence, ego-resilience, responsiveness, problem-solving skills, and peer engagement (Arend, Grove & Sroufe, 1979; Howes, 1991; Kerns, 1994; LaFreniere & Sroufe, 1985; Park & Waters, 1989; Shulman, Elicker & Sroufe, 1994; Waters, Wippman & Sroufe, 1979). By contrast, insecurely-attached children tend to be more aggressive, more often rejected, less competent, and less prosocial; they also tend to elicit fewer positive and more antagonistic responses from others and have more externalising problems (Cohn, 1990; Fearon, Bakermans-Kranenburg, Van IJzendoorn, Lapsley & Roisman, 2010; Youngblade & Belsky, 1992). Intervention research has further illustrated associations between parenting and parental sensitivity on children's attachment security and psychological adjustment, with families in parent-oriented interventions showing increases in parental sensitivity, children's attachment security, and positive psychological adjustment (Dozier et al., 2009; Fisher & Kim, 2007; Kalinauskiene et al., 2009; Svanberg, Mennet & Spieker, 2010).

A second well-established theoretical framework for understanding the mechanisms of transmission of parenting effects on children is coercion theory (Patterson, 1982; Patterson, Reid & Dishion, 1992; Reid, Patterson & Snyder, 2002). According to coercion theory, the primary pathway to child and adolescent psychological maladjustment is through inept parental discipline skills and reciprocal, coercive interchanges between the child and the parent. Within this framework, harsh discipline has been identified as a key factor in accounting for individual differences in child outcomes (Eddy & Chamberlain, 2000; Keiley, Lofthouse, Bates, Dodge & Pettit, 2003). In more extreme cases, harsh discipline involves physical abuse and other forms of maltreatment, which have been linked to a host of child externalising and internalising problems (Aarons et al., 2008; Kim & Cicchetti, 2010). However, the effects of harsh parenting on child behaviour extend to community families, as well as families experiencing maltreatment. For example, Simons, Chao, Conger, and Elder (2001) examined change in delinquent behaviour in a community sample across four years from ages twelve or thirteen to fifteen or sixteen, and found that harsh parenting predicted individual differences in delinquency. Similarly, harsh discipline has been found to increase children's risk for developing internalising problems (Capaldi, 1992; Shaw, Keenan, Vondra, Delliquadri & Giovannelli, 1997). In addition, specific child temperamental characteristics interact with environmental influences to predict individual pathways to child internalising and externalising behaviour. For example, high child inhibition and harsh parenting have been shown to jointly contribute to the development of internalising problems in early childhood (Gilliom & Shaw, 2004); child impulsive/unmanageable temperament was more strongly related to later externalising problems when parents used unrestrictive, non-controlling parenting strategies (Bates, Pettit, Dodge & Ridge, 1998); inconsistent parental discipline was most strongly related to externalising problems for children high on impulsivity (Lengua, Wolchik, Sandler & West, 2000); and parental harsh discipline was more strongly related to increases in girls' externalising behaviour when child impulsivity was high (Leve, Kim & Pears, 2005).

Parenting has also been identified as an important mediator (explanatory factor) underlying links between the interparental relationship and child psychological outcomes, particularly in terms of child antisocial behaviour. For example, evidence from at least three studies suggests that parental transitions (separation-divorce) influence child non-compliance and delinquency via their direct effects on parenting. A study of married and divorced lower- to middle-class families found that the effect of divorce on child adjustment was mediated by mother-child interaction (Pett, Wampold, Turner & Vaughan-Cole, 1999). Similarly, Martinez and Forgatch (2001) measured family transitions, parenting practices, and child adjustment in a sample of 238 divorcing mothers with sons in the first through the third grade (six to eight years of age). Analyses revealed that the impact of the number of family transitions on their son's academic functioning, acting-out behaviour, and emotional adjustment was mediated by parenting practices. Capaldi and Patterson (1991) measured child and maternal antisocial behaviour, parenting practices, and the number of marital transitions in a sample of 206 families with boys during late childhood and early adolescence. Results suggested that the effect of transitions on child antisocial behaviour was mediated through both maternal antisocial behaviour and unskilled parenting practices. Mediational effects of parenting on child adjustment have also been observed for family factors such as interparental conflict and non-maternal care (Belsky, 1999; Fishman & Meyers, 2000; Gonzales, Pitts, Hill & Roosa, 2000). Taken together, this work suggests the importance of effective parenting practices in the context of the interparental relationship.

The role of the interparental relationship in children's psychological development

Research on the role of the interparental relationship and, in particular, the impact of interparental conflict on children has a long and established history (Cowan & Cowan, 2002; Davies & Cummings, 1994; Emery, 1982; Grych & Fincham, 1990; Harold & Conger, 1997). From as far back as the 1930s, it has been recognised that discord between parents has a potentially debilitating effect on children's psychological development (Towle, 1931). Indeed, children of all ages have been shown to be adversely affected by conflict between parents that is frequent, intense, and poorly resolved. Newly born children, as young as six months, have been shown to evidence higher physiological symptoms of distress such as elevated heart rate in response to overt, hostile exchanges between their parents when compared to exchanges between non-parental adults. Infants and children up to the age of five years show signs of distress by crying, acting out, freezing, as well as withdrawing from or attempting to intervene in the actual conflict itself. Children between the ages of six and twelve years (middle childhood) and thirteen and seventeen years (adolescence) also show signs of emotional and behavioural distress when exposed to ongoing, acrimonious exchanges between parents (see Harold, Pryor & Reynolds, 2001).

It is important to note, however, that within the context of a couple relationship, periodic conflict between couples is a natural and normal part of family life. Indeed, it is expected that most children will be exposed to conflict between their parents at some point in their lives without necessarily experiencing adverse effects. With this in mind, researchers have turned to identifying the processes within families, and within children themselves, that explain why some children remain relatively unaffected by discord between parents while others go on to develop long-term and potentially debilitating emotional and behavioural problems.

Interparental conflict: "why, when, and how" children are affected

As already outlined, exposure to frequent, intense, and poorly resolved interparental conflict has been associated with a number of indices of child maladjustment, including increased anxiety, depression, aggression, hostility, antisocial behaviour, and criminality as well as deficits in academic attainment (Harold, Aitken & Shelton, 2007). The processes through which interparental conflict has been shown to exert these effects on children involve (1) disruptions in the parent–child relationship and (2) the negative emotions, cognitions, and representations of family relationships engendered in children as a result of exposure to conflict.

The role of the parent–child relationship: Parents embroiled in a hostile and distressed couple relationship are typically more hostile and aggressive towards their children and less sensitive and emotionally responsive to their children's needs (Erel & Burman, 1995). The first theoretical perspective aimed at explaining the effects of interparental conflict on children hypothesises that the effects of conflict between parents are deemed to occur indirectly through a "spillover" of emotion from the couple relationship to the parent–child relationship. In support of this proposal, there is a robust association between levels of conflict in the interparental relationship and levels of conflict in the parent–child relationship (Erel & Burman, 1995). However, if conflict between parents only ever affected children via disruptions in the parent–child relationship, children would be adversely affected irrespective of whether or not they actually witnessed or were aware of conflict occurring between their parents. That is, children who both witnessed or were aware of conflict occurring between their parents *and* children who did not witness or were not aware of conflict occurring between their parents would be influenced equivalently through disrupted parenting practices. As described below, research evidence does not support this conclusion.

The role of children's awareness of parental behaviour: Research conducted over the past two decades has shown that overt interparental conflict to which children are exposed has a greater impact on child distress than covert conflict to which children are not exposed (see Cummings & Davies, 2002, 2010). This finding has led researchers to consider a second set of hypotheses that focus on the underlying psychological processes (cognitions, emotions) engendered in children who live in households marked by hostile interparental relations. Three primary theoretical perspectives have emerged that emphasise the importance of children's own understanding, interpretation, and expectations pertaining to parental behaviour when explaining the effects of interparental conflict on children's psychological development. In their cognitive-contextual framework, Grych and Fincham (1990) propose that the attributions children assign to their parents' relationship arguments account for effects on well-being. Davies and Cummings (1994) emphasise the importance of attachment processes and highlight the role of children's emotional security as a factor in accounting for variation in well-being. Harold and Conger (1997) offer a family-wide model and propose that the attributions children assign to conflict occurring between their parents (interparental conflict) orient their expectations and representations of conflict occurring between them and their parents (parent–child conflict), which in turn affects their long-term psychological development.

i. *A cognitive-contextual framework*: Grych and Fincham (1990) propose that children's responses to interparental conflict occur through their cognitive (attributional) processing of the conflict. According to this perspective, the impact of conflict on children depends both on how it is expressed and how children interpret its meaning, as well as perceived implications for their well-being. These authors suggest that there are two stages of cognitive processing underlying the link between children's exposure to conflict and their interpretation of its meaning. The first of these, primary processing, is a stage where the child first becomes aware that conflict is occurring and experiences an initial level of arousal. They suggest that specific characteristics of the conflict episode, such as its frequency, intensity, and resolution potential, as well as contextual factors such as the quality of the parent–child relationship(s), child temperament, child gender, and history of exposure to conflict influence this initial stage of appraisal.

This primary stage of processing may then lead to a more elaborate secondary stage, during which the child attempts to understand why the conflict is occurring and what he or she should do in response. Secondary processing involves making sense of the cause of the conflict, ascribing responsibility and blame, as well as calculating how best to cope with the conflict (Grych & Fincham, 1990). Children who view conflict as threatening or who feel unable to cope effectively experience more anxiety and helplessness. Children who blame themselves for parental disagreements or feel responsible for not helping to end them experience guilt, shame, and sadness. If conflict is frequent, intense, and poorly resolved, these attributes are believed to increase children's risk of emotional and behavioural problems (Grych & Fincham, 1990; Grych, Fincham, Jouriles & McDonald, 2000).

Many of the hypotheses drawn from the cognitive-contextual framework have been supported empirically (e.g., Grych, Raynor & Fosco, 2004; Kerig, 1998). In a longitudinal study, Grych, Harold, and Miles (2003) showed that children's attributions of threat and self-blame accounted for (or mediated) the relationship between interparental conflict and children's internalising symptoms (depression, anxiety) and their externalising problems (aggression, hostility). Specifically, girls' threat-based attributions emanating from the conflict exacerbated their symptoms of depression and anxiety (internalising) more so than for boys, while boys' attributions of self-blame and responsibility exacerbated their aggressive, hostile, and antisocial (externalising) behaviours more so than for girls (Grych, Harold & Miles, 2003). These findings have important implications for understanding children's responses to conflict between parents and, importantly, why boys and girls may be differentially at risk in the context of acrimonious interparental relations.

ii. *An emotional security hypothesis*: Davies and Cummings (1994) offer a complementary perspective suggesting that a child's sense of "emotional security" is threatened in the context of interparental conflict. Deriving their idea from attachment theory (Bowlby, 1969), these authors propose that the effects of destructive and badly managed conflict between parents are explained through disruptions to three conceptually related areas of children's emotional functioning. First, feelings of *emotional reactivity* may be affected such that children feel angry, sad, or scared in the context of conflict. Second, their *representations of family relationships* may be affected such that conflict between parents affects children's expectations that conflict will occur elsewhere in the family system (e.g., the parent–child relationship). Third, children may feel motivated to *regulate exposure to marital emotion* so that they directly intervene in, or actively withdraw from, the immediate vicinity of the conflict. The impact of conflict on children is explained by the extent to which one or more of these aspects of emotional security is adversely affected and how well children can manage to regulate overall emotional disruption.

Initial tests of this perspective by Davies and Cummings (1998) found that exposure to interparental conflict led to differences in how emotionally secure children felt, and that these in turn explained the initial impact of conflict on children's emotional and behavioural problems. Specifically, children who felt sad, angry, or scared and who regarded the conflict episode as an immediate and potentially longer-term threat to the quality of other family relationships, showed heightened symptoms of emotional and behavioural distress. More recently, Harold, Shelton, Goeke-Morey, and Cummings (2002) integrated the two perspectives offered by Grych and Fincham (1990: cognitive-contextual framework) and Davies and Cummings (1994: emotional security hypothesis). They showed that children's cognitions and emotions emanating from exposure to interparental conflict work in concert to the extent that the emotional reactions children have to their parents' relationship arguments explain the impact that their cognitive appraisals have on their symptoms of psychological distress. These results highlight the "mental architecture" that underlies the link between interparental conflict and child adjustment and underscore the importance of examining children's interpretations of interparental behaviour in order to better understand its effects on development.

iii. *A family-wide model of inter-parental conflict and its effects on children*: Building on the proposal that children's understanding of interparental conflict is an important factor in determining its impact on their psychological development, Harold and colleagues (1997) offer a "family-wide model" suggesting that both interparental and parent–child conflict sequentially exert adverse effects on children's psychological development. Importantly however, these authors propose that how children perceive their parents to behave towards each other (i.e., interparental conflict) determines how they expect their parents to behave towards them (parent–child conflict), which in turn affects their symptoms of psychological distress. What is significant about this approach is that it combines explanations aimed at accounting for the effects of interparental conflict on children through parenting (i.e., the spillover of negative emotion from the couple relationship to the parent–child relationship (Erel & Burman, 1995)), with more recent theoretical perspectives emphasising the importance of considering children's perceptions of interparental behaviour in explaining effects on development (Grych & Fincham, 1990).

Collectively, these theoretical models highlight the importance of considering the child's individual perspective (understanding) in delineating how exposure to conflict between parents adversely affects their psychological well-being. By highlighting the active role that children's subjective evaluations of interparental conflict plays in determining its effects on their well-being, we may better understand why some children seem relatively unaffected by interparental conflict while others go on to develop long-term, clinically significant emotional and behavioural problems.

Calibrating negative parental behaviour: a categorical or dimensional problem

As mentioned earlier, conflict between parents must be understood as a natural and relatively normal part of family life, with effects on children being influenced more by the expressed intensity, duration, severity, content, and resolution properties employed by parents as compared to the simple occurrence of conflict per se. Historically, consideration of the role of conflict between parents and its effects on children has tended to rely on a categorical definition of parental behaviour. That is, interparental conflict has been considered a threat to children only if it is overt, acrimonious, or hostile in form and content. Indeed, practitioners and policy makers have historically treated conflict between parents as a threat, not only to marital partners, but also to children, if, and only if, conflict behaviours attain such a level of severity that the definition of "domestic violence" may be applied.

Research conducted over the past several decades, however, has highlighted how children's exposure to discordant, but non-violent, conflict between parents also exerts negative effects on child development (Cummings & Davies, 2010; Rhoades, 2008). Indeed, recent research supports the proposal that practitioners and policy makers move away from considering conflict between parents as aversive if and only if behaviours attain a level of severity deemed violent, towards recognising that rather than being viewed as a simple present or absent dichotomy (i.e., violent or not), conflicted behaviour between parents exists across a continuum of expressed severity—ranging from silence to violence. Research findings show that in the context of both maritally intact and separated households, conflict between parents need not be overtly hostile in order to adversely affect children (Amato, 2001; Cummings & Davies, 1994). For example, parents who are embroiled in a relationship that may be described as non-acrimonious, but who are emotionally withdrawn from each other to such an extent that the relationship is devoid of any warmth or affection, may put children as much at risk for long-term emotional and behavioural problems as parents involved in a relationship marked by frequent, intense, poorly resolved, and overtly hostile conflicts.

How parents manage conflict, therefore, may determine children's adjustment to conflict more than the actual occurrence of conflict per se (depending on the level of expressed severity). Indeed, research suggests that the effect of interparental conflict on children depends both upon the manner in which it is expressed, managed, and resolved, as well as the extent to which children feel at fault for or threatened by their parents' relationship arguments (Grych, Harold & Miles, 2003). Furthermore, distinguishing between constructive and destructive conflict management styles may further explain why differences exist in children's adaptive and maladaptive responses to interparental conflict. Destructive conflict behaviours such as violence (Holden & Ritchie, 1991), aggression (Jouriles, Norwood, McDonald, Vincent & Mahoney, 1996), non-verbal conflict or "the silent treatment" (Cummings, Ballard, El-Sheikh & Lake, 1991), and conflicts about child-related matters (Grych & Fincham, 1993) are linked with increased distress or risk for psychological adjustment problems in children. By contrast, constructive conflict expression and management such as mutually respectful, emotionally modulated conflicts (Easterbrooks, Cummings & Emde, 1994), conflict resolutions, and explanations of unresolved conflicts (Cummings, Ballard, El-Sheikh & Lake, 1991) are linked with a lowered risk for child distress and an increased potential for improved social competence and general well-being among children. Resolution of conflict, in particular, has been shown to be a powerful factor in reducing the negative effects of conflict on children. For example, in a study reported by Cummings, Ballard, El-Sheikh, and Lake (1991), children exposed to a condition of unresolved conflict (continued fighting, silent treatment, etc.) responded more negatively than children exposed to partially resolved conflicts (changing topic or submission) who, in turn, responded more negatively than children exposed to resolved conflicts (apology, compromise). This finding emphasises the importance of conflict management and the promotion of positive conflict management strategies at the level of the inter-parental relationship in intervention studies aimed at remediating the adverse effects of family conflict on children (e.g., parental separation and divorce).

Implications of research for intervention programme development

Research findings derived from the literature on interparental conflict and child adjustment provide valuable insight into the effects of family conflict on children that go beyond simply describing what happens when children are exposed to discordant relations between parents, to highlighting the familial and individual processes through which children are adversely affected. While most currently available interventions recognise the importance of the couple relationship as a source of influence on the parent–child relationship, few presently incorporate consideration of the couple relationship as a direct source of influence on children, with fewer still acknowledging the importance of the child's perspective in explaining the impact of conflict between parents on their well-being. Interventions targeting the effects of family stress on children (e.g., family economic pressure, negative parenting, poor parent mental health, parental separation-divorce, domestic violence) therefore need to be revised in light of this evidence base and a debate commenced concerning how best to translate such research findings into policies and practices aimed at easing family stress effects on children—both for the benefit of the present generation of children living in households where interparental conflict is a common feature and the next generation of families that these individuals comprise. As Cowan and Cowan (2002) outline:

> The time has come to design family-based intervention studies that go beyond the simple question of "Does the intervention work?" or the more complex question "What kind of intervention works for particular people or families, under what specified conditions?". We join a growing chorus that advocates the use of theory and existing research to focus on specific intervention targets within the family (e.g., emotion regulation in marital and parent–child relationships) and the inclusion of measures to test whether change in the hypothesized mediator accounts for variation in intervention outcome. This strategy will have two important payoffs: it will contribute to a more differentiated understanding of how family factors affect children's and adolescents' development and it will help to guide clinicians in the design of more effective preventive and therapeutic interventions. (pp. 753–754)

Relevance of research for practice and policy in the UK

As the research reviewed in this chapter suggests, children living in households marked by hostile interparental relations are recognised as being at risk for a variety of adverse psychological outcomes, ranging from low level distress to severe emotional and behavioural problems. The relevance of research pertaining to interparental conflict effects on children has taken on greater significance in the area of child protection and family justice in the UK in light of recent legislative changes (Adoption and Children Act 2002). As such, the definition of significant harm emanating from exposure to conflict and violence between parents has been extended to include "impairment suffered from seeing or hearing the ill treatment of another". While it has been long recognised that discord and conflict between couples is damaging to children, particularly when children are caught up in the adversarial contexts of parental separation and divorce, little real attention has been paid to the effects that conflict between parents causes some children, with even less attention paid to the facilitation of service provision for children who evidence significant psychological impacts (Rivett, Howarth & Harold, 2006).

The review of research presented in this chapter provides an evidence base aimed at remedying this dearth of information, and associated application to practice and policy contexts, in two primary respects. First, by examining processes that underlie individual differences in children's adaptation to hostile interparental relations, evidence is advanced beyond simply noting that interparental conflict is a risk factor for children's psychological development to highlighting what it is that explains resilience to risk (i.e., psychological distress) for some children when compared to others. The value of findings derived from this evidence-based review lie in the contribution to identifying the type and nature of support required for children and parents in the midst of interparental conflict (e.g., parental separation-divorce), thereby allowing service provision to be geared to the particular needs and circumstances of both children and parents.

Incorporating evidence provided throughout this chapter in pertinent policy and practice decision making has the potential to realign thinking in the area of family justice, for example, regarding parental disputes and child welfare away from the present legal focus and mindset towards a more mental health oriented approach (Douglas, Murch & Perry, 1996). Second, by highlighting the mechanisms *through which* interparental conflict affects children's mental health, attention and resource allocation may be directed not only to those children who may benefit from service provision, but also to identifying what particular types of intervention and support may actually benefit those children most in need of support. At present, support for children and parents who are involved in the family justice system in England and Wales is limited. While the Child and Family Court Advisory and Support Service (CAFCASS) in England and Wales has the responsibility to screen applications for orders relating to children and to work with the family throughout the proceedings, the nature of its involvement is facilitative (promoting a settlement of the dispute) or investigative (leading to a report for the court), rather than aimed specifically at capitalising on evidence-based research that would allow identification of those actually at risk from interparental conflict as well as best practice in alleviating adverse effects.

As far as support for a child is concerned, it is unclear whether a court could order that a child receive any kind of therapeutic support to promote child psychological well-being as part of its resolution of a Children Act dispute. The only way in which this might be done is by attaching a condition to a residence or contact order under section 11 (7) of the Act, but there is no judicial authority for using this power for such a purpose. Using the findings from the programme of research described in the present chapter, however, it would be possible to map responses and interventions on to a much broader front. This could have two dimensions—one focused on the family justice system and the other as a general social support mechanism. Initially, CAFCASS officers could utilise information derived from the evidence base described here as part of their assessment procedures in order to identify the children and parents who need particular forms of support as part of either their initial work with a family in response to an application for a Children Act order, or at the point when a parent seeking a divorce files an s. 41 statement of arrangements (as proposed by Murch et al., 1999). This would fit well within the proposed private law pathway model which CAFCASS has been seeking to implement. Within Wales, CAFCASS Cymru have commissioned the development of the Child and Adolescent Welfare Assessment Checklist (CC-CAWAC; Harold, 2009; Pinnell & Harold, 2008), a comprehensive assessment pack for practitioners working with children and families aimed at allowing assessment of the psychological impacts on children and adolescents who have witnessed or who are witnessing interparental conflict and domestic violence. An adaptation of this or a similarly focused psychological risk-assessment protocol focusing on children's experiences of interparental and parent–child conflict within the context of parental separation could be adapted for use by CAFCASS in England. What would then be important would be to develop interventions appropriate to the needs of different children and parents as understood from the findings of the assessment and to incorporate these into the facilities offered (or required) by the legal process, thereby enhancing the dissemination of evidence-based practice into these judicial decisions. One would propose that such evidence-led practice guidance would significantly advance current understanding of parental conflict and implications for children more than has hitherto been the case in relation to the legal process (Trinder, Kellett & Swift, 2008). Eventually it might be proposed that these facilities could be made available to the vast majority of families who do not resort to legal proceedings, either by an expansion of CAFCASS's role, or through initiatives of the Department for Children Schools and

Families (DCSF) in England and the Welsh government in Wales, as an aspect of children's services or health provision.

A last word: summary and synopsis of findings and recommendations

The body of research considered in this chapter highlights the significant role that the couple (interparental) relationship plays in promoting positive or negative developmental outcomes for children. Children living in households marked by high levels of interparental conflict and discord are at elevated risk for a variety of negative psychological outcomes including increased anxiety, depression, aggression, conduct problems, lower levels of social competence, reduced academic attainment, and poor physical health related outcomes. Further, the interparental relationship not only serves as a factor directly related to the psychological well-being of children, but serves as an orienting influence on the experiences and expectations children have of other family relationships, including the parent–child relationship. If there is one additional lesson to be taken away from this research review, it is that the perspective of the child should not be neglected in examining and treating the impact of family relationship experiences on children's psychological development. As Serot and Teevan (1961) argued, the essential relationship between children's well-being and their relationship with their parents is that which exists between the children's perception of the parent–child relationship and their psychological adaptation. Research reviewed in this chapter endorses this perspective, highlighting the importance of children's perceptions of parental behaviour as a key determinant of its effects on their development.

Promoting intervention programmes and assessment strategies that focus on the interparental relationship may therefore pay significant dividends in rectifying the negative consequences of family stress, family conflict, and family breakdown on children and parents in the short term, and help prevent the intergenerational transmission of factors that lead to disrupted family relationships and family breakdown in the long term. As Cowan and Cowan (2008) conclude, the time has come to move away from family focused interventions that emphasise parenting level interventions only, to programmes that keep the family as a system in mind. Programmes that enhance couple relationship skills are in keeping with this proposal and have been evidenced to offer significant advantages to children across maritally intact and separated contexts (Cowan, Cowan & Heming, 2005; Pruett, Insabella & Gustafson, 2005). In a noteworthy overview of the impact of social policy relating to interparental conflict, Emery (2001) was optimistic that the cumulative effects of policy initiatives and educational interventions seeking to foster interparental cooperation and discourage conflict could ultimately produce a cultural change in family processes. With this objective in mind, recognising and acting on the processes through which children are affected by family experiences marked by high levels of interparental conflict and discord are necessary steps if we are to realistically address the needs of children at a time of such continued structural change in the landscape of modern family life, both in the UK and internationally.

References

Aarons, G. A., Monn, A. R., Hazen, A. L., Connelly, C. D., Leslie, L. K., Landsverk, J. A., Hough, R. L. & Brown, S. A. (2008). Substance involvement among youths in child welfare: The role of common and unique risk factors. *American Journal of Orthopsychiatry, 78*: 340–349.

Ainsworth, M. D. S., Blehar, M., Waters, E. & Wall, S. (1978). *Patterns of Attachment: Psychological Studies of the Strange Situation.* Hillsdale, NJ: Lawrence Erlbaum.

Amato, P. R. (2001). Children of divorce in the 1990s: An update of the Amato and

Arend, R., Grove, F. L. & Sroufe, L. A. (1979). Continuity of individual adaptation from infancy to kindergarten: A predictive study of ego-resiliency and curiosity in preschoolers. *Child Development, 50*: 950–959.

Bakermans-Kranenburg, M. J., van IJzendoorn, M. H. & Juffer, F. (2003). Less is more: Meta-analyses of sensitivity and attachment interventions in early childhood. *Psychological Bulletin, 129*: 195–215.

Bates, J. E., Pettit, G. S., Dodge, K. A. & Ridge, B. (1998). Interaction of temperamental resistance to control and restrictive parenting in the development of externalizing behavior. *Developmental Psychology, 34*: 982–995.

Belsky, J. (1999). Quantity of nonmaternal care and boys' problem behavior/adjustment at ages 3 and 5: Exploring the mediating role of parenting. *Psychiatry: Interpersonal & Biological Processes, 62*: 1–20.

Bowlby, J. (1969). *Attachment and Loss: Vol.1. Attachment.* New York: Basic.

Bowlby, J. (1982). *Attachment and loss: Vol. 1. Attachment* (2nd edn.). New York: Basic.

Bretherton, I. & Waters, E. (Eds.) (1985). Growing points of attachment theory and research. *Monographs for the Society for Research in Child Development*, *50* (1–2, Serial No. 209): 3–35.

Capaldi, D. M. (1992). The co-occurrence of conduct problems and depressive symptoms in early adolescent boys: II. A 2-year follow-up at grade 8. *Development and Psychopathology*, *4*: 125–144.

Capaldi, D. M. & Patterson, G. R. (1991). Relation of parental transitions to boys' adjustment problems: I. A linear hypothesis. II. Mothers at risk for transitions and unskilled parenting. *Developmental Psychology*, *27*: 489–504.

Cohn, D. A. (1990). Child–mother attachment of 6-year-olds and social competence at school. *Child Development*, *61*: 152–162.

Conger, R. D., Ge, X., Elder, G. H., Lorenz, F. O. & Simons, R. L. (1994). Economic stress, coercive family process and developmental problems of early adolescents. *Child Development*, *65*: 541–561.

Cowan, C. P., Cowan, P. A. & Heming, G. (2005). Two variations of a preventive intervention for couples: Effects on parents and children curing the transition to school. In: P. A. Cowan, C. P. Cowan, J. C. Ablow, V. K. Johnson & J. R. Measelle, (Eds.), *The Family Context of Parenting in Children's Adaptation to Elementary School*. Monographs in Parenting Series (pp. 277–312). Mahwah, NJ: Lawrence Erlbaum.

Cowan, P. A. & Cowan, C. P. (2002). Interventions as tests of family systems theories: Marital and family relationships in children's development and psychopathology. *Development and Psychopathology*, *14*: 731–759.

Cowan, P. A. & Cowan, C. P. (2008). Diverging family policies to promote children's well-being in the UK and US: Some relevant data from family research and intervention studies. *Journal of Children's Services*, *3*: 4–16.

Crittenden, P. (1995). *The Preschool Assessment of Attachment: Coding Manual*. Miami, FL: Family Relations Institute.

Cummings, E. M. & Davies, P. T. (1994). *Children and Marital Conflict: The Impact of Family Dispute and Resolution*. Guilford Series on Social and Emotional Development. New York: Guilford.

Cummings, E. M. & Davies, P. T. (2002). Effects of marital conflict on children: Recent advances and emerging themes in process-oriented research. *Journal of Child Psychology and Psychiatry*, *43*: 31–63.

Cummings, E. M. & Davies, P. T. (2010). *Marital Conflict and Children: An Emotional Security Perspective*. New York: Guilford.

Cummings, E. M., Ballard, M., El-Sheikh, M. & Lake, M. (1991). Resolution and children's responses to interadult anger. *Developmental Psychology*, *27*: 462–470.

Cyr, C., Euer, E. M., Bakermans-Kranenburg, M. J. & Van IJzendoorn, M. H. (2010). Attachment security and disorganization in maltreating and high-risk families: A series of meta-analyses. *Development and Psychopathology, 22*: 87–108.

Davies, P. T. & Cummings, E. M. (1994). Marital conflict and child adjustment: An emotional security hypothesis. *Psychological Bulletin, 116*: 387–411.

Davies, P. T. & Cummings, E. M. (1998). Exploring children's emotional security as a mediator of the link between marital relations and child adjustment. *Child Development, 69*: 124–139.

Davies, P. T., Harold, G. T., Goeke-Morey, M. C. & Cummings, E. M. (2003). *Monographs of the Society for Research in Child Development, Serial 270, 67*: 41–62.

Department for Children Schools and Families (DCSF) (2002). *The Adoption & Children Act* (s. 120). London: HMSO.

Department for Children Schools and Families (DCSF) (2008). *The Children's Plan: One Year On.* London: HMSO.

Department for Children Schools and Families (DCSF) (2010). *Support for All: The Families and Relationships Green Paper.* London: HMSO.

Department for Education and Skills (DfES) (2007a). *Every Parent Matters.* London: HMSO.

Department for Education and Skills (DfES) (2007b). *Every Parent Matters.* London: HMSO.

Douglas, G., Murch, M. & Perry, A. (1996). Supporting children when parents separate: A neglected family justice or mental health issue? *Journal of Child Family Quarterly Law, 8*(2): 121–135.

Downey, G. & Coyne, J. C. (1990). Children of depressed parents: An integrative review. *Psychological Bulletin, 108*: 50–76.

Dozier, M., Lindhiem, O., Lewis, E., Bick, J., Bernard, K. & Peloso, E. (2009). Effects of a foster parent training program on young children's attachment behaviors: Preliminary evidence from a randomized clinical trial. *Child & Adolescent Social Work Journal, 26*: 321–332.

Dunn, J., Plomin, R. & Daniels, D. (1986). Consistency and change in mothers' behavior towards young siblings. *Child Development, 57*: 348–356.

Easterbrooks, M. A., Cummings, E. M., Emde, R. N. (1994). Young children's responses to constructive marital disputes. *Journal of Family Psychology, 8*: 160–169.

Eddy, J. M. & Chamberlain, P. (2000). Family management and deviant peer association as mediators of the impact of treatment condition on youth antisocial behaviour. *Journal of Consulting and Clinical Psychology, 68*: 857–863.

Emery, R. E. (1982). Inter-parental conflict and the children of discord and divorce. *Psychological Bulletin, 92*: 310–330.

Emery, R. E. (2001). Interparental conflict and social policy. In: J. H. Grych & F. D. Fincham (Eds.), *Interparental Conflict and Child Development: Theory, Research, and Applications* (pp. 417–439). New York: Cambridge University Press.

Erel, O. & Burman, B. (1995). Interrelatedness of marital relations and parent–child relations: A meta-analytic review. *Psychological Bulletin, 118*: 108–132.

Fagot, B. & Pears, K. C. (1996). Changes in attachment during the third year: Consequences and predictions. *Development & Psychopathology, 8*: 325–344.

Fearon, R. P., Bakermans-Kranenburg, M. J., Van IJzendoorn, M. H., Lapsley, A. & Roisman, G. I. (2010). The significance of insecure attachment and disorganization in the development of children's externalizing behaviour: A meta-analytic study. *Child Development, 81*: 435–456.

Fisher, P. A. & Kim, H. K. (2007). Intervention effects on foster preschoolers' attachment-related behaviours from a randomized trial. *Prevention Science, 8*: 161–170.

Fishman, E. A. & Meyers, S. A. (2000). Marital satisfaction and child adjustment: Direct and mediated pathways. *Contemporary Family Therapy: An International Journal, 22*: 437–452.

Ge, X., Conger, R. D., Cadoret, R. J., Neiderhiser, J. M., Yates, W., Troughton, E. & Stewart, M. A. (1996). The developmental interface between nature and nurture: A mutual influence model of child antisocial behaviour and parent behaviours. *Developmental Psychology, 32*: 574–589.

Gilliom, M. & Shaw, D. S. (2004). Co-development of externalizing and internalizing problems in early childhood. *Development and Psychopathology, 16*: 313–334.

Gonzales, N. A., Pitts, S. C., Hill, N. E. & Roosa, M. W. (2000). A mediational model of the impact of interparental conflict on child adjustment in a multiethnic, low-income sample. *Journal of Family Psychology, 14*: 365–379.

Goodman, A. & Greaves, E. (2010). *Cohabitation, Marriage and Child Outcomes*. London: Institute for Fiscal Studies. Available at http://www.ifs.org.uk/projects/318 (accessed 5 January 2011).

Grych, J. H. & Fincham, F. D. (1990). Marital conflict and children's adjustment: A cognitive-contextual framework. *Psychological Bulletin, 108*: 267–290.

Grych, J. H. & Fincham, F. D. (1993). Children's appraisals of marital conflict: Initial investigations of the cognitive-contextual framework. *Child Development, 64*: 215–230.

Grych, J. H., Fincham, F. D., Jouriles, E. N. & McDonald, R. (2000). Interparental conflict and child adjustment: Testing the mediational roles of appraisals in the cognitive-contextual framework. *Child Development*, *71*: 1648–1661.

Grych, J. H., Harold, G. T. & Miles, C. J. (2003). A prospective investigation of appraisals as mediators of the link between inter-parental conflict and child adjustment. *Child Development*, *74*: 1176–1193.

Grych, J. H., Raynor, S. R. & Fosco, G. M. (2004). Family processes that shape the impact of inter-parental conflict on adolescents. *Development and Psychopathology*, *16*: 649–665.

Harold, G. T. (2009). The CAFCASS Cymru Child and Adolescent Welfare Assessment Checklist (CC-CAWAC). Children and Family Advisory Support Service Wales (CAFCASS Cymru), Welsh Government (UK).

Harold, G. T. & Conger, R. D. (1997). Marital conflict and adolescent distress: The role of adolescent awareness. *Child Development*, *68*: 330–350.

Harold, G. T. & Murch, M. A. (2005). Interparental conflict and children's adaptation to separation and divorce: Implications for family law. *Child and Family Quarterly*, *17*: 185–205.

Harold, G. T., Aitken, J. & Shelton, K. H. (2007). Inter-parental conflict and children's academic attainment: A longitudinal analysis. *Journal of Child Psychology and Psychiatry*, 48(12): 1223–1232.

Harold, G. T., Fincham, F. D., Osborne, L. N. & Conger, R. D. (1997). Mom and Dad are at it again: Adolescent perceptions of marital conflict and adolescent psychological distress. *Developmental Psychology*, *33*: 333–350.

Harold, G. T., Pryor, J. & Reynolds, J. (2001). *Not in Front of the Children? How Conflict between Parents Affects Children*. London: One-Plus-One Marriage and Partnership Research.

Harold, G. T., Shelton, K. H., Goeke-Morey, M. C. & Cummings, E. M. (2002). Relations between interparental conflict, child emotional security, and adjustment in the context of cognitive appraisals. In: Davies, P. T., Harold, G. T., Goeke-Morey, M. C. & Cummings, E. M., *Monographs of the Society for Research in Child Development, Serial 270*, *67*: 41–62.

Harold, G. T., Shelton, K. H., Goeke-Morey, M. C. & Cummings, E. M. (2004). Marital conflict, child emotional security about family relationships and child adjustment. *Social Development*, *13*: 350–376.

Hetherington, E. M., Bridges, M. & Insabella, G. M. (1998). What matters? What does not? Five perspectives on the association between marital transitions and children's adjustment. *American Psychologist*, *53*: 167–184.

Holden, G. W. & Ritchie, K. L. (1991). Linking extreme marital discord, child rearing, and child behaviour problems: Evidence from battered women. *Child Development, 62*: 311–327.

Howes, C. (1991). A comparison of preschool behaviours with peers when children enroll in child-care as infants or older children. *Journal of Reproductive & Infant Psychology, 9*: 105–115.

Jouriles, E. N., Norwood, W. D., McDonald, R., Vincent, J. P. & Mahoney, A. (1996). Physical violence and other forms of marital aggression: Links with children's behaviour problems. *Journal of Family Psychology, 10*: 223–234.

Kagan, J. (1999). The role of parents in children's psychological development. *Pediatrics, 104*: 164–167.

Kalinauskiene, L., Cekuoliene, D., Van IJzendoorn, M. H., Bakermans-Kranenburg, M. J., Juffer, F. & Kusakovskaja, I. (2009). Supporting insensitive mothers: The Vilnius randomized control trial of video-feedback intervention to promote maternal sensitivity and infant attachment security. *Child Care, Health & Development, 35*: 613–623.

Keiley, M. K., Lofthouse, N., Bates, J. E., Dodge, K. A. & Pettit, G. S. (2003). Differential risks of covarying and pure components in mother and teacher reports of externalizing and internalizing behaviour across ages 5 to 14. *Journal of Abnormal Child Psychology, 31*: 267–283.

Kcrig, P. (1998). Moderators and mediators of the effects of interparental conflict on children's adjustment. *Journal of Abnormal Child Psychology, 26*: 199–212.

Kerns, K. A. (1994). A longitudinal examination of links between mother-child attachment and children's friendships in early childhood. *Journal of Social and Personal Psychology, 11*: 379–381.

Kim, J. & Cichetti, D. (2010). Longitudinal pathways linking child maltreatment, emotion regulation, peer relations, and psychopathology. *Journal of Child Psychology and Psychiatry, 51*: 706–716.

LaFreniere, P. J. & Sroufe, L. A. (1985). Profiles of peer competence in the preschool: Interrelations between measures, influence of social ecology, and relation to attachment history. *Developmental Psychology, 21*: 56–69.

Lengua, L. J., Wolchik, S. A., Sandler, I. N. & West, S. G. (2000). The additive and interactive effects of parenting and temperament in predicting problems of children of divorce. *Journal of Clinical Child Psychology, 29*: 232–244.

Leve, L. D., Kim, H. & Pears, K. C. (2005). Childhood temperament and family environment as predictors of internalizing and externalizing trajectories from age 5 to age 17. *Journal of Abnormal Child Psychology, 33*: 505–520.

Martinez, C. R. Jr. & Forgatch, M. S. (2001). Preventing problems with boys' noncompliance: Effects of a parent training intervention for divorcing mothers. *Journal of Consulting and Clinical Psychology*, 69: 416–428.

Murch, M. G., Douglas, L., Scanlan, L., Perry, A., Lisles, C., Bader, K. & Borkowski, M. (1999). *Safeguarding Children's Welfare in Uncontentious Divorce: A Study of S. 41 of the Matrimonial Causes Act 1973: Research Series 7/99, Lord Chancellor's Department*. Cardiff, UK: Cardiff University.

National Institute of Child Health and Human Development, Early Child Care Research Network. (2001). Child-care and family predictors of pre-school attachment and stability from infancy. *Developmental Psychology*, 37: 847–862.

Office for National Statistics (2006). Divorces: 1957–2003, Couples, and Children of Divorced Couples, Numbers, Age of Child. London: Office for National Statistics. Available at http://www.statistics.gov.uk/STATBASE/xsdataset.asp?vlnk=7079 (accessed 5 January 2011).

Office for National Statistics (2008a). The proportion of marriages ending in divorce. *Population Trends*, 131: 28–36.

Office for National Statistics (2008b). *Divorce Rate Lowest for 26 Years*. London: Office for National Statistics. Available at http://www.statistics.gov.uk/pdfdir/div0808.pdf (accessed 5 January 2011).

Office for National Statistics. (2009). *Marriage Rates Fall to Lowest on Record*. London: Office for National Statistics. Available at http://www.statistics.gov.uk/pdfdir/marr0209.pdf (accessed 5 January 2011).

Park, K. A. & Waters, E. (1989). Security of attachment and preschool friendships. *Child Development*, 60: 1076–1081.

Patterson, G. R. (1982). *Coercive Family Process: A Social Learning Approach*. Eugene, OR: Castalia.

Patterson, G. R., Reid, J. B. & Dishion, T. J. (1992). *A Social Learning Approach: IV. Antisocial Boys*. Eugene, OR: Castalia.

Pett, M. A., Wampold, B. E., Turner, C. W. & Vaughan-Cole, B. (1999). Paths of influence of divorce on preschool children's psychosocial adjustment. *Journal of Family Psychology*, 13: 145–164.

Pinnell, M., Harold, G. T. (2008). Inter-parental conflict and psychological impacts on children: The development of a CAFCASS Cymru risk assessment toolkit as an example of research into practice. *Seen and Heard*, 18: 21–28.

Pruett, M., K., Insabella, G. M. & Gustafson, K. (2005). The Collaborative Divorce Project: A court-based intervention for separating parents with young children. *Family Court Review*, 43: 38–51.

Pryor, J. & Rogers, B. (2001). *Children in Changing Families: Life After Parental Separation*. Oxford: Blackwell.

Reid, J. B., Patterson, G. R. & Snyder J. (Eds.) (2002). *Antisocial Behaviour in Children and Adolescents: A Developmental Analysis and Model for Intervention.* Washington, DC: American Psychological Association.

Reiss, D., Neiderhiser, J., Hetherington, E. M. & Plomin, R. (2000). *The Relationship Code: Deciphering Genetic and Social Patterns in Adolescent Development.* Cambridge, MA: Harvard University Press.

Rhoades, K. A. (2008). Children's responses to interparental conflict: A meta-analysis of their associations with child adjustment. *Child Development, 79:* 1942–1956.

Rivett, M., Howarth, E. & Harold, G. (2006). Watching from the stairs: Towards an evidence based practice in work with child witnesses of domestic violence. *Clinical Child Psychology and Psychiatry, 11:* 103–125.

Rutter, M. (2000). Resilience reconsidered: Conceptual considerations, empirical findings, and policy implications. In: J. P. Shonkoff & S. J. Meisels (Eds.), *Handbook of Early Childhood Intervention* (2nd *edn.)* (pp. 651–682). New York: Cambridge University Press.

Rutter, M. (2006). Implications of resilience concepts for scientific understanding. In: B. M. Lester, A. Masten & B. McEwen (Eds), *Resilience in Children. Annals of the New York Academy of Sciences* (pp. 1–12). Malden, MA: Blackwell.

Rutter, M., Belsky, J., Brown, G., Dunn, J., D'Onofrio, B., Eekelaar, J., Ermisch, J., Moffitt, T., Gardner, F., Weale, A. & Witherspoon, S. (2010). *Social Science and Family Policies.* London: The British Academy Policy Centre.

Scaramella, L. V. & Leve, L. D. (2004). Clarifying parent–child reciprocities during early childhood: The early childhood coercion model. *Clinical Child and Family Psychology Review, 7:* 89–107.

Serot, N. M. & Teevan, R. C. (1961). Perception of the parent–child relationship and its relation to child adjustment. *Child Development, 32:* 373–378.

Shaw, D. S., Keenan, K., Vondra, J. I., Delliquadri, E. & Giovannelli, J. (1997). Antecedents of preschool children's internalizing problems: A longitudinal study of low-income families. *Journal of the American Academy of Child and Adolescent Psychiatry, 36:* 1760–1767.

Shulman, S. B., Elicker, J. & Sroufe, L. A. (1994). Stages of friendship growth in preadolescence as related to attachment history. *Journal of Social & Personal Psychology, 11:* 341–361.

Simons, R. L., Chao, W., Conger, R. D. & Elder, G. H. (2001). Quality of parenting as mediator of the effect of childhood defiance on adolescent friendship choices and delinquency: A growth curve analysis. *Journal of Marriage and the Family, 63:* 63–79.

Svanberg, P. O., Mennet, L. & Spieker, S. (2010). Promoting a secure attachment: A primary prevention practice model. *Clinical Child Psychology and Psychiatry, 15*: 363–378.

Towle, C. (1931). The evaluation and management of marital status in foster homes. *American Journal of Orthopsychiatry, 1*: 271–284.

Trinder, L., Kellett, J. & Swift, L. (2008). The relationship between contact and child adjustment in high conflict cases after divorce or separation. *Child Adolescence and Mental Health, 13*: 181–187.

Waters, E. & Cummings, E. M. (2000). A secure base from which to explore close relationships. *Child Development, 71*: 164–172.

Waters, E., Wippman, J. & Sroufe, L. A. (1979). Attachment, positive affect, and competence in the peer group: Two studies in construct validation. *Child Development, 50*: 821–829.

Youngblade, L. M. & Belsky, J. (1992). Parent–child antecedents of 5-year-olds' close friendships: A longitudinal analysis. *Developmental Psychology, 28*: 700–713.

COMMENTARY ON CHAPTER TWO

Susanna Abse

A commonly held belief, supported by therapists' experience, theories of psychopathology, and systematic research, is that without intervention, troubling or negative intergenerational patterns will be repeated in the next generation. Couple relationships play a central role in maintaining or breaking intergenerational cycles. Furthermore, preventive interventions focused on strengthening the couple relationships of parents of young children have the potential to affect the parents' relationship quality and their children's social, emotional, and academic development. (Carolyn Pape Cowan and Philip A. Cowan, 2005)

Developing a dialogue across different languages is never an easy task, especially if like me you are a monoglot. Nevertheless, a passionate shared concern is often enough to make people learn a new language, and in the case of the relationship between Professor Gordon Harold and the Tavistock Centre for Couple Relationships (hereafter referred to as TCCR), this indeed has been the case. In my response to Harold and Leve's chapter, I will attempt to make a bridge between their world of developmental psychology and TCCR's psychoanalytic approach.

Harold and Leve carefully and comprehensively address how and why conflicted and cold parental relationships impact on children. Children are not all the same and react to the negative impact of unhappy parents in different ways. Some withdraw from family life, retreating to cold bedrooms and computer games, while others never leave the scene, watching vigilantly for trouble and intervening by being naughty or super helpful in an attempt to divert parents from their ongoing war. Harold and Leve detail the arduous scientific psychological research that shows the evidence for this. Having practised for twenty years, I find that the qualitative evidence I have gathered in the consulting room largely confirms the findings of these research studies.

Harold and Leve's chapter helpfully provides answers to important questions about children's outcomes in relation to the couple, but there are many questions that remain. What accounts for some children being more resilient than others to difficult experiences of parenting? Harold and Leve address this question, outlining the field of resilience research which focuses on understanding protective factors which may explain differences in children's responses to adverse life events. In my response I will attempt to describe some of the theoretical developments that I think relate to these questions. I will also describe how these conclusions have led us at TCCR to develop a new intervention, just as Harold and Leve indicate the need for, at the end of their chapter.

The couple relationship is the crucible where things can go very wrong but it is also the crucible within which negative intergenerational patterns can be broken, through the healing influence of a developmental partnership. All the therapeutic interventions at the TCCR, some specifically targeted at young families, aim to strengthen the couple relationship and thereby improve children's social, emotional, and academic development.

Concern for children's well-being continues to be high up on the policy agenda, and policy makers in central government on both sides of the House seem to have begun to digest the evidence that Harold and Leve outline. A wider recognition of the importance of couple relationships to children's outcomes is now underway (DCSF, 2010), but there is a long and rough road ahead. While the children's workforce now agrees and understands that parenting does matter, understanding that the interparental relationship is crucial may be a far more difficult message to digest. Reaching a hand into family life is a complex business for governments and attending to the couple relationship can seem like poking that hand into what is felt to be a very private and sensitive area. Experience has taught those of us who are involved in this area of policy that there is considerable resistance to accepting that what we do with our partners might be a matter for public concern. Just as Oedipal prohibitions obscure our capacity to think clearly about our parents' relationship, so have these Oedipal anxieties prevented policy makers and practitioners from really getting to grips with this area of family life.

A foundational theoretical construct at the TCCR is that the experience of our parents' relationship is central to how we function in our own adult partnerships. Whilst it is now universally agreed that childhood experiences of parenting impact on psychological development, psychoanalytic methodology has been interested in detailing these impacts through exploring historically the relational field *between* parent and child. This exploration has led to a key belief within psychoanalysis that the influences are bi-directional. TCCR has extended the idea of this bi-directional parental influence beyond the simple trajectory of parent ↔ child to the more complex idea that the experience of the relationship *between* the parental couple has an enduring and profound influence on an individual's own psychological development. And whilst I shall not elaborate on this point, it is also true that psychoanalytic couple therapists would expect bi-directional influences to prevail here too, with children affecting the couple relationship in the same way that the couple relationship affects them.

Harold and Leve in detailing these effects show how it is not only the parent's capacity to parent effectively in the midst of marital unhappiness that is the problem but the child's experience of *witnessing* this which impacts on development. In particular, they explain that the child will attempt to make sense of what he or she is observing between their parents and from this, a range of conscious and unconscious beliefs about the cause of this unhappiness are formed. Psychoanalytic practitioners would expect that where they are unconscious, their impact is no less and indeed may be more pervasive and difficult to modify as the child develops and grows. While Harold and Leve focus on the impacts on children, couple therapists at TCCR will be further interested in the longitudinal impacts these beliefs have on the individual's capacity to develop and sustain an adult relationship of their own.

Jenny is the elder of two children. Her parents, Mr and Mrs J had an explosive relationship which would erupt in great tides of ill humour and occasional mutual violence. Jonathan, her younger brother, was asthmatic and would regularly need rushing, breathless to hospital with a life-threatening attack. Jenny, my patient, believed that it was her job to keep everyone safe. From an early age, she adopted behaviour in order to keep the household calm and secure; managing her parents and serving their needs so that the stress and impact of her and her brother did not tip them into angry and frightening exchanges. What emerged in her therapy was her belief that Jonathan's birth had been the end of an idyllic time in the family, and that while Jonathan was the cause of all the problems between her parents, it was Jenny's role to be the family saviour. In this way, she tried to prevent family conflict and so placed herself as the indispensable heroine of the family.

Jenny's childhood experiences led to a marriage where she sacrificed her own needs and wishes in order to maintain an illusion of harmony and peace between her and her husband. This extreme compliance imploded soon after her own children left home and, full of anger and resentment, she ended her marriage.

The way that we *respond* to our parent's relationship is just as important as how that relationship functions and operates, and this response, as we see from Jenny's experience, then shapes how we respond and relate in our own adult partnerships. These "ghosts from the nursery" made Jenny anxious about conflict and led to a mode of relating that was more a response to childhood concerns and fears than a realistic adult response to her husband. Patterns of relating in the couple, therefore, can be clearly linked to the beliefs and attributions about relationships formed in childhood. Morgan (2010) develops the theory of how unconscious beliefs, described by Britton (1998), are created about the nature of relationships and that these form and influence a couple's life together. Morgan explains that "Unconscious phantasies are the stories we create to explain our experiences of relating externally and internally. The explanation provides the best way of managing the event and feeling that you are taking some control …. These phantasies accumulate in our unconscious and affect how we experience reality." While unconscious phantasies can be modified by reality, some remain fixed in the unconscious and take the form of firmly held beliefs.

Where these beliefs dominate the interaction between couples, the capacity for uncertainty, curiosity, and modification of patterns of relating becomes restricted. All these notions build on early psychoanalytic theories of couple interaction (Bannister & Pincus, 1965) and, most importantly, they also link to the attachment literature. This describes how repeated patterns of interaction in childhood become "internal working models" (Bowlby, 1988) within the psyche. These internal working models then operate as templates which we use to pattern our understanding of the world of relationships. The development of a coherent internal working model within the individual is vital for psychological health; without these internal structures, an individual struggles to make sense of a world that seems senseless and chaotic. Internal working models, however, are not the same as beliefs, but rather potential templates and patterns that are taken in through repeated experience and used to structure our understanding about relationships. Beliefs, rather than offering a potential template for understanding, become the "truth" about a person or a relationship. Capacity for uncertainty is lost and the belief then colours and shapes the individual's experience of reality with little room for revision or modification.

Understanding that the quality of the adults' relationship is central to psychological health for children and adults, and knowing too from the research that conflict pertaining to children seemed to be particularly problematic, we began at TCCR to develop a new service to address these concerns. We knew that some couples might find seeking help for their parenting concerns more acceptable than seeking help for their more intimate difficulties. With this in mind, TCCR set up a new service in 2007 called, optimistically, Parenting Together (Hertzmann & Abse, 2009). The parents accessing this fledgling service were those in conflict over their children and seemed particularly upset and emotional, which made us wonder whether a traditional psychoanalytic approach would be efficacious. We also came to realise that many of our referrals were separated parents, who had no desire to spend months exploring the complex web of unconscious preoccupations and beliefs that had caused, and continued to cause, serious difficulties between them.

In working with parents in our new Parenting Together service, our clinical experience and our growing interest in attachment theory led us to wonder about the particular way that difficulties with the children seemed to activate the attachment system. Much of parenting is instinctive and driven by primitive biological impulses. While this is problematic in some ways, it also ensures that humans override natural self-protective or self-centred drives in order to care for highly dependent infants. It does, however, mean that the ways we respond as parents-for example, if our children or our relationship with them is threatened-may be less rational and less considered than in relation to other parts of our life. We noticed that this more primitive, irrational way of responding was common to many of the parents we were treating. Discussions about the children seemed to arouse very strong feelings, with heightened emotions and greater dysregulation, which made thoughtful reflection particularly difficult. Indeed many of these parents reminded us of borderline couples we had treated, and as the referrals stacked up we realised a good proportion of our parents were functioning in this way. As they were preoccupied with their beliefs about past wounds and betrayals and had visceral fears about their children, we increasingly spent our clinical time with angry, hostile parents locked into repetitive cycles of accusation and blame. Given this, my collaborator, Leezah Hertzmann suggested we explore the use of "mentalization based therapy" (Bateman & Fonagy, 2006) as a therapeutic tool to address these parents' concerns.

This approach, developed by Fonagy and collaborators, aims to increase an individual's capacity to regulate emotional states through developing and strengthening the ability to reflect on one's own and others' inner states of mind and feelings. Mentalising is not only the capacity to accurately read one's own or another's inner state of mind and feeling, but also a way of approaching relationships that expects that one's own thinking and feeling may be enlightened, enriched, and changed by learning about the mental states of other people.

This attitude is characterised by:

- An inquiring and respectful stance in relation to other people's mental states
- An awareness of the limits of one's knowledge of others
- Reflecting a view that understanding the feelings of others is important for maintaining healthy and mutually rewarding relationships.

Mentalising involves an expectation that we will hear and take into account other people's perspectives, needs, and feelings and that they will respond in similar ways to our perspectives, needs, and feelings. When we mentalise, we are naturally and spontaneously curious and respectful of the thoughts, feelings, goals, and beliefs that we sense and recognise in ourselves and in other human beings. We approach relationships with the expectation that our mind and their mind may change as a result of the interaction.

Most crucially, the capacity for mentalising helps us to regulate our own emotions. Being able to mentalise allows us to spontaneously and intuitively make sense of our own actions and those of others. It gives us the capacity to question our thoughts and beliefs, to wonder what the other is thinking or believing, and because of this we are less locked into an unchanging set of unconscious beliefs that drive our behaviours in rigid and powerful ways. With this capacity, we can allow for change and we can allow for differences of opinion. We can imagine, for instance, that our version of events might differ from someone else's and indeed we might modify our version in the light of this new information. Because of this, we may get less upset, and less likely to apportion blame or believe we are being wounded or attacked. We will naturally want to try to make sense of things that seem unfair or unjust. We will want to know *why* someone is cross or rejecting. We will see ourselves as having agency in a relationship; not merely victims of others' actions or beliefs.

Being able to operate in this way makes life generally less problematic. Indeed, this capacity seems to have enormous protective qualities and is likely to be a crucial component of "natural resilience" to the challenges of psychosocial stress and adversity. Does this capacity therefore explain the differences in children's responses to their parents' conflict and unhappiness? Can the child's ability to mentalise on their parents' relationship or their parents' relationship breakdown lead to more adaptive ways of dealing with these challenging life experiences? If so, then helping children to develop this capacity is bound to be a key part of addressing the disadvantage that poor parental relationships can inflict on children's development. Indeed, Harold and Leve are specifically pointing to the need for interventions that can modify children's attributions to parental discord, helping children to understand, for instance, that the conflict they are witnessing is not their fault. Our assertion would be that these interventions need to enhance mentalisation in children because this capacity offers protection against adverse life experiences such as parental conflict.

A key aspect of mentalisation is the capacity to grasp mental states. This becomes evident in the second year of life and it continues to be refined over the whole course of our lives. In the process of development, as the nature of mental states is grasped with increasing sophistication, the perception of others' behaviour takes on greater complexity and richness. But how do children develop this capacity? Fonagy and his collaborators describe how a child's understanding of their own psychological experiences is learnt from their parents' understanding of them. Where children are accurately mirrored by a parent, their inner worlds begin to build a coherent picture of their own and others' experiences. If they have a hunger pain in their tummy and they are responded to accurately, they learn the nature of that pain, where it is located, what is its cause and, indeed, how much anxiety to attribute to it. This development is acquired by observing the responses of their carer. If their distress is not accurately mirrored, a coherent understanding of their own experience is not developed, leading to a chaotic and uncontaining internal experience. Nurturing and improving this understanding strengthens a child's ability to control and manage feelings and to express them in more effective, less impulsive ways. For normal development, a child needs to experience a mind that has his/her mind in mind, and is able to reflect his/her feelings and intentions accurately. Given this, children need parents who can reflect and mentalise on their feelings and, given that the relationship between the parents seems to be so crucial for future development, children need parents who can do this mentalising together.

If parents do not mentalise together, children cannot form a representation in their mind of a couple which is positive and constructive and where differences can be negotiated and resolved. Indeed, the representation that the child forms may be an internal working model of a couple where feelings cannot be managed or resolved but rather are acted out destructively. The individual parent's capacity to mentalise is likely to have an enormous impact on their ability to parent together. Without this capacity, parents struggle to establish a co-parenting relationship which is secure, effective, reciprocal, and one where both parents trust the other to parent safely and effectively. Instead, parents become caught up in self-reinforcing and self-perpetuating cycles of non-mentalising coercive interactions which undermine each other's parenting, and in the worst scenario, the relationship the child has with each parent.

Those who mentalise strengthen the capacity for mentalising in those around them. Just as mentalising therapists can foster this capacity in their patients, mentalising parents foster this capacity in their children *and* in their co-parent. And conversely, non-mentalising in one parent dysregulates and increases non-mentalising in the other.

Jane and Tariq had been having considerable difficulties parenting their five-year-old daughter, Millie. They had never lived together but when Jane had become pregnant early in their relationship, they agreed to go ahead with the pregnancy and take shared responsibility for the baby. Things had gone reasonably well for the first five years as the couple collaborated in a friendly and amicable way around their daughter's needs. This was despite both having considerable difficulties of their own. Tariq had a long-term and enduring mental health problem and Jane continued to struggle with her addiction to alcohol. They came into the service following months of angry exchanges about Jane's new boyfriend, who Tariq felt was a dangerous and threatening presence for their daughter.

In our fourth session, both seemed calmer and more thoughtful and they spent the first twenty minutes discussing Millie's new school and Tariq's difficulties around his shift work and how this impacted on the time he could spend with Millie now she was at school full time. Tariq said he would try to pick Millie up at least twice a week but that work was unpredictable at times and he couldn't be sure that he could always get there on time. Jane, responding to this uncertainty and her internal image of an abandoned Millie waiting alone at the school gate, briefly lost her capacity to mentalise and countered by saying that her boyfriend had agreed to pick Millie up on those days anyway so Tariq wasn't needed after all. Quickly the interaction became angry and accusatory as both Tariq and Jane began to blame the other. Jane asserted that Tariq was unreliable and controlling and he responded by saying that she had no judgement about people because she was a mad drunk.

At this point, the therapist intervened by slowing down the interaction and asking the parents to question and reflect on how they had slid into this interchange which did not seem to help them, or more importantly Millie. After a few minutes where the therapist and couple rewound the session back to where they had become upset, Jane was able to identify how upset she had been by Tariq's uncertainty about the pick-up time from school. She described her concerns about Millie being left alone and Tariq was then able to reassure her that if he was going to be late, he would let her and the school know. He also was able to talk about how worried he was that he might let Millie and Jane down and how frightened he was that if he did, she would withdraw his contact with Millie.

When both parents are engaged in conflict—whether overt or silently hostile—their feelings are often running very high, making it hard for them to reflect on their own or anybody else's mental state, including their children's. When parents are engaged in negative, ongoing conflict, particularly when it is child-focused, they are less able to keep their child's mind in mind. The overall aim of the Parenting Together service, or more accurately mentalisation based interparental therapy, is to help both parents foster their capacity to consider their own difficulties in co-parenting, while simultaneously considering their child's experience. An important aspect of this is to be able to differentiate between their child's own feelings and what parents assume or would like to think is in their child's mind. This Parenting Together approach would not have developed if it were not for the groundbreaking work conducted at the Anna Freud Centre by Professors Peter Fonagy and Mary Target, together with the work of Fearon et al. (2006), who devised and developed mentalisation based family therapy—a treatment for whole families.

Parents, whose co-parenting relationship is conflicted, will often hold firm beliefs about their child's feelings for the other parent. For example, where parents are separated, they often say that their child has expressed a wish not to see the other parent. Parents take this as a concrete desire which has to be acted on and may then feel that denying the other parent's access to the child is their way of protecting them. Where these beliefs pertain, mentalisation may be absent with a resulting loss of capacity to explore what the child might mean by expressing this wish and indeed what might be the child's role and wishes in relation to their parents' relationship. Children can have complex wishes and feelings with respect to their parents' relationship and can, at times, split parents so that the alliance is felt to be firmly with them.

Harry and Charlene had been separated for over four years. They had been involved in numerous court appearances which they both seemed rather baffled by. These ongoing battles seemed to have a life of their own with neither taking any responsibility for the very expensive and time consuming processes they were involved in. They were in constant touch with a range of professionals including CAFCASS, social services, and the staff of the contact centre, and their children had been briefly on the child protection register as a result of allegations by Charlene that their four–and-a-half-year-old daughter had said that Daddy had let her kiss his willy. Harry did not see his daughters for more than a year from that point, but extensive investigations and assessments by professionals did not conclude that any abuse had taken place. Eventually Harry was given permission by the courts to see his daughters, but interestingly, because of Charlene's continued beliefs and fears, this was allowed only in the context of a contact centre.

They came into the Parenting Together service at the behest of the judge. At the first session, Charlene brought her brother to the centre to "protect" her from Harry. A confusion ensued at reception as to who were the two parents, but eventually the brother was left downstairs and Harry and Charlene settled into a deeply acrimonious and bitter fight in my consulting room that I found very difficult to contain.

However, after several fruitful individual sessions, Harry and Charlene were able to begin some work together, and I was able to identify a problematic pattern of relating in which Charlene believed fervently that Harry was a threat and a danger to the children. In turn, Harry, driven to distraction by these accusations and the ongoing loss of his children, behaved in a confirming hostile and aggressive manner which pressed home to Charlene that she must do all that was necessary to prevent his access to the children.

In the Parenting Together service at TCCR, we have frequently seen this pattern of relating, where attributions or beliefs about a partner have led to negative and hostile cycles of relating. Charlene's belief that Harry was dangerous led to her preventing him from seeing his children. Harry's experience of this loss activated his attachment system, resulting in a flight/fight mechanism where he would alternate between abandoning and threatening behaviour, confirming for Charlene that he was, as she believed, a very bad lot.

Intervening in this cycle involves the therapists encouraging parents to examine their attributions, feelings, and behaviour. Using a mentalising approach, we slow down the interactions, put them under the microscope and ask parents to pause and reflect on their feelings and beliefs, allowing new thoughts to come into play and old thoughts and beliefs to be questioned. With this case, I suggested that they took time to get to know each other again, to really explore whether their beliefs about each other were realistic. For both parents this meant taking a huge risk, but I encouraged these parents by outlining clearly the negative effects their ongoing war was likely to be having on their two little girls.

> A picture began to emerge which illustrated the intergenerational nature of these difficulties. Indeed, the experience of their own parents' coupling was, it emerged, deeply related to their current difficulties. Harry described how his own parents' marriage had broken down when he was seven. His father had left the family home and had been "encouraged" not to visit his children. His mother married again and this relationship, too, was unhappy and also violent. Harry described how he was often bullied by his stepfather and scapegoated in the family as a troublemaker. As a result he left home at fifteen and joined the army as soon as he could. In the army he found a boundaried and ordered home, but he left at twenty-five as he could no longer bear the feeling of being controlled and ordered about.
>
> Mrs Charlton's parents were still together though she acknowledged that both she and her brother wondered if they would not have been better apart. Towards the end of the therapy she explained that her mother had spent most of her childhood complaining to her about her father and, as a result, to this day she had an aversion to him.

While these patterns of relating were spontaneously described by the parents during the therapy, the work did not focus on delving into these concerns. Rather, the therapists encouraged the parents to explore and question their own thoughts and attributions in the "here and now". Each parent at moments of stress or challenge would lose their capacity to mentalise and tend to revert back to old beliefs, based in part on their negative experiences of each other, but also based on experiences from their own childhood. Over and over again, these beliefs were challenged and questioned as to their relevance in the "here and now" and the parents began to listen to each other respectfully, adjusting their views and behaviour as uncertainty about their own rightness came into play.

In work with parents such as these, and indeed in work with any deeply conflicted couple, the wish is for the therapist to act like judge and jury and determine who is right (Vincent, 1995). In the Parenting Together service we studiously avoid taking up this role and we actively discourage looking back at old wounds and grievances. The intervention is brief, so we ask parents to focus on the "here and now" and whether these old wounds and grievances serve any purpose in relation to their children's present needs and well-being. As the work with Harry and Charlene progressed, they began to really talk about their children and I noticed how pleasurable they found this. Discussion about their daughters' likes and dislikes, strengths and difficulties lit up both their faces and a freshness of speech and attitude came into play that was a world away from their earlier interaction.

Gordon Harold's work on interparental conflict and the work of TCCR's long-term collaborators, Philip and Carolyn Cowan on interventions with parents, has encouraged TCCR to engage with and explore new ways to intervene with unhappy and conflicted parents. Drawing on the research of developmental psychologists, attachment theorists, and psychoanalysts we have begun to advance new ways of working with parents which take into account the complexity of couple relating and the complexity of children's developmental processes. Attempting a creative "marriage" of ideas drawn from these paradigms is challenging, but we believe that the in-depth understanding of the couple relationship that TCCR has developed will be usefully enhanced by new ideas and new research. Understanding that children are deeply affected by their parents' unhappiness is one thing; working out how to respond effectively quite another. And in order to do this, we will continue to gratefully draw on and learn from the work of researchers such as Professor Harold and Dr Leve.

References

Bannister, K. & Pincus, L. (1965). *Shared Phantasy in Marital Problems*. London: Institute of Marital Studies.

Bateman, A. W. & Fonagy, P. (2006). *Mentalization-Based Treatment for Borderline Personality Disorder: a Practical Guide*. Oxford: Oxford University Press.

Bowlby, J. (1988). *A Secure Base: Clinical Application of Attachment Theory.* London: Routledge.

Britton, R. (1998). *Belief and Imagination: Explorations in Psychoanalysis.* London: Routledge.

Cowan, C. P. & Cowan, P. A. (2005). Two central roles for couple relationships: breaking negative intergenerational patterns and enhancing children's adaptation. *Journal of Sexual and Relationship Therapy, 20*(3): 275–288.

Department for Children Schools and Families (DCSF) (2010). *Support for All: The Families and Relationships Green Paper.* London: HMSO.

Fearon, P., Target, M., Sargent, J., Williams, L., McGregor, J., Bleiberg, E. & Fonagy, P. (2006). Short-term mentalization and relational therapy (SMART): an integrative family therapy for children and adolescents. In: J. G. Allen & P. Fonagy (Eds.), *The Handbook of Mentalization-Based Treatment.* Chichester, UK: John Wiley.

Hertzmann, L. & Abse, S. (2009). *Parenting Together. Mentalization Based Inter-parental Therapy—a treatment handbook* [unpublished].

Morgan, M. (2010). Unconscious beliefs about being a couple. *Fort da, 16*(1): 56–63.

Vincent, C. (1995). Consulting to divorcing couples. *Family Law,* December: 678–681.

CHAPTER THREE

How couple therapists work with parenting issues

Mary Morgan

C ouple psychotherapy as it has been developed over the last sixty-three years within the Tavistock Centre for Couple Relationships (TCCR) does not have parenting as its primary focus but the couple relationship itself. This does not mean that couples who come for therapy do not get help with parenting. On the contrary, this comes from developing insight into the couple relationship and helping the couple develop the kind of relationship in which effective parenting can take place.

The TCCR model of couple psychotherapy

The TCCR's inception as the Family Discussion Bureau in 1948 followed growing political concern about the breakdown of marriage and family life in post-war Britain. It has since that time given its attention to understanding the couple relationship and developing a psychoanalytic approach to helping couples in difficulty, knowing that couple relationships are at the heart of family life. None of this has changed, though today we might extend the concept of the couple relationship further to include an internal capacity for couple relating and also acknowledge the many different and complex forms that family life takes in the twenty-first century.

At the beginning the TCCR model started in an exploratory way, using what was already known, described thus in the first publications: "The dynamic theory of behaviour offered by psychoanalysts seemed especially appropriate for marital problems. In recognizing the importance of unconscious forces in mental life, it gave a basis for understanding and dealing with the irrational and emotional elements in personality which often proves so intractable in family tangles" (Bannister et al., 1955; also cited in Ruszczynski, 1993). There was always an atmosphere of exploration and discovery as psychoanalytically informed work with each partner led to an understanding of the couple's unconscious fit and their projective and introjective system. As understanding developed of the interplay between the intrapsychic and the interpersonal, the couple's conscious and unconscious relationship, there was a move towards more joint work (the couple seen together) that provided a unique opportunity to study these processes. This also enabled the "reflection process" (Mattinson, 1975) or "marital countertransference" to be studied to gain a fuller picture of the couple's internal world (Ruszczynski, 1993).

Couple psychoanalytic psychotherapy is distinguished from other forms of couple therapy by its emphasis on developing an understanding of the unconscious aspects of couple interaction and helping couples by making this understanding explicit. In the process of developing and sharing this understanding, attention will be given to those aspects of interaction that bear on a couple's capacity to parent. For couple psychotherapists, parenting issues are addressed within the context of the adult couple relationship manifested in all its conscious and unconscious forms.

The aim of couple psychotherapy

It is difficult to talk about the aim of couple psychotherapy as if this might lead to prescribing what a couple relationship should be. However, it is important to think about what kind or quality of psychological relationship enables a couple to function well, both as a couple and as parents to their children. Warren Colman (1993) has written about marriage as a "psychological container" in which each partner is psychologically contained by the relationship they create. "The relationship itself becomes the container, the creative outcome of the couple's union, to which both partners can relate. It is an image of something the couple are continually in the process of creating, sustaining and maintaining, while at the same time feeling that they exist within it—are contained by it." It is this experience of feeling contained by the relationship that fundamentally supports the couple as parents to their children. James Fisher (1999) has described the move from "narcissism", a state of mind antithetical to being in a relationship, to psychological "marriage", a state of mind shared by both partners who support and care for one another in a reciprocal way. Of course, this is not always sustained even in the strongest partnerships and at times partners may separately or together move into withdrawn and angry states of mind characteristic of the paranoid-schizoid position described by Klein (1946).

At the TCCR's 50th Anniversary Conference in 1998 Stan Ruszczynski and I (in collaboration with Philip Stokoe) presented the idea of the "creative couple", which was subsequently developed in a paper (Morgan, 2005). The creative couple is a concept which locates the adult couple relationship in psychic development and distinguishes it from the couple relationship between mother and baby. It explores what becomes possible in this kind of intimate adult relationship if it is functioning well. In contrast to the primary relationship in which there is an idea (eventually) of "self and other", in the creative couple relationship, it is possible, because of developments that have occurred since, to have the idea of "self, other (my partner), *and* our relationship". The working through of the early Oedipal situation (Figure 1) and the creation of what Britton (1989) describes as a "triangular space" in which we can see ourselves in interaction with others, entertain another point of view, and also retain our own, is one of the important steps in this development. In the creative couple the triangular configuration is now one in which the relationship held in mind by both partners functions as a third position (Britton, 1989) (Figure 2). Each partner can take this third position and observe him or herself interacting with the other, rather than remaining in a place where only his or her own internal states, as impacted on by the other, are experienced.

The relationship also feels to be a potentially creative entity where each partner recognises and builds up experience of the fact that an intercourse between two separate and different people can be creative. The outcome of creative intercourse is not known until it takes place but the couple increasingly gain a sense that it is possible to discover

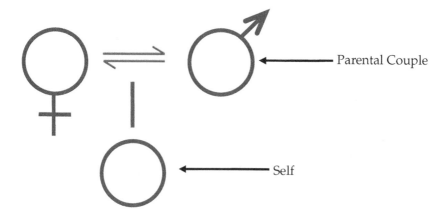

Figure 1. The Oedipal triangle.

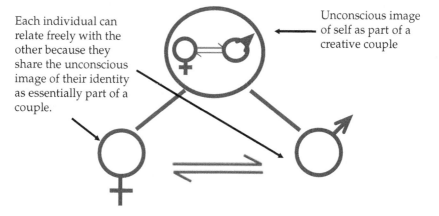

Figure 2. The creative couple.

something new by thinking together. The relationship is then valued as a resource for the two individuals within it. This capacity is fundamentally a state a mind that adults need, both inside themselves and in relation to other people. Being part of a couple might foster this psychological development in the adult or even bring it into being, though being in a couple relationship is not in itself necessary to this development. What is clear, however, is that this capacity is an essential feature of a well functioning relationship.

I think it will be obvious why this kind of development is fundamental to parenting. Parenting requires the acquisition of certain capacities, which are developed partly from past personal experience of being parented but are also drawn from the experience of others as parenting unfolds. Parents learn from a variety of sources—midwives, health visitors, family members, friends in similar circumstances, but especially from each other. However, to be fully able to utilise these kind of resources one has to have a sense inside oneself of relationships being something from which one can get help, in which it is alright not to know or understand, in which it is possible to acknowledge getting things wrong, and in which it is possible to share one's uncertainties in reasonable safety. For those helping parents to develop skills in parenting, such a non-judgemental, creative exchange may be difficult to achieve. The couple therapist looks at how this kind of creative couple relationship can be established, within which parenting can occur. If this is established this does not mean that outside help with parenting will not be sought—from friends, family or professionals, but it does mean that the help can be received and properly thought about.

Taking this developmental view I will describe some areas in which the development of a creative couple relationship has become stalled, the implications of this for parenting, and thoughts about how this might be addressed by the couple therapist.

A parent's need to be parented

One of the most common issues that interfere with the capacity to parent one's children is one's own need to be parented. The adult couple relationship is one of the few other relationships that has the intensity and intimacy of the primary mother–baby relationship. A partner's unmet needs in that early relationship can lead to an attempt to gratify them in the adult relationship. In fact, when one explores the unconscious beliefs of couples coming for help (Morgan, 2010) it is surprising how often they hold these primitive beliefs, e.g., "He is responsible for my unhappiness"; "She should meet all of my needs", just like a young baby might expect from the mother. Such a relationship is unlikely to support the parenting of children.

This kind of relationship is also what one might describe as a two person relationship in which the adult couple, either each partner in relation to each other, or mother or father in interaction with the children, cannot step into a third position and think about what is happening between self and other and how the needs of both partners and the children can be met. Without having a third position it is not so easy to manage the child's needs and demands which may be experienced as an attack on limited resources.

When parents feel so needy themselves there may also be pressure on the children to meet the parents' needs, for love, attention, acceptance, and so on resulting in serious psychological difficulties. These can range from problems for the child in separating from the parent, to being a "parentified child" where the roles of parent and child are inverted, and to breaches of boundaries which can lead to being a confidant to the parent or, in extreme circumstances, to sexual abuse.

In couple psychotherapy the couple can get help to work through and come to terms with these deficits in their own childhood. They can obtain support and containment for themselves to enable them to give more freely to their children. Over time, they also have the possibility of developing a reflective capacity, which runs in parallel with a confidence of being in an enduring relationship. This capacity and confidence, which I have earlier described as a "third position", is internalised by being able to trust in the relationship with the therapist and to identify with the quality of reflective thinking that the therapy encourages. What is so important here is that, integrated into the help the couple get as parents, is some help in understanding and working through the deficits in the parenting each had as children, so that their unmet needs do not completely distort their attempts to parent.

Bill & Emma

Having a child threw Bill and Emma's relationship into a crisis from which it was very difficult to recover. Both of their own mothers had been, in different ways, very ill. Bill's had suffered from a psychotic illness and Emma's from a serious physical illness throughout her early childhood followed by her mother's death when she was seven. Emma longed for a child and the couple committed to being together when they found she had become pregnant. Prior to this, the couple each felt the other met their needs in a very parental way; they were each other's "baby". Once Emma became pregnant she formed an exclusive bond with her actual baby and Bill felt completely pushed out.

The therapy with this couple helped them to work through their earlier losses and challenged their belief that they could get the parenting they needed from each other or, in Emma's case, from their child. Their unconscious attempts to get these needs met in these ways were carefully picked up by the therapist through many examples of incidents occurring in their daily lives, until the couple could become more aware of these themselves. They also benefitted from the experience of the therapist as a "third" who was able to take a position in which their needs as a couple alongside the needs of the baby could be thought about. Through mourning the loss of re-finding a parent in each other, the couple were able to begin to develop a more mature dependency on each other which helped them to be better equipped to attend to the needs of their baby.

Being both a couple and parents

Another common difficulty, coming developmentally later than the one just described, is in being able to be both a couple *and* be parents. Unresolved Oedipal issues may mean that one is left with the unconscious belief that either there is only a parental couple from which one feels excluded, or there is a denial of the parental couple and a belief that the sole relationship is that between parent and child. Sometimes such an internal situation is reinforced by family experience. This can lead to problems so that either the couple find it hard to feel themselves still to be a couple following the birth of the children, or defensively become "so much" a couple because the children are experienced as such a threat. This is a problem for the children both because they are deprived of the warmth and intimacy of the parental couple and because they do not have the benefit of a parental couple who can think about them and manage including and excluding them appropriately.

Susan & Robbie

The therapy with this couple revealed an unconscious belief that there was not room in their relationship for both a couple and children. Robbie had grown up with a mother devoted to him and his brother at the cost of his parents' relationship. When he, as the youngest, married, his mother sunk into a severe depression. Susan grew up knowing her mother adored her father, so that she and her siblings had to tiptoe and fit around her parents' relationship as best they could. When this couple got together they were both desperate for some space and freedom, and although they had passing thoughts about having children, they had never discussed this properly and it remained unexplored and unresolved. At the point of coming for therapy they presented with extremely ambivalent feelings about the wish to start a family, wanting it as much as fearing it. The fact of his early life being overly child centred and hers overly parent centred led to an unconscious belief that there was not room for both a couple and children. Without the therapy, which enabled them to become conscious of their beliefs and thus less driven by them, this couple may have repeated the model of family life which they brought into the relationship—in which children were overly included or excluded.

Being a couple

Another area of difficulty is the move from the stage of adult autonomy, in which there is a feeling of independence, to being able to be in relationship and dependent on another. The dependence described here is that which Fisher describes as "marriage"—"the passion for and dependence on the other", in contrast to "narcissism", "in which there is intolerance of the independent existence of the other" (1999). This kind of dependence is such a different place to be from the helpless dependence of the infant on the mother although anxiety about the recreation of this infantile state may be great. What is different about the creative couple relationship is that the mutual dependence between the couple follows the capacity for *independence* so that instead of a return to a mother–baby relationship there is an intercourse between two adults where the capacity to be separate and different fosters creativity.

Eva & Steven

Eva and Steven came for help because they felt continually let down by each other in ways that made them feel quite despairing about the relationship. The couple were married and had one child, Nina, aged eight. Both parents had busy professional working lives but they were able to provide between them quite a lot of time to look after Nina. They did try to work together as parents—very hard in fact, but this had a very flat uncreative quality. The sessions with them were very busy too with very little time for reflection. Sometimes the therapist felt it was possible to make emotional contact with them and begin to understand their experience and what might be leading to these difficulties, but mainly there was this other feeling of working hard but not getting anywhere. The emotional quality of the therapy captured the feeling between the couple in their daily lives. The therapist experienced them as making very little contact with each other; they were too busy just trying to manage. There was also no sense of there being space for more than one emotional reality so that differences could not be valued or find creative expression.

Nina seemed to be a rather isolated child, with no particular friends at school and could be extremely clingy with Eva. Steven seemed to feel that this was normal, "A child needs her mother", but it was clear that he also felt excluded and blamed Eva for this. The school was concerned that Nina was not achieving her potential and seemed always to be quiet and withdrawn. The therapist had the impression that she was a rather depressed little girl. On the other hand, she could be quite a handful at home, in ways that amounted to her demanding a lot of direct contact from her mother. Steven would occasionally try to intervene, but he felt that nothing he did was ever right, and his sensitivity to that feeling made him quickly give up and withdraw. Eva was also very anxious and very organised and related to Steven rather as a junior work colleague, giving him lists of things that needed doing. He would try his best and never succeed. Unconsciously, his anger at being related to as an appendage to Eva led to a sabotaging of arrangements, which infuriated Eva and led her to become even more controlling.

In one session they were arguing about arranging a first sleepover for Nina with a school friend. Eva was in an anxious and controlling state of mind, as she often could be, and had a whole list of instructions for Steven to hand to the friend's mother. Steven felt this was completely unnecessary and refused. Eva felt angry and despairing with Steven, whom she felt was being so oppositional. They sat in the session in silence, neither able to think.

At this point the couple were very far away from being able to value and make use of their relationship. Neither partner had the belief that engaging with the other would help in understanding what was making them so anxious and how these anxieties might be addressed in an appropriate way. The opposite was the case. Steven felt obliterated by Eva and Eva felt abandoned and made to feel unsafe by Steven.

This is an example of a couple struggling with each other and, consequently, finding it difficult to parent their unfulfilled and, possibly, depressed child. For these two individuals, engaging thoughtfully with each other felt very threatening. They were aware that they needed the other's help but the only way they could conceive of helping one another was by propping each other up, not through having a reciprocal and mutual exchange of valued ideas—an intercourse. As a consequence both seemed to feel like a single parent. Eva felt she was the main parent with an inadequate "nanny/helper" in Steven and he felt like a very inadequate father with a severe and controlling super ego in the form of Eva. While they were stuck in this position there was no conception of the idea that they might be able to help each other, think together, and find ways forward together.

Despite very stuck moments in this session they were able, with help, to see that some of the anxiety that was bouncing between them was Nina's anxiety about separating from Eva which, in turn, was being fuelled by Eva's own anxieties about separating and facing the fact that Nina was growing up and beginning to establish more of her own life. The couple was also helped to see how the idea of Nina growing up and away was unconsciously disturbing their couple equilibrium as if the idea of them functioning happily together without Nina there was impossible to imagine.

In relation to parenting I would suggest that no amount of information they had access to about how to parent, from professionals, friends, or self-help books would be of use to this couple. Eva in fact sought advice from everywhere but responded to it by adding it to her endless lists of what to do, which led to an increased sense of being overwhelmed. For Steven, whose state of mind was one in which he felt inadequate and was always getting things wrong, advice only made him feel worse, confirming his negative view of himself as a parent.

The therapist's approach to this couple was to help them see how deprived they each made themselves of a position where they could think together and thereby provide a truly dynamic container for their daughter. Without this containment they were not enabling Nina to contemplate an experience of being excluded from a clinging relationship to her mother, mourn that loss and work through to a more appropriately autonomous way of relating.

The therapist's understanding of this couple's difficulty came largely from the emotional experience of engaging with them in the course of their therapy. To start with, the experience of the sessions was one in which, although very busy, little came out of any exchange between the couple or between them and the therapist—in other words there was very little creative intercourse. The shift from this arid state with its negative implications for parenting began to occur as the relationship to the therapist developed and strengthened. As Eva began to experience the therapist as someone who might help contain her anxiety and Steven experienced her as less critical, they allowed more mutual emotional contact. The sessions started to feel less arid. It was then possible to help the couple begin to understand their emotional experience and what might be leading to these difficulties. For example, it became possible to understand and think about why Eva had such difficulty relying on another and why Steven felt he had nothing to offer. In addition, it was helpful that the therapist was able to take a reflective or "third position", where she was able to focus on the couple and their relationship and, in doing so, help them value rather than demean their relationship. The sessions came fully alive when not only the therapist, but the couple themselves, were able to find a "third position". They could then, as it were, stand in that place and look at their relationship.

Conclusion: creative parenting

The development towards the creative couple state in which parenting can occur is like all developmental steps in that it involves a loss of previous states of mind. In developmental terms the baby has to relinquish the longed-for primary relationship to the mother and painfully accept the reality of the differentiation of himself from others; what in other terms is described as weaning as an emergent self develops. In later development, the young adult has to give up the much prized position of believing he or she is autonomous and accept what, at that moment, and from that perspective, appears to be a weaker position, of needing someone else. Often the avoidance of a developmental step is linked to a fear of depression: the emotional accompaniment to loss, which is often believed to be a mire in which one can become trapped because there has been no help to work through loss at an earlier stage of development. In this case it seems very significant that "depression" appeared to afflict Nina, particularly when she was away from Eva: it was as if she were demonstrating the unconscious belief that loss leads to becoming stuck in depression.

If childhood development has gone well, forming an adult couple relationship becomes less problematic. It will be challenging, as all developments are, but some of the building blocks will be in place. There is then the discovery of the creative potential of being part of a couple which, as I suggested earlier, is essential to a well functioning relationship. This internal capacity and conviction is important in different circumstances. Parents are not always around together to parent, yet having the awareness of an absent partner's views means that they can be represented during his or her absence. Nor, contrary to popular belief, is it always helpful when they are together that they "join forces" and hold a "united front", although there is a place for this. In other words joining forces does not always mean holding exactly the same view but might mean giving the child an experience that the parents can bring together their different views in a creative tension. Allowing this to happen requires that parents know their relationship can survive and, indeed, flourish on the back of their different opinions and ideas.

What is so important in parenting is that parents have inside themselves a creative couple state of mind, in which it is possible to take into account another perspective, alongside their own, so that an internal dialogue takes place from which new thinking can arise. This is dynamic responsive parenting and, while describing it in this way may make it appear to be a laborious and impossible task, in everyday parenting this way of relating and thinking often takes place in a flash and, often, unconsciously. Moreover, having this capacity does not mean that good parenting always prevails, though with this capacity in place, one knows when it has not. Ignoring one's partner's views, being too internally preoccupied, being temporarily overwhelmed, or caught up in the emotions of others are temporary states, from which it is possible to recover. What is essential to parenting is that one can be aware of these destabilizing experiences and recover from them, towards a more thoughtful, creative couple capacity.

References

Bannister, K., Lyons, A., Pincus, L., Robb, J., Shooter, A. & Stephens, J. (1955). *Social Casework in Marital Problems.* London: Tavistock.

Britton, R. (1989). The missing link: parental sexuality in the Oedipus complex. In: J. Steiner (Ed.), *The Oedipus Complex Today: Clinical Implications.* London: Karnac.

Colman, W. (1993). Marriage as a psychological container. In: S. Ruszczynski (Ed.), *Psychotherapy with Couples: Theory and Practice at the Tavistock Institute of Marital Studies.* London: Karnac.

Fisher, J. (1999). *The Uninvited Guest: Emerging from Narcissism towards Marriage.* London: Karnac.

Klein, M. (1946). Notes on some schizoid mechanisms. *International Journal of Psychoanalysis, 27*: 99–110.

Mattinson, J. (1975). *The Reflection Process in Casework Supervision.* London: The Institute of Marital Studies (republished 1992).

Morgan, M. (2005). On being able to be a couple: the importance of a "creative couple" in psychic life. In: F. Grier (Ed.), *Oedipus and the Couple.* London: Karnac.

Morgan, M. (2010). Unconscious beliefs about being a couple. *fort da, 16*(1): 56–63.

Ruszczynski, S. (Ed.) (1993). *Psychotherapy with Couples: Theory and Practice at the Tavistock Institute of Marital Studies.* London: Karnac.

COMMENTARY ON CHAPTER THREE

Lynne Cudmore

In response to Mary Morgan's paper, "How couple therapists work with parenting issues", I am writing from the perspective and experience of my dual professional identity as a couple psychotherapist and a child and adolescent psychotherapist who works in both generic and specialised child and adolescent mental health services (CAMHS) in the UK National Health Service (NHS). It is perhaps salient to note that, although my training and experience as a couple psychotherapist has been used extensively in the development of couple based interventions with a range of parents, I am employed as a child and adolescent psychotherapist and, as far as I know, there are no couple psychotherapists employed in CAMHS though a number of child psychotherapists are now undergoing further training as couple psychotherapists. This is a welcome development and one that will promote a dialogue and new ways of working for two professional groups who share a psychoanalytic framework but whose focus in work with parents has traditionally been different: the couple relationship remaining central in couple psychotherapy and the parent–child relationship in child psychotherapy.

Before I discuss the contribution of couple psychotherapists to thinking about work with parents, an important dimension of Morgan's paper is the clear description of the psychoanalytic framework within which understanding of the couple/parent relationship at TCCR takes place. The paper's emphasis on the unconscious processes and beliefs that permeate psychic life and family entanglements, the distinction between infantile and adult states of mind, and the worker's use of the countertransference in understanding the interaction between couples locate the contribution of psychoanalytically trained practitioners— child, adult, and couple—within the discourse on parenting. As Rustin (2009) has described, we live in an era where public and governmental preoccupations with parenting are high and where there is an emphasis on the need to educate, provide information, and "skill up" parents. While these interventions can be extremely helpful the approach out- lined in this chapter with its emphasis on listening, receptivity, explora- tion, and the search for meaning is different.

As Morgan describes, couple psychotherapy at TCCR does not have parenting as its primary focus but the couple relationship itself. For many couples seeking help from this specialist service their relation- ship as parents may not be their primary focus either. However, as cou- ple psychotherapists and parents know, it is often the case that when the couple relationship is in difficulties the relationship between them as parents is affected adversely. This often has an impact on the rela- tionship between parents and children and children will be affected in a variety of ways. Parents vary in their degree of concern about this and many of those that are concerned might make their way to a special- ist couple service such as TCCR to work on this boundary crossing. However, infants and children are usually the ticket of entry to CAMHS services but behind their presenting problems their parents' couple dif- ficulties are often revealed.

The relationship between "partnering" and "parenting" has often been referred to as a "missing link". Although policy documents such as *Every Child Matters* (DfES, 2003) and *Every Parent Matters* (DfES, 2007) have highlighted the important part parents play in achieving good outcomes for children, there is little mention in these documents of the significance for children of the partnership between parents. However, in the 2006 (round 2) guidelines for projects supported by the Parenting Fund, support for couple relationships is included as a funding criterion for the first time. As Clulow (2010) has commented, the earlier discon- nection between parenting and partnering at the policy level may have reflected the struggle that many parents have in attending both to their children and to the needs of their relationship as a couple. In this paper, the unconscious beliefs that may underpin this struggle are explored. Working in a CAMHS setting I am also aware that many practitioners fear that attending to the couple's relationship will leave the children "out of mind" and this is often cited as a reason why working with couples is not appropriate in this setting. Work with the couple relationship is not often seen as the province of CAMHS.

The aims of couple therapy as outlined in this chapter are to help the couple develop insight into their relationship and the ways in which they each function within it. Developing the capacity in each partner to think and reflect upon their emotional experience and developing their capacity "to take a step back" and observe their interaction hopefully contributes to the development of the kind of relationship where they can feel supported by each other and where they can think together while respecting their differences. Developing and strengthening these adult capacities promotes their functioning as parents and creates an environment where the emotional and physical needs of their children can be considered.

A central idea in this chapter is the concept of the creative couple (Morgan, 2005) which locates the adult couple relationship in psychic development and distinguishes it from the early couple relationship between mother and baby. It explores what becomes possible in this kind of intimate adult relationship if it is functioning well. In contrast to the primary relationship in which there is an idea of self and other, in the creative couple relationship it is possible to have the idea of me, the other (my partner), and *our* relationship. The relationship held in mind by both partners functions as a "third position", and a place from where each partner can observe him or herself interacting with the other in the relationship. The relationship is experienced as a potentially creative entity where each partner recognises and builds up experience of the fact that an intercourse between two separate and different people can be creative. Morgan sees this kind of development as fundamental to effective parenting, the bedrock for a creative relationship between parents.

How might child and adolescent mental health services incorporate this important dimension of the couple relationship in their work with parents? Within these services there is a broad church of professionals from different theoretical backgrounds, offering a range of short- and long-term interventions carried out in clinical and outreach settings that come under the umbrella "work with parents". For example, parents are seen when their children are in individual therapy in order to give the therapist a sense of the child's development in the family and at school, as well as to give the parents an opportunity to enquire about their child's progress in the therapy (Rustin, 1998, 2009). Work with parents of late adopted or fostered children who have often had a traumatic start in life and who present their parents with many complex problems is another growing area of work. Parental couples are likely to be seen in both these contexts and attention will fall on each parent's relationship with the child and the impact on them as a parental couple of their child's difficulties, but the couple's relationship will not be the "patient". However, other parents, individually or as a couple may be seen more with the aim of exploring ways in which their parental functioning is disturbed by unconscious aspects of their perception of their child (Bailey, 2006; Rustin, 1998). This kind of work is more on the boundary between individual and couple psychotherapy and parent work.

Colleagues at TCCR have undertaken many research projects which have had a direct relevance for CAMHS work. These include the seminal study of couple interventions in a social services department (Mattinson & Sinclair, 1979), the study on the transition to parenthood (Clulow, 1982), the impact of infertility on the couple relationship (Cudmore, 1996) and the impact of a child's death on the couple relationship (Cudmore & Judd, 2001).

I have picked out one area of work (though there are more) where I think that a couple perspective, working with and holding the couple in mind, is an added value intervention. Many children are referred to CAMHS with behavioural problems and emotional distress when their parents are either separated acrimoniously or unable to separate because of the acrimony. These children are so often caught up in the crossfire between their parents that it is difficult in the context of blame and recrimination for parents to hold their children's needs and distress in mind. The parents have lost their capacity to reflect on their own experience and emotions, have lost the capacity to reflect on their partnership as parents, and have often lost their concern about the impact of their couple difficulties on their children. Very often they may be trying to get rid of the feelings they cannot bear in themselves, into their partner or into their children. Although working with the couple relationship seems essential it is also important for the therapist to hold the "real" children in mind and to help the parents, who themselves are so often dominated by a more infantile state of mind, to face this reality too. The following is an example of a clinical intervention with a separated couple.

Clinical vignette

Molly, aged two-and-a-half, was referred with her mother by her GP at the mother's instigation. The referral letter described Molly as a usually bright and happy little girl who had been affected by her parents' recent separation. She was wetting herself, tearful, and frequently hit out at her mother. The GP said that father was undermining of mother's attempts to set up a routine to make Molly feel more secure. I first met Molly's mother, Andrea, who was in a very anxious and fragile state of mind, burdened by the volatile relationship with her husband and the legal complications following separation. The family flat was in her husband's name and she was concerned that they would lose their home. While acknowledging the huge emotional strain they were all under, I also said that, because of the adversarial interaction between her and her ex-husband Paul, I could imagine how difficult it was to put their battles to one side and think about their daughter and her need for parents who could think together about her and her worries. I talked about Molly's incontinence and tantrums being a symptom of her distress in this turbulent situation between her parents and a communication to them both about what she was finding intolerable and could not bear. I thought that she and her husband did need to come together to talk about Molly and to recognise that their difficulties had "leaked" into their role as parents.

When I met Paul he was initially very defensive and anxious to give me his side of the story. He denied there was a problem with Molly; he said his wife was exaggerating, using Molly as part of the marital vendetta to stop him seeing her. When he realised that I was not there to criticise, blame, or to take sides, he began to tell me about Molly's anxieties about going to bed and to sleep at night and how unsure he felt about looking after her now that he didn't have Molly's mother to help him. He hadn't thought before our meeting that Molly's difficulty sleeping might be related to her worries about her parents and all the changes in her life. I saw this couple for seven months. For many weeks the sessions resembled a court room: accusations and counter accusations, attack and defence, mutual suspicion and distrust dominated the exchanges. They either sat tight-lipped or let all their hatred out on each other. There was no space to think. However, in time, feelings of distress and helplessness emerged from behind the anger and blame. As they became more contained by the sessions and had regained their capacity to think they were able to be more sensitive to Molly and to think with her about her feelings, and they were able to do this individually and as a parental couple.

Seeing parents together when they have separated seemed to some of my colleagues an unusual intervention but training in couple psychotherapy provides the theoretical framework and equips the worker for this difficult task. Many of the couples I see at CAMHS would not seek help from a couples service and for this reason I very much hope that the couple dimension of work with parents will continue to develop.

References

Bailey, T. (2006). There's no such thing as an adolescent. In: M. Lanyado & A. Horne (Eds.), *A Question of Technique. Independent Psychoanalytic Approaches with Children and Adolescents*. Hove, UK: Routledge.

Clulow, C. (1982). *To Have and to Hold: Marriage, the First Baby and Preparing Couples for Parenthood*. Aberdeen: Aberdeen University Press.

Clulow, C. (2010). Developing the couple perspective in parenting support: evaluation of a service initiative for vulnerable families. *Journal of Family Therapy*, 32(2): 142–168.

Cudmore, L. (1996). Infertility and the couple. In: C. Clulow (Ed.), *Partners Becoming Parents*. London: Sheldon Press.

Cudmore, L. & Judd, D. (2001). Traumatic loss and the couple. In: C. Clulow (Ed.), *Adult Attachment and Couple Psychotherapy*. Hove, UK: Brunner-Routledge.

DfES (2003). *Every Child Matters*. London: HMSO.

DfES (2007). *Every Parent Matters*. London: HMSO.

Mattinson, J. & Sinclair, I. (1979). *Mate and Stalemate: Working with Marital Problems in a Social Services Department*. Oxford: Blackwell.

Morgan, M. (2005). On being able to be a couple: the importance of a "creative couple" in psychic life. In: F. Grier (Ed.), *Oedipus and the Couple*. London: Karnac.

Parenting Fund (2006). http://www.parentingfund.org/history

Rustin, M. (1998). Dialogues with parents. *Journal of Child Psychotherapy*, 24(2): 233–252.

Rustin, M. (2009). Work with parents. In: M. Lanyado & A. Horne (Eds.), *The Handbook of Child and Adolescent Psychotherapy*. London: Routledge.

CHAPTER FOUR

The role of the family court system of England and Wales in child-related parental disputes: towards a new concept of the family justice process

Mervyn Murch

Introduction

This chapter considers ways in which the family justice system of England and Wales approaches so-called "private" child-related parental disputes. I argue that in the light of behavioural science research concerning children and high conflict parental breakdown, as well as the likely impact of the economic downturn on public services including the courts, the time has come for a major rethink of our conventional approach to these matters. In doing so I focus primarily on the litigation process as carried out at first instance in our currently divided administration of local family courts and their related welfare support services, now principally provided by the Children and Family Court Advisory and Support Service (CAFCASS). Thus in this context I will omit reference to the important role played by gatekeepers to the system (i.e., solicitors) and those mediators and conciliators involved in alternative dispute resolution (ADR).

This chapter falls into four parts. First, for those unfamiliar with the work of the family courts, I summarise the key features of this specialist interdisciplinary part of the civil justice system. Second, I briefly refer to some of the research covered by Professor Harold in Chapter Two as it concerns family justice practice. In addition, I outline some key socio-legal research concerning the reactions and views of children and parents who have experienced the litigation process. Third, in the context of this growing body of empirical research I consider some important contemporary policy issues and attempt to show how these might be better addressed and understood in the light of changing conceptions of the family justice system. These view it as much from a community mental health as a legal perspective. This is because the system interacts with families under stress undergoing critical structural change during the litigation process which, in its impact on families and children, has significant social, psychological, and educational sequelae. I have termed this approach "participant family justice" in order to distinguish it from the more conventional legal view of the process. I shall touch on the social and psychological significance of symbolic legal ritual, judicial authority, and the scales of justice, all of which can be linked conceptually to notions of psychological balance/ stability and disequilibrium in family relations. In this respect I shall argue that the resort to the family justice system in cases of high conflict parental dispute can be viewed, in part at least, as a search for a new and better emotional equilibrium to correspond to a just/fair basis upon which to base the family's post separation/divorce life. Finally, I shall suggest that the current economic downturn and anticipated major cuts to the budgets of family courts and related services provide a golden opportunity to reform the structure of a system which has been reluctant to change.

PART I: GROUND CLEARING—THE DISTINGUISHING FEATURES OF THE FAMILY JUSTICE SYSTEM

Evolving law and social change

As this book is primarily intended for front line clinicians dealing with couple relationships, psychotherapists, and social policy makers, some of whom may not have a working knowledge of the family justice system, a number of scene-setting points need to be made for it may not be realised what a rapidly expanding and developing subject family law is. It is no longer the sole domain of lawyers but rather now depends on close interdisciplinary teamwork between judges, lay magistrates and their legal advisers, advocates, court social workers provided by CAFCASS and some voluntary agencies, and a variety of child and mental health specialists and paediatricians called upon to provide expert evidence. Moreover, family law itself is constantly developing and adapting to rapid social change and an evolving and sometimes conflicting mix of social values (Murch, 2009). (Note that family law also has a growing and important international dimension—not considered in this chapter.)

The foundations of family justice—the rule of law and the separation of powers

To appreciate the significance of the work of the family justice system, particularly in dealing with parental disputes concerning children, one must first understand the central tenets of the rule of law and the constitutional principle of the separation of powers and the independence of judges upon which the family justice system of England and Wales is based. (Note that the Constitutional Reform Act (2005) provides, in s. 17(1), that on taking office the Lord Chancellor must swear to respect the rule of law and the independence of the judges.) In our times, the most lucid and scholarly exposition of the term "the rule of law" has been advanced by Lord Bingham (2010). Observing that the concept of the rule of law evolves over time in response to new views and situations, Bingham suggests that the core of the principle is: "that all persons and authorities within the state, whether public or private, should be bound by and entitled to the benefits of laws publicly made, taking effect in the future and publicly administered by the courts" (p. 8).

Within this broad definition are a number of subsidiary principles such as that the law should be accessible to all citizens (including children); equality before the law; that ministers and public officers of the state must exercise the powers conferred on them in good faith and fairly without exceeding the limits of their powers and not unreasonably; and that the law must afford adequate protection of fundamental human rights. On this last point it will be remembered that the Human Rights Act 1998 gave direct effect in this country to the European Convention on Human Rights 1950. As far as the practice of family law is concerned, this has two key articles: the right to a fair trial (Article 6); and the right to respect for private and family life (Article 8). Later in this chapter I will examine the application of these principles to two contemporary policy issues concerning the way the family justice system approaches family disputes: first, the search for an effective means for resolving such disputes without excessive cost and unnecessary delay when parents are unable to resolve the dispute themselves; second, the importance of the constitutional principle of the separation of powers which distinguishes the work of the family courts from executive aspects of the state. It is this principle which, as we shall see, goes to the heart of the controversy about the future role of the Child and Family Court Advisory and Support Service (CAFCASS).

The scale of the family law courts' private law workload

All the evidence suggests that while the number of divorces continues to decline, applications to family courts affecting children in so-called private law proceedings, particularly concerning contact or residence, continue to rise. Thus, while in 2004 there were 166,010 divorce petitions filed, by 2008 that figure had dropped to 128,837 (HM Government, 2009, Table 5.5 p. 96). By contrast, family courts received a steadily increasing number of applications concerning children in private law proceedings, from 104,470 in 2002 to 113,590 in 2008 (ibid., Table 5.1 p. 91). In that year the great majority of these applications, generally in connection with divorce or parental separation, were filed in the County Court (93,390) rather than the Magistrates' Court's Family Proceedings Court which cannot hear divorce cases (19,360), with a further 850 filed in the High Court—all three types of court have the same jurisdiction with respect to applications under s. 8 of the Children Act 1989 concerning residence or contact. (Note that the Childrens Act 1989 s. 8 also provides for orders concerning prohibited steps—for example, to stop a parent taking the child to another country. It also provides for a specific issues order determining specific aspects of the child's upbringing—for example, religion.) Thus, in 2009 there were about 45,000 s. 8 applications for residence orders, a rise of 11% over the previous year and about 53,000 for contact orders, a corresponding increase of 23% (Ministry of Justice, 2011a, para. 5.8). (Note that these figures may over-represent the numbers of children involved, as a single child subject to multiple orders may be counted several times.)

Domestic violence is also, of course, a serious and long-standing social problem. The Family Law Act 1996 provides for two types of order which can be made in either the Family Proceedings Court or in the County Court—a non-molestation order and an occupation order which can define or regulate a right of occupation of the home.

Numbers of such applications to the County Court fell slightly between 2004 and 2008 from 27,813 down to 24,879 (op. cit., note 5 Tables 5.8 and 5.9). Nearly all these cases result in an order being made, very often with a power of arrest being attached which may become operative if the order is infringed. (It should be noted that as from July 2007 the Domestic Violence, Crime and Victims Act 2004 came into force, which made breaching a non-molestation order a criminal offence.)

Popular myths about family law

Family law is also a subject about which there is currently a good deal of myth (Maclean & Eekelaar, 2009, pp. 4–8). Thus in the popular British press one regularly encounters the widely held view that lawyers milk the system for all they can get and that they help to perpetuate an adversarial system of justice which aggravates stressful family conflict and divides disputing couples into "winners and losers"—a stereotypical view which in my experience is sometimes shared by marital and family therapists and medical practitioners. Of course such a view is given credence by the publicity given to high profile celebrity divorce cases such as that of the McCartneys. But it is certainly not so for the bulk of both "public" law (i.e., cases of child neglect and abuse involving the local authority) and "private" law child-related proceedings which make up the everyday hurly-burly of work in the local family courts. (See also Maclean & Eekelaar, 2009—a research-based book which provides a graphic picture of the complex, emotionally hot messes of human distress and conflicting interests which courts have to deal with on a massive scale.) Rather than aggravating and profiting from family conflict, most family lawyers and the courts bend over backwards to get the parties to settle their disputes, as a number of recent studies have shown; even to the extent that some parents feel unduly pressurised to do so (Hunt, 2010).

Another over-simplified myth, often held by well-meaning reformers, lawyers, and those policy makers seeking to find economies is that disputed litigation over children's issues is invariably bad for the children's welfare. Like all myths there is, of course, some truth in this. But given that recent behavioural research suggests that it is the degree and frequency of parental conflict itself which for many children is damaging (Harold, Pryor & Reynolds, 2001; Harold, Shelton, Goeke-Morey & Cummings, 2004), it is more difficult in our present state of knowledge to point the finger specifically at court proceedings as a prime cause, even though the way they are handled may aggravate matters in a number of cases.

Those who argue against court hearings in private law cases look to alternative dispute resolution in the form of mediation as a better and cheaper mechanism if parents cannot settle their differences by negotiation, with or without the help of their solicitors. Mediation has an important role to play in the family justice process, broadly defined either as the "out of court" variety provided by voluntary services or by CAFCASS officers following an initial court hearing (now termed a First Hearing Directions Resolution Appointment before a county court district judge, usually assisted by a CAFCASS officer) (see President of the Family Division's Practice Direction *The Revised Private Law Programme* effective from 1 April 2010). But, as I shall argue later, mediation is not a panacea.

Interdisciplinarity

Another preliminary point to be emphasised is the decidedly interdisciplinary character of the family justice system. Thus, while judges in the County Court's family hearing centres and care centres are legally trained, and while the lay justices in the Magistrates' Court's Family Proceedings Court are assisted by a legally qualified adviser (formally termed a clerk to the justices), child welfare reports under s. 7 of the Children Act and a certain amount of in-court conciliation are provided by qualified social workers employed by CAFCASS. (Note that CAFCASS, 2009, p. 17 indicates that in 2008/09 the service was involved in a total of 38,449 private law cases, mostly concerning disputes about contact and residence, some 20,000 of which involved welfare reports under s. 7 of the Children Act 1989.) In certain complex and protracted cases CAFCASS staff may also act as guardians working in tandem with specially trained children's lawyers, when a judge decides that the child's interests need to be separately represented (under r. 9.5 of the Family Proceedings Rules 1991). This is still a somewhat controversial provision (see further below) which occurs in rather less than 10% of disputed cases (CAFCASS, 2009 p. 19). Nevertheless, the demand for this type of case increased by 30% with 1,804 cases in 2008/09 compared to 1,388 in the previous year.

One way of conceptualising the interdisciplinary nature of the family justice system is to see its fabric as having a warp still largely comprised of orthodox jurisprudential thinking concerning reciprocal rights and duties, as defined in substantive family law by statute and judicial precedent under our traditional adversarial common law approach; while into the weft are woven various strands of sometimes conflicting political, philosophical, social, and psychological ideas. This gives the evolving system a dynamic creative tension and, under the influence of judicial discretion in particular cases, helps to adapt it to rapid social change and increases its impact on modern family life.

Funding the system

A further important feature that needs to be appreciated by those unfamiliar with the workings of the system is that its funding is based on a complex mix of public and private provision. As Auerbach (1985) has pointed out: "It is social context and political choice that determines where the courts or alternative institutions can render justice more or less accessible—and to whom" (pp. 114–145).

Thus one contemporary policy issue, aggravated by the current economic downturn, is whether and to what extent the state should provide legal aid and advice to parents and children in private family law proceedings. Additionally, there is a set of economic questions currently concerning government funding for family courts, CAFCASS, voluntary agencies providing alternative dispute resolution services, and court welfare support services such as supervised contact centres (Murch, 2010). I consider some of these matters further below.

The court's settlement seeking function

As already mentioned, perhaps most important of all, the structure and machinery of courts are increasingly being adapted to promote settlement, particularly in private law disputes between estranged parents. As Sir Roger Ormrod, a distinguished Lord Justice of Appeal with medical training pointed out years ago: "… this turns the advocate into the negotiator and the judge into a problem-solver or honest broker and enables the parties to adjust themselves to the situation as it is … imposed solutions are sometimes unavoidable but they are better avoided" (1974, pp. 15–25).

This raises a point about the psychological significance of judicial authority in the handling of family litigation—a matter I consider more fully below.

The participation of children in the family justice process

Another major feature of the modern family justice process is the increasing recognition being given to the voice of the child. As has been pointed out elsewhere (Lowe & Murch, 2001):

> Historically the great shift in English law governing parent and child was the move from the position where children were of no concern at all to one where their welfare was regarded as the court's paramount concern ... traditionally, under English law, children's futures have been decided upon the views of the adults, that is, of parents and professionals. In other words the welfare principle itself is adult-centred and paternalistic. Even so, what we have been witnessing over the last decade or so is the equally significant cultural shift in which children are no longer seen as passive victims of family breakdown but increasingly as participants and actors in the family justice process.

The paramountcy of the welfare principle under the Children Act 1989, the primary statutory provision concerning child-related proceedings in both public and private law, is augmented by a checklist which has to be applied in *all* contested s. 8 applications. Thus s. 1(3)a provides a mandatory direction to family courts to take account of the child's own wishes and feelings. In the majority of disputed cases between divorced or separated parents this is done through the intervention of a CAFCASS family court adviser who will interview the child and make a report to the court. But as will be considered more fully later, CAFCASS has been under economic pressure to reduce the resources devoted to report writing in order to create capacity for in-court conciliation. This means in effect that there are now many children and young people who are not given an opportunity to express their views to the court. Some argue that this goes against the principle contained in Article 12 of the United Nations Convention on the Rights of the Child 1989.

Moreover, Article 9(2), which in public debate has received less attention, also provides that in any proceedings concerning the separation of a child from his/her parents: "... all interested parties shall be given the opportunity to participate in their proceedings."

This raises the question whether the children should be regarded as "parties" as distinct from merely having an interest by being the subject of proceedings. In law, the issue is whether the child should be "joined" as an additional party with the right to be separately represented by a lawyer and/or a court appointed guardian. As is well known, following the Maria Colwell case and other child abuse tragedies in the 1970s, it became standard practice in *public* law cases involving local authorities to separate the interests of children from that of their parents and to provide a child with a guardian ad litem working with a specially appointed children's solicitor. (See, for the history of this provision, Timms, 2009.) Gradually this practice of separate representation for children became extended to private law cases involving serious parental child-related disputes under the provision of r. 9.5 of the Family Proceedings Rules 1991—a provision which, as we have seen, although still relatively unusual, is increasingly used particularly in high conflict cases. (For more detailed discussion of the legal and practice issues, see Douglas, Murch, Miles & Scanlan, 2006.) Unfortunately, the recent Interim Report of the Family Justice Review, while acknowledging the principle that the voice of the child should be heard in family proceedings (Ministry of Justice, 2011a para. 20) makes no mention of it in its chapter on private law proceedings. This could mean that political pressure has been to prioritise the representation of children in public law proceedings at the expense of children involved in parental disputes (ibid., Chapter Five, pp. 142–183).

This is a suitable point at which to turn next to socio-legal research concerning the well-being of children, family conflict, and the voice of the child.

PART II: CHILDREN AND PARENTAL LITIGATION

The well-being of children—the general picture

Before considering recent research concerning the experience and views of children involved in legal proceedings resulting from their parents' divorce or separation, it is necessary as a backcloth to point up some more general family issues and trends concerning the well-being of children in the UK.

The broad picture is clearly presented in a recent landmark report from the Good Childhood Inquiry convened and funded by the Children's Society (Layard & Dunn, 2009). Drawing on findings from a UNICEF report indicating how children are faring in twenty-one of the world's richest countries, it shows that on a number of measures children in the UK rank "bottom of the class", with the United States next.

Since then the picture has remained relatively stable although we have fallen well behind other European and Scandinavian countries. As the report states (Layard & Dunn, 2009):

> Britain and the US have had more broken families than other countries and our families are less cohesive in the way they live and eat together … family breakup affects children in all classes as do the commercial and peer pressures that encourage risky lifestyles. (p. 4)

As to the underlying causes, the Children's Society report echoes an earlier consultation study by the Joseph Rowntree Foundation in pointing to an emerging culture of "excessive individualism" which it is claimed contributes to family breakdown in terms of parental conflict, separation, and divorce.

Drawing on various studies (Ford & Goodman, 2005) the Children's Society report points out that while the majority of children lead happy lives "a minority are seriously troubled or disturbed" (op. cit., note 27, p. 43). While there are many contributory causes, the report states:

> When all positive factors are looked at simultaneously, key factors which directly affect mental health include living apart from your father (which increased the risk of difficulties for over 40%), family conflict, poor mental health of a parent, living in rented housing and more than two adverse life events.

It is of course the issue of parental conflict, separation, and divorce which so often brings the family into contact with the machinery of justice. Yet family proceedings and family courts are not immediately associated in the public's mind with community mental health matters: an oversight which needs to be strongly addressed since family law and mental health are inextricably connected (as I will explain further below).

Children and the breakdown of parental relationships

In the not so distant post-war period, it was often asserted that divorce was harmful for children's social, psychological, and physical development. But under the influence of more recent behavioural and social science research, that view has become modified. True, children of divorced or separated parents are found to be at significantly greater risk of adverse outcomes in social, psychological, and physical development and in relation to their educational attainment than children whose parents remain together. But in various longitudinal studies it has been found that levels of behaviour and educational difficulties are higher where parents later separate than in those whose parents do not. As Pryor and Rogers indicate in an authoritative research review for the Joseph Rowntree Foundation, such findings show that "poor outcomes are in place before separation suggesting other or additional causes of long term disadvantage" (Pryor & Rogers, 2001, p. 73). (Pryor and Rogers reviewed eighteen major studies including several longitudinal investigations concerning children's adjustment to parental separation from the UK, US, New Zealand, and Australia.) Even so, there is no doubt that children generally are affected when their parents separate, although as the Children's Society report states (Pryor & Rogers, 2001):

> Many of the problems dissipate over time ... the majority (at least two thirds) appeared to be developing without psychological scars. (note 27, p. 23)

Even so, one should not ignore the disruption to children's education resulting from parental discord and separation, the disadvantages of which may be cumulative and long term.

Moreover, as has been pointed out elsewhere (Harold & Murch, 2005), for many of these children divorce and separation of their parents is not the only major family change they will experience: the majority of their parents will subsequently live with new partners (who may themselves have children from previous relationships). Some may well remarry and others may have a series of temporary partners. All such events may be experienced by children as troublesome and stressful and at least temporarily impact adversely on their education and social well-being.

More recently research by Professor Harold and others suggests that a central consideration in accounting for children's adaptive and maladaptive responses to their parents' separation is not simply the degree of hostility and conflict that occurs between parents but the perceptions and attributions that children ascribe to the source, content, duration, and level of intensity of their parents' conflict (Harold, Pryor & Reynolds, 2001; Harold, Shelton, Goeke-Morey & Cummings, 2004). As Harold and Leve have developed these points in their earlier chapter, I only wish here to emphasise that the voice of the child is a critically important dimension which reinforces the parallel movement in family law to accord greater importance to the views and experiences of children.

Children's views of the litigation process

The most authoritative general text concerning the participation of children in family proceedings is an Australian study by Parkinson and Cashmore (2008) which I strongly recommend. Because I co-directed several researches into children's perception and experience of the litigation process arising from the Cardiff Children in Divorce Research Programme, fully written up elsewhere (Butler, Scanlan, Robinson, Douglas & Murch, 2003; Douglas, Murch, Miles & Scanlon, 2006; Murch, Douglas & Scanlan, 1999) and already summarised in a recent policy paper (Murch, 2010), I want here just to highlight three critical needs of children who are the subject of family litigation: information, support, and impartial judicial authority and continuity.

i. The need for reliable information
    First, invariably parental separation constitutes a major crisis in children's lives, characterised by an acute sense of shock, disbelief, and emotional distress. My colleagues and I use the term "crisis" in a specific Caplanian mental health sense to describe their reaction to sudden loss or threat of loss that temporarily overwhelms the child's normal coping mechanisms (Caplan, 1961, 1964, 1989). At such times, children require reliable information to help them cope and come to terms with their parents' separation and divorce, with resulting changes in family structure (i.e., the acquisition of a possible stepparent, their parents' new and possibly temporary partners, other children they may have, etc.), and with any ensuing litigation concerning contact or residence.

It was noted (Butler, Scanlan, Robinson, Douglas & Murch, 2003, p. 186) that: "Those who were well informed appeared better able to buffer the impact of the crisis and to have stronger self esteem and capacity to understand and manage their lives."

By contrast, lack of information and confusion added to children's uncertainties and, sometimes, seemed to have longer-term adverse repercussions (for example, in relationships with their parents and any new partner). Here it is also worth noting that the younger the child the greater the likelihood of their not being told anything about the parents' separation or divorce (Butler, Scanlan, Robinson, Douglas & Murch, 2003). (In a representative sample drawn from court records, only 52% of the children between seven and ten could recall being told anything by either parent.) The Cardiff r. 9.5 study mostly involved children who were subject to protracted and hotly disputed litigation, often involving a number of separate court proceedings. Their needs for reliable information were even more pronounced. Those who did not receive it were generally left feeling excluded, isolated, depressed, and angry.

It is therefore gratifying to report that in its Interim Report the government-appointed Family Justice Review endorsed the view that in family proceedings "children and young people must be given age appropriate information which explains what is happening" and that the proposed Family Justice Service (probably incorporating CAF-CASS England) should have a clear role in ensuring that the voice of children and young people is heard. Nevertheless, doubt remains whether the Review intended this to apply equally to litigated cases involving parental disputes (see footnote 26 at p. 6). (For reference to the Family Justice Review, see further below.)

ii. The need for passage agent support
    The second point to emerge strongly from the Cardiff studies was the need for many children to have empathetic "impartial passage agent" support throughout the proceedings, particularly for children in high conflict situations. My research colleagues and I define this term as a: "concerned impartial person accessible to children who can support and help them manage the critical family transitions following the breakdown of their parents' relationship".

    Those children involved in high conflict child-related litigation described a heightened need for emotional comfort and impartial support throughout the litigation process. While the study found that some of them received this kind of support from the court appointed guardian or solicitor, nevertheless (Murch, 2010):

> There were other children who had not found anyone they could trust or relate to. They appeared lost, withdrawn and depressed, intimidated or angered by their contact with the family justice system, particularly if they felt the court's guardian had misrepresented their views. (note 40, p. 42)

iii. The need for impartial judicial authority and continuity

The third important point to emerge, particularly from the r. 9.5 study, was that most of the children believed that if their parents could not resolve their differences, then some sort of impartial judicial authority was needed. Even so, many regarded courts as "scary places" where some believed that the judge would punish their parents, even send them to prison, for behaviour for which the children themselves felt responsible, such as refusing contact visits. Many of these children wanted more "child-friendly" courts which worked in such a way that if they wanted to they could put their views to the judge directly. Thus they wanted the setting and the judge to be sufficiently approachable for them to do so.

In this respect it is worth noting that interviews with the children's parents confirmed the general views of the children. Moreover, a number of the r. 9.5 parents wished the guardian had been appointed much earlier to help them short-circuit escalating conflict and costly litigation. They too wanted courts with a less intimidating atmosphere, as many previous studies of parental perspectives of family justice have found (Hunt, 2010, note 13). They also wanted greater judicial continuity so that if they had to return to court, for example following adjournments, the same judge would deal with the case. Indeed, lack of judicial continuity has been found to be a serious organisational issue under current arrangements—a point recognised by the recent Family Justice Review (see further below).

PART III: CONTEMPORARY FAMILY JUSTICE POLICY ISSUES

i. The prospect of major cuts in resources

Overshadowing all contemporary and often long-standing family justice policy issues is the prospect of major financial cuts resulting from the new coalition government's need to correct the deficit in the nation's finances arising from the global economic downturn and the banking crisis of 2008/09.

An indication of how the Lord Chancellor and Secretary of State for Justice, Kenneth Clarke, himself a lawyer, was approaching the matter can be gleaned from a speech he gave to the Centre for Crime and Justice Studies on 30 June 2010. He talked of trying "to turn financial stringency into some constructive and sensible policies"; of needing to "reconcile drastic and necessary cuts in public spending with positive policy making". Although the speech was mostly concerned with penal affairs, he gave a clear indication that major reform would be needed in two areas affecting the family justice system: the courts and legal aid.

With respect to the reform of the courts, the government had already announced on 23 June 2010 a "consultation" on a proposed reduction in the number of local magistrates' courts and county courts (Hunt, 2010, note 13). This suggested that out of a combined total of 530 courts, 103 of the former and 54 of the latter could be closed on the basis that their number and location no longer reflected changes in population.

With respect to legal aid, Kenneth Clarke stated: "It is clear to me that we must make major changes in the system of legal aid". While acknowledging the right and desire of people to use the law to settle disputes and to assert claims, he indicated that people might very well have to pay more from their own resources. And in a very significant comment on family law he observed:

> Nor am I convinced that in many private family cases the traditional adversarial system is necessarily the best for the parties involved or the best use of public funds. In the worst cases, bitter disputes between spouses and partners are actually, in my opinion, made worse by repeated and fruitless battles between lawyers in court hearing after court hearing. Might we be better off focusing on better and less legalistic ways of seeking to resolve highly charged emotional disputes between former partners in broken relationships?

ii. Reductions in civil legal aid and its impact on "private" family law proceedings

Following the government's Comprehensive Spending Review in November 2010, the Ministry of Justice, which has to reduce its budget by 23% over four years, issued a consultation paper concerning legal aid (Ministry of Justice, 2010). This proposed to remove it from most routine divorce disputes concerning property, money, and arrangements for children. However, it will continue to be available to fund legal representation in court in cases of domestic violence and child abduction. The overall aim is to divert as many cases as possible to mediation which the government will fund, also providing a limited amount of legal help (£150) for a solicitor's advice during the mediation process and afterwards in order to formalise and give effect to any agreements reached. Parents who can afford to pay for legal representation will of course still be able to commence litigation in court as before. (Note that new legal aid provisions to this effect became operative from April 2011.) It is hoped to increase the number of Legal Services Commission contracts for "quality assured family mediation services" from the existing 740 locations to 979 from 2011 onwards.

Understandable though these reforms are, given the current need to correct the fiscal deficit, there are fears that where mediation has not been successful, lack of legal aid will lead to more litigants in person. This may well increase pressure on courts' administration and on the judiciary. Moreover, when one parent can afford to be represented and the other not, there may be a temptation by the latter to make allegations of domestic violence merely in order to qualify for legal aid in order to secure the help of a lawyer.

Children are of course the law's paramount concern. Here too there are worries about the government's proposals. Diverting cases away from the courts risks reducing the number where the child's welfare ought to be ascertained according to the Children Act's welfare checklist. Moreover, there may be less chance that the voice of the child will be heard since many mediation services still do not involve them directly in the process. True, in the most extreme cases coming to court, judges may continue to order that the children should be separately represented under r. 9.5 of the Family Proceedings Rules 1991. In such cases the government has agreed to provide them with legal aid to fund their legal representation.

Only time will tell whether these problems will arise. According to the Minister, Jonathan Djanogly (2010): "These measures are only our first steps. Next year we will need to understand fully the conclusions drawn from the Family Justice Review."

The Review's interim report was published in March 2011 and its final report is expected to be completed in autumn 2011 (see further below).

iii. What is the public interest in private law proceedings?

In his lecture in June 2010, Kenneth Clarke raised the key question of what it is about so-called "private" family law proceedings that is in the public interest. This fundamental question has to be addressed head on.

It is all too easy to take a superficial view and argue that these child-related parental disputes are still in essence an adversarial contest between two adults and as such the state should not be expected to pay for an essentially private dispute (as family justice practitioners themselves unfortunately term them to distinguish them from "public law" disputes).

In family matters such a view needs to be firmly rejected for the following reasons. First, it effectively downplays if not ignores the interests of children. In this respect it is contrary to the statutory principle enunciated in s. 1 (1) of the Children Act 1989 that the child's interests are paramount. (Note that this lays down the cardinal principle that "When any court determines any question with respect to (a) the upbringing of the child and (b) the administration of a child's property or the application of any income from it, the child's welfare should be the court's paramount consideration." (For an elaboration of the meaning of the welfare principle, see Lowe & Douglas, 2007, Chapter One.) As we have mentioned, this fundamental principle applies to *all* children whether they are the subject of public or private law proceedings.

Secondly, I take the view that in the light of all we know about the potential impact on children of parental conflict and parental separation, the state has a clear interest in promoting their well-being and minimising any harm or disadvantage. The definition of harm includes serious psychological and educational harm as well as the risk of physical abuse or neglect. Moreover, access to justice in the family courts is every bit as much the child's right as that of its parents, especially as the court's welfare service in the form of CAFCASS exists to support and safeguard their interests during the course of proceedings.

Thirdly, it is significant that, as we have seen, a number of children and young people who have themselves been subject to contested proceedings arising from their parents' separation recognised that if their parents cannot reach a settlement, then some kind of impartial judicial authority is needed. The state should not ignore the views of many of its younger citizens who speak so powerfully from bitter experience.

iv. Diversion to conciliation—is it the answer?

As one who has been associated with the mediation/conciliation movement from its earliest pioneering days (Murch, 2004, pp. 21–32), I am sure that it has a key part to play in the range of family justice services dealing with private child-related parental disputes. Over the last forty years it has developed from small beginnings, largely supported by voluntary effort which initially received little official encouragement and financial support, into a widely accepted sophisticated professional activity with various specialisms. Moreover, its practice has spread from the family courts to become a recognised part of the wider civil justice system under the label of alternative dispute resolution (ADR). (Note that Ministry of Justice, 2011a, para. 5.123 suggests that the term "alternative dispute resolution" should be rebranded as Dispute Resolution Services in order to minimise a deterrent to their use.) Nevertheless, as mentioned above, mediation is not the panacea that many hope for.

First there is some evidence to suggest that unless both parents are willing to give it a go, it will fail (Davis, 1988, 2004), at least in terms of avoiding subsequent resort to the courts. Even when parents are willing to engage in the mediation process and therefore reach agreement, research evidence suggests that many of these agreements do not last very long—survival rates over six months ranging from 45% for one study (Magistrates' Court Service Inspectorate, 2003) and 39% for another (Trinder, Connolly, Notley & Swift, 2006).

Much depends on how one assesses the value of conciliation. The most recent research review of these matters by Joan Hunt for the Family Justice Council (2010) commented that:

> Many, perhaps most parents do not feel they have any real choice about participating in the process and a substantial minority feel under pressure to reach agreement. Conciliation is probably less

traumatic than a contested hearing but it is still a very stressful process.

This may be particularly so in cases where there is evidence of domestic violence. (Note that s. 29 of the Family Law Act 1996 requires prospective legal aid applicants to have first explored the mediation option.)

Moreover, Hunt observes that while:

> There is some evidence that conciliation does appear to be quite effective in restoring contact where it has recently broken down and increasing the amount of contact and the likelihood of children having overnight stays with their non-resident parents … but there is little evidence that conciliation equips parents with the skills to negotiate agreements in future without professional help or that it has much impact on parental relationships.

A major difficulty in all this under current practice is how to determine which cases will settle through negotiation, which need the intervention of a neutral mediator, and which will inevitably end up as hotly disputed high conflict cases being litigated in courts, despite all efforts to divert them to alternative dispute resolution mechanisms (see further below).

v. CAFCASS—is it fit for purpose?

CAFCASS has been plagued with organisational and resource difficulties ever since it was established in April 2001. The aim was to combine the previous civil court work of the probation service, the children's work of the Official Solicitor for the High Court, and that of the independent panels of guardians ad litem originally set up in 1984 to provide effective separate social work and legal representation for children mainly in public law care proceedings (see further Timms, 2009). Professor Judith Masson has recently commented these aims were optimistic:

> CAFCASS was under-staffed and under-funded. It was mired in conflict with former self-employed guardians who successfully challenged their new contracts in the courts. There were huge delays in appointing guardians and the chief executive was dismissed.

In retrospect, one can see that throughout its brief history there has been a crippling tension between bureaucratic managers and its professional social work staff, particularly those who came from the previous panels of guardians who, unlike the service's former probation officers did not have a line-managed service.

One major issue concerned accountability: were guardians and family court advisers to be primarily regarded as officers appointed by the court or chosen and primarily accountable to CAFCASS managers? Moreover, over the last ten years increasingly tight financial resources aggravated the triangular tension between a professionally trained workforce working in tandem with specially appointed children's solicitors (wishing to exercise professional discretion in the interests of the children), CAFCASS management keen to control expenditure and to develop a more uniform national service, and the family courts which were experiencing severely increasing workloads and wanted rapid response from their CAFCASS officers. In recent years, in some areas delays have been chronic and have required special measures to deal with the backlog. (Note that during the last decade the service has been subject to various adverse comments from official bodies such as the Parliamentary Constitutional Affairs Committee, Her Majesty's Magistrates' Court Inspectorate and Ofsted, all of which have been concerned about delay.)

Moreover, from August 2009 the service has been on an emergency footing dealing with the flood of public law cases which followed the publicity given to the Baby P case. Since then it has only been able to offer "a minimum safe standard". (Note that the revised Private Law Programme—which asserts that the overriding objective is that the child's welfare is the court's paramount concern, and was issued by the President of the Family Division in consultation with CAFCASS in July 2009—was extended until 30 September 2010. This emphasised the importance of parties being helped to reach agreement and requires the court at the First Hearing Dispute Resolution Appointment to "deal expeditiously and fairly with every case in ways which are proportionate to the nature, importance and complexity of the issues; ensure that parties are on an equal footing and save unnecessary expense". It sets out a number of procedural steps that the CAFCASS officer must take before the First Hearing, all designed to speed up the process.) This further increased the tension between front line staff wishing to exercise their professional discretion while performing their statutory duty to give consideration to the best interests of the child, and centralised line managers having to ration very limited financial resources.

Thus, by midsummer 2010 serious questions, aggravated by the economic downturn, hung over the future of CAFCASS in its present form. Would the Family Justice Review endorse its present management structure or would it suggest radical change, possibly a regionally devolved structure incorporated into a system of unified local family courts where the CAFCASS officer would be primarily accountable to the court and function as part of an interdisciplinary team of court support services? (See further below.)

vi. Has the time come to unify local family courts?

The split in responsibility between the Family Proceedings Court and the County Court has been a recurrent source of controversy well documented in Stephen Cretney's magnum opus (2003). (See particularly Chapter Twenty One, pp. 741–775. See also Murch, 2009.) The germ of the idea can be traced back to 1909 when Lord Gorell, who chaired the Royal Commission on Marriage and Divorce, suggested the removal of magistrates' domestic jurisdiction to the superior courts. At the time this was regarded as impractical. It resurfaced again in the 1950s in a suggestion to the Royal Commission on Marriage and Divorce (the Morton Commission) and was again rejected (Royal Commission on Marriage and Divorce, 1955, Cmnd. 9678). However, in the 1960s something of a family court campaign had built up, although with various ideas about how it should be organised. All this came together in 1974 in the socio-legal analysis made by the Departmental Committee on One-Parent Families (Finer Committee, 19 74, vol. 1, Cmnd. 5629). This endorsed the concept of a local family court as a judicial institution administering family justice according to law and not as a branch of social welfare. The Committee proposed the abolition of the Magistrates' Court's domestic jurisdiction because of its stigmatic association with criminality.

As explained elsewhere (Murch, 2009, note 1), Finer's proposals were not implemented. Nevertheless, a major strategic step was taken some years later when the Lord Chancellor in the Thatcher government, Lord Mackay of Clashfern, succeeded in transferring ministerial responsibilities for magistrates' courts from the Home Office to the Lord Chancellor's Department (now the Ministry of Justice). Also at the time the reform of child care law, which led to the Children Act 1989, fostered the concept of interdisciplinary collaboration and the recognition that the processes of family courts need to be rationalised, even if not unified, hence the notion of concurrent jurisdiction which has been explained earlier.

So, where are we today? Are we any nearer to achieving a unified structure, and, if so, on what basis? Those arguing for the maintenance of the status quo always assert that the transitional cost of change will be prohibitive, without, as far as I know, there ever having been a detailed economic study of the costs of maintaining the existing divided structure or any serious attempt to see whether unification would produce major medium- to long-term cost savings. Superficially, one might think that a bench of lay magistrates is cheaper than a professional judge whether working as a district judge in the Family Proceedings Court, as occasionally happens, or as a full time judge in the County Court. But this view fails to take account of the respective administrative costs of the two kinds of court, assuming that they can be separately distinguished and quantified from other areas of work in the respective courts. It might further be argued that while unification might in theory be worthwhile and even save public money once established, the reorganisation and start up costs of a unified local family court would not be justified, particularly while the country is facing a serious economic downturn with major cuts in public expenditure. Moreover, current reductions in the size of the civil service risk reducing resources available for planning reform: turkeys do not vote for Christmas!

I take a contrary view both on economic grounds and more importantly for child welfare and family support reasons. Dealing with the question of cost first, I suspect that court efficiency, whether in the Magistrates' Court or the County Court has a great deal to do with the speed of case throughput and the avoidance of delay (which has an obvious knock-on impact on the legal aid budget). For example, research which I conducted in the 1980s for the Lord Chancellor's Department and Home Office suggested that some county courts had a faster throughput than magistrates' courts and vice versa (Murch, Borkowski & Copner, 1987). A great deal depends on how rigorous judges and magistrates are in their case management by strict timetabling, avoiding unnecessary adjournments, and interim orders in part heard cases, etc.

One aspect of this is the degree of priority that existing courts can give to family cases, particularly when they have other pressing cases to be heard, such as crime in both levels of courts and a range of other civil and commercial matters in the County Court. Again, I suspect that a more streamlined specialist family court would provide a more suitable administrative structure.

Furthermore, as Judith Masson has recently pointed out (2010), despite much exhortation to limit the workload of the higher courts in order to reduce delay and to start nearly all public law cases in the Magistrates' Court: "There has been a steady drift away from the Family Proceedings Courts to the County Courts" (p. 53).

She offers a number of reasons for this. First, "The idea that proceedings that frequently lead to a child being separated from parents were suitable to be heard at the lowest level of court was not universally supported by children's lawyers and guardians."

Second, because the criteria to transfer cases up from the magistrates' courts to the county courts were easy to satisfy, cases likely to last more than a day were transferred to the county courts even if this contributed to further delay.

Third: "As more cases were transferred both experience and professional confidence in family proceedings courts declined."

Given all these contributory factors, one can only hope that the recently appointed Family Justice Review, charged with considering management and administrative structures, will undertake the necessary in-depth investigation to appraise the economics of the existing arrangements as well as making reliable estimates of cost saving which could be achieved with a unified structure.

vii. The Family Justice Review 2010

As we have seen, Kenneth Clarke concluded his comments on court reform and legal aid by referring to the Family Justice Review, announced in the final days of the previous Labour government in January 2010 (Department for Children Schools and Families, 2010, Cmnd. 7787). Its task is to undertake a critical examination of the shortcomings of the traditional adversarial system and, in the Minister's words: "to search for more civilised ways of handling disputes over children, property and some of the most important aspects of people's lives".

Accordingly, it will examine the effectiveness of the family justice system and the outcomes it delivers and make recommendations for reform. Its specific aims are to:

• Examine both public and private law cases.
• Explore if better use can be made of mediation and how best to support contact between children and non-residential parents and grandparents.
• Examine the processes (but not the law) involved in granting divorces and awarding ancillary relief (matters concerning children, money, and property).
• Look at how different parts of the family justice system are organised and managed.

In March 2011 the Review, chaired by David Norgrove, issued an interim report (Ministry of Justice, 2011a). Although issued "for consultation" this gave a clear indication of the overall reforms which its members had in mind. Nothing less than a complete fundamental structural reform of the system was proposed. In broad outline this prioritised the needs of children and families and was in accord with the constitutional principle of the separation of powers, ensuring a politically independent judicially led system.

As far as the courts were concerned, the Review members were appalled by their existing administratively fragmented, muscle-bound structure and their related welfare support services. They were astonished by the archaic state of the management information system, remarking that "information flows around the system as though computers and the internet had not been invented" (Ministry of Justice, 2011a, para. 2.62), "with vast disorganised court files moved around in supermarket shopping trolleys" (Ministry of Justice, 2011a, para. 3.137).

Because the existing arrangements are so complicated "with overlapping structures and a lack of shared goals and objectives" (Ministry of Justice, 2011b), children are left for months if not years in limbo while their cases are being resolved. Chronic delay is a particularly acute problem in public law cases involving allegations of neglect or child abuse, where children can remain for ages on a series of interim care orders, being passed around from one short stay foster home to another. Because chronic delay also applies to many high conflict cases concerning contact and residence, this too can play havoc with children's attachments and add to their insecurities and anxieties. The lack of a modern management information system of course masks those courts and related welfare services which are particularly slow and disorganised. Moreover, delay adds to costs. But as many of us have known for years, such is the appalling state of management information that it has been impossible to accurately relate legal aid expenditure to case flow rates. One can only wonder what interests have been served by perpetuating this appalling state of ignorance.

Having made a careful analysis of the flaws underlying the existing structure, the Family Justice Review makes a number of radical proposals for root and branch reform with the twin goals of prioritising the welfare of children and saving substantial amounts of public money. Thus it proposes a unified local family court system (Ministry of Justice, 2011a, note 69, para. 3.151) and wants to see more specialist judges to hear cases from start to finish and exerting effective case management with the help of court-based social workers and specialist family court administrators operating modern IT systems (Ministry of Justice, 2011a, para. 3.142). It proposes to bring all of these services within a new Family Justice Service led by a national Family Justice Board and a system of local boards, all within the auspices of the Ministry of Justice, but with close links with the Department for Education, currently responsible for CAFCASS in England, and the Welsh government which separately funds CAFCASS Cymru (Ministry of Justice, 2011a, paras. 3.27–3.43).

The Review recognises that structural changes alone will not be enough. They will have to be accompanied by a change of culture which will modify previous mindsets and modes of work. It follows that if there is to be much closer inter-professional teamwork within the system, with an accompanying recognition that family law is an interdisciplinary activity which needs to further synthesise legal thinking with mental health and child welfare considerations, there will have to be considerable investment in cross-disciplinary professional education. This will require a properly resourced and well-structured system of continuing professional development at all levels of the operation. This is perhaps the one area where the interim report holds back from making firm recommendations, waiting to see what emerges from the consultation process. (Note that the final report from the Family Justice Review will, unfortunately, not emerge until after this book goes to press. But it is to be hoped that those working therapeutically in the field of family and couple relationships will make a positive educational contribution to the creation of the new system of continuing professional development in the family justice system whatever its eventual structure.)

Will the coalition government accept the proposals of the Family Justice Review? At the time of writing it is impossible to tell. The omens are quite good although only when new legislation is framed and the resource implications of proposed changes have been finally calculated will the chances of reform emerge. The Review's final report was published in November 2011 while this book was in press but its main recommendations were substantially the same as appeared in its earlier interim report.

PART IV: TOWARDS A NEW CONCEPT OF FAMILY JUSTICE

In considering reform of the interdisciplinary machinery of family justice, a great deal depends on how one understands its purpose and mode of working. Many lawyers will take a fairly orthodox view, seeing it as essentially just another branch of civil justice, the purpose of which is to resolve disputes using traditional adversarial procedure to test the evidence produced by the parties, with the judge or tribunal "holding the ring", impartially seeing that the applicable law and rules of procedure are complied with. But as has been explained in Part I, it is increasingly recognised that family justice is evolving into a hybrid interdisciplinary system which has many other features. These are slowly adapting it to meet the particular needs of children as well as parents in conflicted families—families who in the main are looking for a fair resolution to their disputes, whether internally or with the welfare authorities of the state. In addition to which, the family courts have a clear duty to apply the law to protect the vulnerable, as in the case of domestic violence and child abuse, and to regard the interests of children as paramount in both public and private law proceedings. Moreover, family courts have a range of enforceable powers which can strike at the very heart of family life by separating children from one or both parents and regulating who shall live in the family home. They also have the power in divorce and separation proceedings to determine the division of family property and the form of financial support. The crucial point to remember is that all such matters inevitably affect the emotional well-being of intra- and extra-family relations: for example, externally in relationships with other relatives, friends, and work colleagues and, for children, in their relationships and performance at school—a critically important issue which often seems to get overlooked in family court proceedings. Inevitably, therefore, the family justice system gets engaged, albeit temporarily, with the psychodynamics of family life.

For these reasons I have come to the conclusion that the family justice process has to be thought about not only in legal terms but from the perspective of what the late Professor Gerald Caplan and others termed community mental health (or as some would call it, population-oriented preventive psychiatry) (Caplan, 1961, 1964, 1974, 1986, 1989). I want therefore to conclude this chapter by outlining some of the ways that Caplan's ideas help us understand the psychosocial aspects of family justice.

i.   Family justice as a community support system
     In using the term "support" and "support system" I use the approach summarised by Caplan. He writes:

> The idea that a person receives support or is in need of support usually carries the connotation that he is weak. From this point of view the term is unfortunate, because what we have in mind is not the propping up of someone who is in danger of falling down but rather the augmenting of a person's strengths to facilitate his mastering of his environment .... "Support system" implies a pattern of enduring or intermittent ties that play a significant part in maintaining the psychological and physical integrity of the individual over time." (1974, note 66)

ii. First responders
     The best known and most ubiquitous support system in our society is the family group and its wider kinship network. The problem is that when family members get embroiled in serious conflict with each other, very often they try to initially keep it secret to themselves or split into partisan camps. Sometimes relatives just do not want to know or get involved. For example, in a study of undefended divorce petitions which I directed in the 1970s, out of a sub-sample of 105 women divorce petitioners, twenty-two had experienced serious domestic violence. The majority had initially turned to relatives and friends who, although they had provided support and sometimes temporary accommodation, often made it

clear to the women that in the longer term they did not want to get involved in the couple's domestic problems.

iii. Second responder

Most of these women had been to their GP who had prescribed anti-depressants and/or tranquillisers. As was reported (Borkowski, Murch & Walker, 1983):

> Seven said the GP had listened carefully and offered useful advice, but another seven said that the GP had been unsympathetic. A few said that once they had arrived at the surgery they had felt too ashamed to talk to the doctor about the violence. (p. 6)

Although this study was a long time ago and GPs' attitudes and understanding may have since changed, it is now generally recognised that among the formal care giving services, GPs are often the first to be turned to, particularly by women.

One should bear in mind that partnerships that deteriorate to the point of breakdown may have a long career of conflict and serious violence during which the couple's needs may change. Again, studies in the 1970s showed that at first many battered wives were likely to want their relationships to continue, even though the police may have been called and injuries resulted in hospital treatment (Dobash, Dobash & Cavanagh, 1985). Solicitors, the gatekeepers to the family justice system, tend to come into the picture only when one or both partners consider the relationship has reached the point of breakdown.

As far as children whose parents separate and/or divorce are concerned, it is only more recently that research has begun to explore their use of informal and formal support systems (Butler, Scanlan, Robinson, Douglas & Murch, 2003). A second line of responder used far less often by children is to be found among community services, including occasionally their school teachers. More recently internet websites established by some children's charities and telephone help lines such as Childline can be viewed as falling within this category of support services. We shall have to see whether, and if so, how such services are affected by forthcoming cuts in public provision.

The concept of primary, secondary, and tertiary prevention

In the health service we are accustomed to thinking in terms of preventive medicine provided by primary healthcare teams, and of secondary preventive backup provided by health trusts that also have responsibilities to mitigate the effects of serious illness with the provision of long-term support services. By analogy, this is another useful conceptual framework to think about the family justice system and its response to family break-up. This is because the notion of prevention focuses on ways of mitigating and buffering the destructive element in family conflict at various stages. With respect to children it aims to boost their resilience and ways of coping with the resulting worries and stresses, particularly at times of family crisis (see Butler, Scanlan, Robinson, Douglas & Murch, 2003, note 37).

As these writers have written (2003, pp. 184–206), if parents are unable to provide the support they (the children) need, because of their own emotional difficulties and inability to communicate, it may be a matter of chance whether children find a suitable channel to express their fears and feelings.

The family court as a tertiary support system

In this chapter I have focused primarily on the litigation process in family courts, which in this respect can be seen as the equivalent of a secondary or tertiary preventive support system. In this respect it is worth remembering that when CAFCASS was established in 2001 its title included the words "support", although many now think that subsequent policies prioritise risk of child abuse and have thus placed the emphasis on surveillance rather than support (Murch, 2009, note 1). Even so, there is evidence to suggest that a number of children caught up in high conflict family litigation, who were represented by a guardian trained in social work, working in tandem with a specially appointed children's solicitor, found the experience supportive and strengthening—enabling them to cope better with the upheavals and uncertainties associated with court proceedings.

The participant model of family justice

i.   The primary task
     From a lawyer's perspective a less orthodox way of thinking about the process of family justice is to view it from the standpoint of the psychodynamics of group relations—particularly the approach pioneered in the 1960s by Bion, Miller, Rice and others, many of whom were associated with the Tavistock Institute of Human

Relations (Bion, 1961; Miller, 1976; Miller & Rice, 1967). Applied to family justice in private family law proceedings, this model, which I propounded some years ago (Murch, 1980, pp. 223–228), starts from the assumption that there is a common objective about which all parties could reach agreement. The aim is that of arriving at a fair and reasonable basis upon which the family can reconstitute itself following parental separation or divorce, paying due regard to the interests of the children. In their hearts, few would disagree with this objective even though they may differ as to the means of reaching it.

ii.   Membership of the conflict resolving system
Once it is accepted that there is such a common, albeit elusive, objective, all the actors within the machinery of justice—judges, solicitors, barristers and CAFCASS officers, as well as the family members themselves, including children who wish to have a voice, can be perceived as being bound together in a common pursuit of an agreed aim. As I explained some years ago (Murch, 1980):

> This becomes the task and each actor within the system has a responsibility to work towards a common goal. To a large extent therefore the task of working towards a common goal becomes itself the authority from which the actors derive their responsibility and by which their roles are defined and differentiated. (note 77, p. 223)

The key point which lawyers often fail to understand is that this way of viewing the family justice process involved working *with* the family rather than doing things *to* it, which is why I have termed it participant family justice. Also, it is a good deal less paternalistic in approach.

It also involves a recognition that the great majority of litigated cases involve a process over time rather than a one-off appearance in which a judge "hands down" a decision as in the case of many other civil disputes. In fact the average length of child-related private law cases is thirty-three weeks, but within a wide range. High conflict cases, not surprisingly, take longer and sometimes run over several years. It also means that although current proceedings are still framed in accordance with the common law adversarial model of justice, as far as children's welfare is concerned, for a number of years the court has relied on inquisitorial elements, for example, through the use of welfare reports and those from child and mental health specialists. Moreover, pure adversarial process as applied to family proceedings has long been criticised as inappropriate since it can so easily aggravate family conflict, fostering an unhelpful winner/loser mentality.

iii. Basic assumption activity and the family justice system
Theoretically there is much more to this approach than I have space to explain here, except to add a word or two about what Bion termed basic assumption activity, that is to say aspects of interpersonal behaviour which sometimes assist but also often hinder the rational purpose of the work. The term "basic assumption" is used because it is as if group members (family justice practitioners and family members) develop unconscious assumptions and beliefs about each other. As Miller and Rice put it (1967, note 76), these transcend the purposes "by which they have met" and may undermine the pursuit of the primary task.

Nevertheless, there is a sense in which institutionally the family justice system depends on certain kinds of basic assumption to advance the work, even though paradoxically the dynamic can become self-defeating. In this respect three basic assumptions have been identified.

i. That in which one member is ascribed dominant power and authority, relieving others of their share of responsibility to work at the task. This occurs, for example, when it is assumed that the whole future of the case depends on what the judge or the CAFCASS officer preparing a report decides.

ii. When it is assumed that the outcome depends almost entirely on a dominant pair or partnership within the system, for example, an agreement negotiated by two legal representatives, or a combination of CAFCASS officer and parent who have identified closely with each other.

iii. When the system's energies are largely focused on the conduct of emotional conflict or fight to the extent that the nature of the primary task is lost sight of. In its most obvious form, the conduct of adversarial litigation channels energies into emotional dispute so that the parties and their advocates get obsessed with "winning" to such an extent that the interests of children get marginalised or overlooked. Thus the dynamic of fight/flight can too easily take over—flight manifesting itself in task avoidance when the system fosters unnecessary delay or gets bogged down in largely irrelevant procedural matters or when one of the parties prevaricates with diversionary tactics.

There is clearly much more that one could say about the approach of group dynamics to the practice and processes of family law. Here I merely want to emphasise one further point: namely that in high conflict parental disputes where the family members are likely to be highly stressed and may, to use a psychoanalytic framework, suffer from weak ego (albeit temporarily) and resort to a fight/flight psychological defence, there may well be a need for a strong containing impartial judicial figure upon which to project compensatory ego functioning, that is, mobilising in a positive way the dependence basic assumption. This takes us on to my final area of hermeneutic ideas, namely the important culturally symbolic aspects of family justice practice.

Psychological significance of symbols in the family justice process

Of all social institutions, with the exception of religious organisations, the law has evolved over centuries if not millennia more rituals and symbols than any other profession that I can think of. In our postmodern age, particularly when major economies are being sought, it is very tempting to dismiss the "trappings of justice" as unnecessary expensive ritual which only serve to alienate the public and mark the law out as some kind of exclusive esoteric world apart from the rest of us. No wonder in family law children and parents find going to court a strange, intimidating experience. No wonder too that sometimes reformers want judges to dispense with wigs, robes, and gowns, and wish to cut out many of the formalities in the courtroom such as the raised bench, the royal coat of arms above the judgement seat, and the need to take the oath—particularly the practice of holding family proceedings in traditional court buildings where criminal trials are also held.

Yet, there are in my opinion aspects to legal symbols and ritual which may well serve important, if implicit, psychological purposes in the management of family conflict. I mention just two: the symbol of the scales of justice and the symbolic authority ascribed to the judge.

Scales of justice, psychological balance, and disequilibrium, and psychosocial homeostasis in family relationships

I assume that readers of this book who work psychotherapeutically in the field of couple and family relations will be familiar with the concept of homeostasis, originally derived from physics and physiology. This refers to the self-regulating principle which preserves the intactness and continuity of the human organism. Transposed by Nathan Ackerman (1958) and others in the 1950s to family group relations, it explains the normal capacity of families to maintain effective coordinated psychosocial functioning under constantly changing conditions.

As many psychotherapists will know, this line of thought led on to what became known in the 1960s as the crisis model of mental health, particularly as developed by Caplan. It also contributed to what has become known as family systems thinking. The term "crisis" was used in a very specific sense to mean a period of emotional turmoil and stress which temporarily disturbs normal psychological equilibrium or homeostasis, that is, the reasonably steady state of everyday life. At an individual and family systems level, this may be temporarily disturbed by critical life-changing events like separations and broken attachments, giving rise to strained and conflicted family relations which may very well end up in litigation. It is my contention that particularly in high conflict parental disputes concerning children, the resort to justice usually contains within it an implicit search to restore or discover a new equitable equilibrium in the families' relationships. Moreover, I argue that the clue to this largely unconscious search can be found in the archetypal symbol of the scales of justice.

Those interested in the history of this symbol, often signifying a court building, will find that there are two historical routes. One concerns the Goddess of Justice, sometimes called Lady Justice, holding a two-edged sword in her right hand and the scales in the left—a motif derived from Greek and Roman times. Sometimes Lady Justice is blindfolded to signify impartiality. The second route is linked to the idea of the last Judgement or Doom which is to be found in Christian theology developed by St Paul and Augustine of Hippo. This depicts St Michael, master of all angels holding the scales of justice. Religious paintings on this theme first appear across Europe in the fourteenth century. In medieval wall paintings, it is often Mary Mother of God who is depicted as holding the scales weighing the soul. Usually the devil tries to tilt one end down as the burden of the soul's sins weighs it down. The Virgin Mary (Queen of Heaven) puts her rosary into the other in recognition of the soul's usually feeble attempt at piety. Tina Beattie, a professor of theology at Roehampton University, once explained to me the point here being that "the smallest act of charity or devotion is enough to tilt the scales of judgement in the soul's favour and mercy is more powerful that sin".

While it is generally believed that the Divorce Reform Act 1969 replaced the concept of the matrimonial offence with a more secular notion of irretrievable breakdown of marriage, the so-called "facts" of desertion, adultery, and unreasonable behaviour (formerly cruelty) used to prove breakdown linger on in English law. Indeed, bitter and angry parents still commonly hold ideas of moral blameworthiness. Even though lawyers and social workers and marital therapists might now view matters differently in more neutral non-judgemental ways, cultural beliefs about good and evil, justice and injustice, still creep into the conduct of family proceedings up and down the country on a daily basis. Thinking pictorially about the scales of justice one can see how St Paul's ideas of spiritual damnation and salvation, rather than concepts of balance and return to stability, have dominated our legal culture until comparatively recently, as of course they still do in the criminal jurisdiction.

Nevertheless, my argument is that this traditional view has tended to obscure the symbolic significance of the more mechanical aspects of the scales, namely the principles of balance and return to stability when the process of weighing during litigation has been completed—at least when the parties and their children can accept that a fair, just resolution has been found so that they can get on and rebuild their lives. In this sense, the family justice system can be viewed as a form of natural "therapy".

Symbolic authority of an impartial judge

I turn now finally to my second feature of family justice, namely the impartial authority figure of the judge. As I have suggested, in the whole drama of litigation, there is at work here what an American judge, Jerome Frank, once termed a degree of modern "legal magic". One only has to think of all the rituals which, particularly in relation to the adversarial mode of trial, attach to the judicial role and serve to enhance its authority, including judicial robes and wigs and the advocates' use of legal jargon and forms of address such as "My Lord", "Your Honour", or in respect of magistrates, "Your Worships" (the similarity with church rituals are obvious here). One could of course develop this theme and discuss it in the context of reforms designed to make courts more child and family friendly. Here, suffice to say that I consider that the more inflamed and recurrent the degree of conflict and hostility in the case, the more symbolically powerful needs to be the authority of the court in order to exert a containing and restraining influence, and in order to allow the parties, their legal advisers, and the court welfare support staff (which collectively I have termed the "family justice team") sufficient time to work with the family in pursuit of the objective of finding an acceptable resolution. Setting strong and realistic time boundaries and limits for this task is part of the impartial judge's case management role—a task greatly assisted by the principle of judicial continuity and by the judicially led family court teams' capacity to keep the focus on the interests of the child—both points endorsed in the Family Justice Review's interim report (Ministry of Justice, 2010, paras. 3.60–3.65).

Conclusion

In this chapter, my purpose has been to show that the family justice system in England and Wales has been evolving as a distinct system of civil justice and that it serves important preventive psychosocial purposes in the management of parental disputes concerning children. I have outlined a number of behavioural science frameworks or schools of thought which, I argue, assist our understanding of this relatively new jurisprudence. I have written the piece at a time when the British government intends to find major economies in the legal system as a whole and when there is serious danger that a lack of understanding of these distinctive features of family justice will lead to irreparable damage to a hybrid system that has the potential to enable thousands of children and their parents to cope better with the aftermath of family breakdown. The threat of cuts in financial provision for public services in general will affect community mental health services as well as family justice. This threat may well lead practitioners in these services to retreat into their respective traditional professional "ghettos" in order to protect their particular intellectual domains. This would run counter to the need to develop much-needed cross-disciplinary understanding, training, and collaboration in the family justice field—just at the time when increasing numbers of families will be experiencing stress and conflict resulting from the downturn in the economy. I hope therefore that in the next few years, those working in the field of couple relations will contribute positively to the reform of the family justice system and assist family lawyers in their understanding of the important community mental health aspects of their family work.

References

Ackerman, N. W. (1958). *The Psychodynamics of Family Life*. New York: Basic.

Auerbach, J. S. (1985). *Justice Without Law: Resolving Disputes Without Lawyers*. Oxford: Oxford University Press.

Bingham, T. (2010). *The Rule of Law*. London: Allan Lane.

Bion, W. R. (1961). *Experiences in Groups*. London: Tavistock.

Borkowski, M., Murch, M. & Walker, V. (1983). *Marital Violence: the Community Response*. London: Tavistock.

Butler, I., Scanlan, L., Robinson, M., Douglas, G. & Murch, M. (2003). *Divorcing Children—Children's Experience of their Parents' Divorce*. London: Jessica Kingsley.

CAFCASS (2009). *Annual Report and Accounts 2008-09*. London: The Stationery Office (TSO).

Caplan, G. (1961). *An Approach to Community Mental Health*. London: Tavistock.

Caplan, G. (1964). *Principles of Preventive Psychiatry*. London: Tavistock.

Caplan, G. (1974). *Support Systems and Community Mental Health—Lectures in Concept Development*. New York: Behavioral Publications.

Caplan, G. (1986). Recent developments in crisis intervention: The prevention of support systems. In: M. Kessler & S. E. Goldston (Eds.), *Decade of Progress in Primary Prevention*. Hanover, NH: University Press of New England.

Caplan, G. (1989). Prevention of psychopathology and maladjustment in children of divorce. In: M. Brambring, F. Losel & H. Skowronek (Eds.), *Children at Risk—Assessment, Longitudinal Research and Intervention*. Berlin: Walter de Gruyter.

Cretney, S. (2003). *Family Law in the Twentieth Century*. Oxford: Oxford University Press.

Davis, G. (1988). *Partisans and Mediators*. Oxford: Clarendon.

Davis, G. (2004). A research perspective. In: J. Wescott (Ed.), *Family Mediation, Past, Present and Future*. Bristol, UK: Jordans Family Law.

Department for Children Schools and Families (2010). *Support for All: the Family and Relationships Green Paper*. London: The Stationery Office (TSO).

Djanogly, J. (2010). *Lucy Faithfull Memorial Lecture—National Family Mediation*, 29 November. Available from http://www.nfm.org.uk/component/jdownloads/finish/60/314

Dobash, R. E., Dobash, R. P. & Cavanagh, K. (1985). Contact between battered women and social and medical agencies. In: J. Pahl (Ed.), *Private Violence and Public Policy*. Boston: Routledge & Kegan Paul.

Douglas, G., Murch, M., Miles, C. & Scanlan, L. (2006). *Research into the Operation of r. 9.5 of the Family Proceedings Rules 1991*. Available from http://www.dca.gov.uk./family/familyprocrules_research.pdf

Finer Committee (1974). *The Report of the Committee on One-Parent Families*. London: HMSO.

Ford, T. & Goodman, R. (2005). *Mental Health of Children and Young People in Great Britain*. London: Office of National Statistics.

Harold, G. & Murch, M. (2005). Interpersonal conflict in children's adaptation to separation and divorce—research and implications for family law, practice and policy. *Children and Family Law Quarterly*, 17(2): 187.

Harold, G., Pryor, J. & Reynolds, J. (2001). *Not in Front of the Children? How Conflict Between Parents Affects Children*. London: One Plus One Marriage and Partnership Research.

Harold, G., Shelton, K. H., Goeke-Morey, M. C., & Cummings, E. M. (2004). Child emotional security about family relationships and child adjustment. *Social Development*, 13(3): 376.

HM Government (2009). *Court Statistics*. London: HM Stationery Office.

Hunt, J. (2010). *Parental Perspectives on the Family Justice System in England and Wales: a Review of Research*. Available from http://www.family-justice-council.org.uk/publications.htm

Layard, R. & Dunn, J. (2009). *A Good Childhood: Searching for Values in a Competitive Age*. London: Penguin.

Lowe, N. & Douglas, G. (2007). *Bromley's Family Law* (10th edn.). Oxford: Oxford University Press.

Lowe, N. & Murch, M. (2001). Children's participation in the family justice system—translating principles into practice. *Child and Family Law Quarterly*, 13: 137–158.

Maclean, M. & Eekelaar, J. (2009). *Family Law Advocacy—How Barristers Help Victims of Family Failure*. Oxford: Hart.

Magistrates' Court Service Inspectorate (2003). *Seeking Agreement: a Thematic Review of CAFCASS Schemes in Private Law Proceedings*. Magistrates' Court Service Inspectorate.

Masson, J. (2010). Judging the Children Act 1989: the courts and the administration of family justice. *Journal of Children Services*, 5(2): 53.

Miller, E. J. (1976). *Task and Organisation*. London: Wiley.

Miller, E. J. & Rice, A. K. (1967). *Systems of Organisation*. London: Tavistock.

Ministry of Justice (2010). *Proposals for the Reform of Legal Aid in England and Wales*. Available from http://www.justice.gov.uk/consultations/legal-aid-reform.htm

Ministry of Justice (2011a, March 31). *Family Justice Review Interim Report*. Available from http://www.justice.gov.uk/publications/policy/moj/family-justice-review.htm

Ministry of Justice (2011b, March 31). Children deserve better from existing family justice system. Available from www.justice.gov.uk/news/press-release310311a.htm

Ministry of Justice (2011c, November 3). *Family Justice Review Final Report*. Available from www.justice.gov.uk/publications/policy/moj/family-justice-review-final.htm

Murch, M. (1980). *Justice and Welfare in Divorce*. London: Sweet & Maxwell.

Murch, M. (2004). The germ and the gem of the idea. In: J. Westcott (Ed.), *Mediation: Past, Present and Future*. Bristol, UK: Jordans Family Law.

Murch, M. (2009). Cultural change in the family justice system. In: G. Douglas & N. Lowe (Eds.), *The Continuing Evolution of Family Law*. Bristol, UK: Jordans Family Law.

Murch, M. (2010). The voice of the child in private family law proceedings—time to rethink the approach. *Seen and Heard, NAGALRO*, 20(1): 36–48.

Murch, M., Borkowski, M. & Copner, R. (1987). *The Overlapping Family Jurisdiction of Magistrates' Courts and County Courts—a Study for the Socio-Legal Centre for Family Studies*. Bristol, UK: University of Bristol.

Murch, M., Douglas, G. & Scanlan, L. (1999). Safeguarding children's welfare in uncontentious divorce: a study of s. 41 of the Matrimonial Causes Act. *Lord Chancellor's Department*, 99(7).

Ormrod, R. (1974). The role of the courts in relation to children—Sixth Hilda Lewis Memorial Lecture. *Child Adoption*, 75(1): 15–25.

Parkinson, P. & Cashmore, J. (2008). *The Voice of the Child in Family Law Disputes*. Oxford: Oxford University Press.

Pryor, J. & Rogers, B. (2001). *Children in Changing Families—Life after Parental Separation*. Oxford: Blackwell.

Royal Commission on Marriage and Divorce (1955). *Report of the Royal Commission on Marriage and Divorce*. London: HM Government.

Timms, J. (2009). Twenty-five years of guardians. *Seen and Heard, NAGALRO*, 19(2): 41–53.

Trinder, L., Connolly, J., Notley, C. & Swift, L. (2006). Making contact happen or making contact work? The process and outcomes of in-court conciliation. *The Department of Constitutional Affairs Research Series*, 3(6).

COMMENTARY ON CHAPTER FOUR

Christopher Clulow

W hy should family courts be of the remotest interest to those working in the field of mental health? Are they not the product of an arcane legal system that is far removed from the realities of family life? Do they not come on the scene too late to be helpful for those in trouble, sometimes making a bad situation worse? Is there any reason to believe that family courts are motivated to respond more closely to the needs of family members? And do those working in mental health services have anything to say that would improve the way family courts operate?

Mervyn Murch has answers to these questions. Drawing on more than forty years' experience of working in the family justice system—a term he was instrumental in coining (Murch & Hooper, 1992)—he has a unique perspective on the slowly changing ways in which separation and divorce have been managed in this country. Poacher turned gamekeeper (he started his professional life as a social worker and is now an emeritus professor of law), he has been at the forefront of interweaving an understanding of the psychodynamics of family life with a keen knowledge of legal process, to signal directions of change that might enhance community well-being. In particular, he has identified the importance of interdisciplinary working if families undergoing stressful change are to be empowered to behave responsibly.

At the heart of his thesis is the observation that families undergoing divorce interact with judicial procedures for managing conflict, and the outcome of that encounter will depend on the kind of relational system they construct together. He uses the systems concept of homeostasis to describe the challenges facing families during separation and divorce, arguing that those who resort to the family justice system to resolve parental disputes can be viewed, in part, as searching for "a new and better emotional equilibrium" for life after divorce. For me, this is a crucial statement, because it places the way people feel about what is happening to them at the centre of the drama of family restructuring. From a mental health perspective I would assert that attending to the emotional dimensions of change is the key to unlocking the secrets of family behaviour. Accepting this premise implies that helping to regulate feelings (encouraging their expression when suppressed and containing them when they get out of hand) is an important function of the family justice system, one that has the potential to secure outcomes that are both just and protective of the welfare of vulnerable family members.

It is one thing to assert the centrality of emotions to family justice, quite another to translate this into systems and procedures that can secure creative outcomes for family change. What constitutes a new and better emotional equilibrium for one family member might constitute just the reverse for another. Homeostasis is an essentially conservative concept, often implying a rebalancing process that restores the status quo ante. This matches the state of mind of some going through divorce (and, perhaps, also, of some who manage the divorces of others). Often one party in the family, whether adult or child, does not want change and will do anything to turn the clock back. Attempts to achieve a new balance in the family are then resisted, fuelling conflict between parents that can find expression in child contact and residence disputes.

Evidence for this comes from many sources, including a study conducted by the Tavistock Centre for Couple Relationships in the 1980s. This research found that an inability of one or both partners to accept the ending of their marriage formed a very important part of the emotional context for disputes over children in 83% of the core sample of welfare enquiries examined (Clulow & Vincent, 1987). A subsequent study conducted at the Centre revealed unconscious transference pressures operating during psychotherapy with divorcing partners to make judges (and servants) of therapists in order to ease the pain of emotional conflict associated with separation and loss (Vincent, 1995). This is just one example of the influence families can exert on extra-familial systems, and during divorce it is the family justice system that will be unconsciously targeted. Partners who feel betrayed, rejected, abused, and unfairly treated may want a legal representative who will prosecute their case and a judge who will vindicate their complaint. The different kinds of anxiety that can drive family conflict during divorce will find their way into the behaviour of family justice practitioners: for example, separation anxiety can feed paranoid-schizoid states of mind that demand adversarial/adjudicative systems of jurisprudence (Clulow & Vincent, 2003).

All of this poses a challenge to those of us who champion the private ordering of conflict associated with family change through processes such as mediation and the model of participative family justice proposed by Murch. If there is a fit between adversarial, investigative, and adjudicatory judicial procedures and the psychological processes affecting many parents at some stage in the divorce process, how can the system change?

The question, as so often is the case with family matters, is whether the reasoned arguments based on research findings and common sense can be translated into an action plan without being subverted along the way. For example, a criticism directed at some forms of mediation is that through privileging "rational" negotiation about practicalities over "irrational" emotional experience they attempt to "sanitise divorce", with the consequence that agreements reached may not last for very long (Sclater, 1999). On the other hand, we know that many families benefit from alternative dispute resolution procedures, not least because they support rather than override parents in exercising their responsibilities. So we are likely to be facing a tension between potentially conflicting opposites in every proposal for managing change: reason versus emotion, past versus present, support versus safeguarding, rights versus responsibilities, and so on. These tensions need balancing, and family courts have a part to play in this.

Murch speculates about the symbolic function of the scales of justice appearing outside many courts, suggesting they might depict the role of the judiciary as achieving balance in the resolution of family conflict (although this is most likely to be perceived not in systemic but judicial terms—achieving fairness and justice in resolving disputes). Colman (2008) makes a helpful distinction between symbols (representations of something unconscious and unknown) and signs (which are essentially conscious and known). Signs, he says, point us in a particular direction, whereas symbols mediate between opposites and allow for an element of surprise about outcomes as we apprehend our situation more fully. He describes symbols as "the clothing of affect in image", and argues that they hold out the hope that something that is not yet known might be discovered. My guess is that when people are feeling anxious their attention is most likely to be drawn to the figure of Lady Justice, and that she will be perceived as a sign of what the future will hold rather than a symbol. She will be the one to decide on whose fate is held in the balance and what the outcome will be. Less apparent might be her role in holding in balance the conflicting realities, concerns, and priorities of the protagonists (of which she is one because of the public interest in child welfare). Taking this view she can be seen as containing all the potential aspects of a dispute, and by doing so encouraging those in conflict to do the same. In psychoanalytic terms we might say she holds a "third position" (Britton, 1989), which, when taken up, can transcend and transform the conflict between polar opposites. Her authority derives from the role she has been given (most likely perceived in terms of the powerful sword she wields rather than her role in holding opposites in balance), her impartiality (the blindfold), and perhaps her female form (inviting associations of maternal care). What, we might ask fancifully, would be the impact of her place being taken by a child? Might that symbolism refocus the protagonists in the way they view their differences and how they should be settled? Might it encourage/shame them into taking up a third position in relation to the disputes in which they have become locked?

Murch's reference to Bion's work with groups is very useful in this context. Bion (1961) observed that work groups have a function that can be subverted by basic assumption mentalities. Such mentalities act as (unconscious) defences to manage anxiety in group members that might threaten the cohesion both of the individuals and the group, or sub-group, to which they feel they belong. It is a telling analogy to draw with the family justice system. Task avoidance associated with basic assumption mentalities (for example, awaiting the arrival of a saviour to resolve problems, or fostering pairing between members of the system) acts against the principle of collaborative justice in so far as it takes responsibility away from individual members rather than supports them in playing their appropriate part.

In this context we have to ask whether the second symbol Murch refers to, the authority of the judge, promotes or inhibits participative justice. If the unfamiliarity of court surroundings acts like a "strange situation" test for family members (Ainsworth, Blehar, Waters & Wall, 1978), we might assume that the trappings of the court, including the dress of judges and legal representatives, will raise rather than reduce anxiety. Raised anxiety leads to raised defences, which, in turn, inhibit the capacity to use symbols and to think. Without a capacity to think there is an increased likelihood that feelings will be enacted rather than contained. It can be argued, and Murch does so, that the legal trappings of court dress and procedure increase the perception of power, and that this can check the behaviour of those who set out to exploit their position. This is a point worth considering. But we know that proceedings in family disputes can continue over years, suggesting that the external trappings of judicial power are less effective than might be supposed, and exposing the ultimate impotence of courts in the face of determined players of the system. Fostering the illusion of omnipotence through costume drama may have the unintended consequence of playing into basic assumption dependency states, or encouraging fight-flight responses. It may also tip the balance of perception away from the court's role in balancing a civil settlement and towards a sense of being judged in connection with a matrimonial offence—a regressive step that evokes the troubled history of our divorce laws and makes way for increasing a public law safeguarding mentality. This is not a climate conducive to participative justice.

The concept of participative justice implies the formation of a group or system whose task is to ensure a constructive outcome to family change. Mobilising Caplan's (1961) three-stage model of preventive community psychiatry (as Murch does), we might conceive of this group as a unified local family court geared up to regulating the emotional experience of those who use its services as the primary means through which its task is achieved. The first tier of response for such a model would be to provide information for those who requested it about the various issues that need to be thought about in connection with the divorce process. This would be aimed primarily at parents, in order to furnish them with the resources to make informed decisions about their family relationships and those they might form with different "players" in the family justice system. Information would also be available for any children affected by family change so they know what is going on and how they might contribute to the process. Because information is power, and power reduces anxiety, the emotional climate is then one that is conducive to a participative process.

The next tier of response would be access to a range of services that might support family members in working out the best way to achieve the outcomes they seek or must accept. Legal advice, counselling help, and mediation services would play their part in this process, with the aim of enabling proposals (including parenting plans) for managing life after divorce to be worked up in ways that take account of the views of parents, children, and the public interest. Implicit in this process is the need to work with the emotional as well as practical details highlighted by drawing up proposals for change.

The third tier would involve a specialist family court judge, assigned to specific families in order to provide continuity of care, whose role would be to review family proposals in terms of justice and child welfare, endorsing them as appropriate. Only where families were unable to come up with workable proposals, or where their proposals failed the tests of justness and child welfare, would the participative process be replaced by investigation and adjudication. It is in this context that CAFCASS would come into play as the investigative arm of the court.

This model, which Murch has indicated through highlighting Caplan's model of preventive psychiatry, would differ from existing procedures (and those proposed but jettisoned when the 1995 Family Law Act was being debated) mainly in terms of involving children in the process, providing a unified court system, ensuring greater continuity of contact between families and family justice practitioners, and allowing sufficient but not too much time for due diligence by the parties principally concerned—the family members who will be affected by proposed changes and the judge who represents the community's stake in post-divorce arrangements. It would take as its core assumption that restructuring family relationships involves rebalancing feelings. The implication of this is that creative outcomes from separation and divorce rely on fostering emotional awareness and containment among all those who come together to form the relational system of family justice.

References

Ainsworth, M. D. S., Blehar, M., Waters, E. & Wall, S. (1978). *Patterns of Attachment: A Psychological Study of the Strange Situation*. Hillsdale, NJ: Lawrence Erlbaum.

Bion, W. R. (1961). *Experiences in Groups*. London: Tavistock.

Britton, R. (1989). The missing link: parental sexuality in the Oedipus complex. In: R. Britton, J. Steiner & E. O'Shaughnessy (Eds.), *The Oedipus Complex Today: Clinical Implications*. London: Karnac.

Caplan, G. (1961). *An Approach to Community Mental Health*. London: Tavistock.

Clulow, C. & Vincent, C. (1987). *In the Child's Best Interests? Divorce Court Welfare and the Search for a Settlement*. London: Tavistock/Sweet and Maxwell.

Clulow, C. & Vincent, C. (2003). Working with divorcing partners. In: M. Bell & K. Wilson (Eds.), *The Practitioner's Guide to Working with Families*. Basingstoke, UK: Macmillan Palgrave.

Colman, W. (2008). *The Symbolic Process*. Lecture given at the Society of Analytical Psychology, London, 8 March.

Murch, M. & Hooper, D. (1992). *The Family Justice System*. Bristol, UK: Jordans Family Law.

Sclater, S. (1999). *Divorce: a Psychosocial Study*. Aldershot, UK: Ashgate.

Vincent, C. (1995). Consulting to divorcing couples. *Family Law, 25* (December): 678–681.

CHAPTER FIVE

Working therapeutically with high conflict divorce

Avi Shmueli

Jo and Ted were powerfully drawn together. They met by chance and quickly began an intense and passionate affair. Jo unexpectedly fell pregnant. Keeping the child was never questioned and she resigned her unfulfilling job. Ted had recently left a vacuous marriage and in the more distant past had, in the normal course of events, suffered the bereavement of his parents. As soon as their child was born a battle for care of the baby ensued. It was ferocious, with application leading to counter-application, claims of violence on both sides, and hearing following hearing. By the time their daughter was aged five, the courts had had enough and were threatening to ban all further petitions for a substantial length of time unless the couple sought some therapeutic help. At this time, Jo was afraid to be in the same room as Ted, while Ted travelled continuously, only ensuring he was present for contact with his daughter.

The field of couple psychotherapy is a rich and complex one which usefully allows different schools of analytic thought to sit alongside each other as, for example, in the now classic *Mate & Stalemate* (Mattinson & Sinclair, 1979). As such, it provides a good forum for what Joseph Sandler (1983) termed the "elasticity" of theoretical concepts necessary to explain observed phenomena and, thereby, to develop psychoanalytic theory. This chapter attempts to illustrate and conceptualise psychoanalytic work with couples who are engaged in high conflict or entrenched divorce and separations. The ideas are developed from the work of the Divorce and Separation Unit (DSU) of the Tavistock Centre for Couple Relationships (TCCR) and the long tradition of psychoanalytic couple psychotherapy developed within TCCR. This chapter describes some of the central ideas in working psychoanalytically with divorce and separation and also provides one approach to working with high conflict couples in particular.

The main argument of this chapter is that the high levels of conflict associated with divorce can be understood as the result of changes occurring in three different psychological domains. These are termed the environmental domain, the pre-conscious normative domain, and the unconscious idiopathic domain. Each exerts an influence on the other two with the unconscious idiopathic domain holding greatest sway in situations of high conflict. The consequence may involve an erosion of identity leading to a pathological regression for one or both partners. In these circumstances, an individual's capacity for reflective and balanced thinking becomes highly restricted. This limitation of the capacity to think in a mature and reasonable way sets difficult challenges for practitioners attempting to help resolve conflict. I suggest some ways in which standard therapeutic technique may need to be modified in these circumstances.

Defining high conflict divorce

The term "high conflict" originated in the USA but, in the UK, is often referred to as "entrenched conflict" and predominantly, although not exclusively, involves difficulties in agreeing post-separation arrangements for children. Paradoxically, while the term can make intuitive sense, a seminal definition has not evolved (Lauter, 2009; Stewart, 2001), and attempts to do so have invariably focused on the actions or "external markers" displayed by the divorcing couple, such as several changes of solicitor, the number of repeated applications made suggesting one partner is a vexatious litigant, and the time taken for a case to settle. The difficulty in the definition arises in no small part from the absence of a baseline measure for expected conflict between the couple at the point of separation (Stewart, 2001). Even so, many practitioners in the family justice system will be familiar with those divorcing couples where conflict characterises all communication, has a self-perpetuating quality, and takes on a life of its own; "The form of the custody dispute becomes their new pattern of relationship" (Johnston & Campbell. 1988, p. 12). Indeed, these conflictual patterns are so prevalent that typologies of "divorce decision making" seek to locate them within the overall patterns of divorce breakdown. Kressel, Jaffee, Tuchman, Watson, and Deutsch (1980), for example, identified the autistic, disengaged, direct, and enmeshed patterns that can define a couple's interaction in the divorce process. In their study it was the enmeshed category that showed high levels of unremitting conflict. In another study, Johnston (1994) identified a variety of dimensions centrally involved in the divorce process. These included the "domain dimension" involving property and financial support, the "tactics dimension" for informal attempts to resolve disputes, and the "attitudinal dimension" referring to the degree of covert and overt hostility between the partners.

To those witnessing the painfulness of unremittingly conflictual and angry break-ups, these typologies are helpful in beginning to make sense of what might seem like inexplicable and overwhelmingly distressing behaviour, made more so when the needs of children for stability seem to be disregarded. Moreover, in these situations, it is all too easy to forget that the current combatants seeking divorce were once a courting pair and lovers. In those early days it is highly likely that each couple had high hopes for creating a happy and fulfilling life together yet, in high conflict divorce, these characteristics of cooperation, mutual concern, and development are absent and seem impossible to rekindle. While the ongoing conflict may demand immediate attention from professionals, friends, and relations who are pressured to take sides, the origin of the conflict lies in the couple relationship itself and it is this that may most fruitfully offer ways of understanding the present crisis.

The central value of couple relationships

The psychoanalytic model of couple relationships (Bannister et al., 1955; Ruszczynski, 1994) developed at TCCR was an essentially optimistic one. Based on the recognition that a relationship signified by legal marriage was one in which each partner made significant emotional investment, early writings emphasised its developmental and creative potential. The degree of psychological investment in marriage allowed for a parallel to be made with the investment that occurs between mother and infant and thus allowed for the development of many theoretical strands. In present times when committed adult relationships take a variety of forms, including marriage, the theory retains its developmental potential but balances this with recognition of the defensive and at times destructive impulses that comprise human nature and which are inevitably present in all couple relationships.

The model proposes that relationships between future partners develop on the basis of conscious and unconscious attractions but because of the opportunities for regressive behaviour to be experienced through sexual, physical, and emotional intimacy, adult coupling provides the possibility of reworking unresolved past conflicts within the arena of the couple relationship. The subtle differences in behaviour that can be subjectively observed when on one's own in comparison to being in the presence of a loved partner serve as evidence for the presence and power of a relationship, holding two individuals together and allowing a process to unfold between them.

As each partner unconsciously brings wishes for their own development to the relationship, so also does each unconsciously bring their defences to bear in order to defend against the psychic pain of conflict resolution and development. In this way, the couple relationship is the forum for the balance between developmental and defensive wishes. Each partner acts and reacts to the other as they jointly try to resolve their now joint struggles. The relationship, if it is functioning well, is therefore akin to Anna Freud's notion of the analyst acting as an auxiliary ego to the patient, helping the latter bear what was previously unbearable in the service of resolution and development (Sherick, 1983), with the added notion that this has now become a mutual process. The central aim for both is to gain conscious understanding and insight into what was previously intolerable and effectively repressed. In this way, certain arguments between couples become repetitive because they represent important underlying themes for one or both.

> Betty and Frank always argued over making tea. Should the spoon used to make the tea be washed immediately or could it be left on the side till later. Who would have thought that a teaspoon could encompass issues of power, authority, and feared subjugation? April and Leslie, on the other hand, had long teasing arguments over who drooled the most and for longest when they first met. Anxieties over desire and dependency could be jointly and safely worked with and expressed in their banter.

Every couple establishes between them an unconscious cycle of projections through which they try to resolve each of their own past struggles and to develop further. Conflict is therefore part and parcel of the couple relationship just as it is in the unconscious mind of every individual. Past and current developmental struggles and conflicts find tangible and concrete representation within the couple relationship wherein lies the hope for resolution. The balance within the relationship between defensive and developmental tendencies, coupled with the strength of the relationship to bear the associated tensions, determines the degree of developmental work that can be undertaken. While some authors view marriage as having a number of specific "tasks" (e.g., Wallerstein, 1994), in my view the central value of the relationship lies in it allowing for a process of psychological working through (Winnicott, 1975) and thus the development of aspects of each individual that could not be previously attended to. Gradually, and not without struggle or psychic pain, insight can lead to psychological growth.

The stress and nature of divorce and separation

While different relationships have different trajectories depending upon the central unconscious dynamics (Mattinson & Sinclair, 1979), sometimes the relationship itself can lead to differing levels of development, and these differences can become too great to be held and contained by the relationship. At these times, crisis may ensue and a breakdown in the form of separation and divorce may follow.

> Anna was in her early fifties and Brad was just sixty when they married. It was Anna's second and Brad's first marriage. Anna's previous marriage had ended painfully with her husband leaving her for another woman and a bitter divorce ensued. She was attracted to Brad's attentiveness and caring during their courtship but she found that when married his behaviour became controlling and excluding rather than loving and involving. The behaviour played into her fears that she had no "voice" in relationships with men. Brad, who had been a single man all his adult life, found it hard to relinquish a bachelor's mindset for the requirements of sharing a life together with a wife. Through therapy Anna found her "voice" and, in the face of Brad's unwillingness to be less dominant and more of a partner, she left the marriage seriously contemplating divorce.

Separation and divorce are deeply stressful events. The now classic and still definitive list of stressful life events by Holmes and Rahe (1967) was initially developed to examine the relationship between life events and illness. It was based on the examination of 5,000 medical records and was then followed by a number of reliability studies, such as Rahe, Mahan, and Arthur (1970). In the list of identified stressful life events, divorce was placed second, being only less significant than the death of a spouse. Separation was ranked third and considered more stressful that imprisonment. It is noteworthy that aspects involving the end of intimate adult relationships occupy the top three places and significantly outrank loss of employment or personal injury in terms of their contributory "score" towards the link between stress and illness.

Divorce shares with other major life events the requirement that those involved manage change on a grand scale. Change involves a balance of losses and gains which are likely to be experienced differently according to whether the changes are wished for or resisted. The many and various connections that bind couples together in a partnership, such as the intimacy of shared living, bonds between parents and children, shared assets of money and property, networks of friends and family, and established patterns of employment will change. Understanding the impact of divorce therefore requires a conceptualisation of the nature of the changes required.

The magnitude and impact of separation and divorce operates on three independent but mutually influencing domains of experience. The first of these may be termed the "environmental domain". This involves having to manage very conscious and tangible factors such as personal finance and property, living arrangements, contact arrangements with children, and the adversarial legal process itself. In the course of separation and/or divorce, changes in this domain are inescapable. For example, anyone seeking a divorce in the U.K. will have to provide a comprehensive and detailed account of their financial position by completing a 'Form E' which is statement of each partner's income, outgoings, assets, and liabilities, both at present and as far as is known in the future, for example, pending proceeds from a trust, pension plans, invested sums. It is, in effect, a "spot balance" of their entire financial situation including a prediction of the future situation as far as this can be predicted. The Form E for each party is a sworn statement, the content of which has to be substantiated by documentary evidence.

The parties then disclose their forms to each other and can challenge each other's statement. Accuracy is, therefore, at a premium in order to avoid future cross examination in court.

What may therefore initially appear to be a purely administrative process is in actuality a complex and demanding task in many ways. First, it requires the assessment of expenses and assets on an individual basis rather than on the basis of a couple. Second, it requires a level of detail that usually has not formed part of couple functioning prior to the separation and divorce. Third, the requirement for future prediction necessitates envisioning a future alone rather than as part of the present marriage or a future relationship. These intellectual tasks, while complicated enough, also require the individual to emotionally recognise the reality of the divorce process as Form E is often the first document required to be completed: divorce is no longer an abstract notion, but a concrete reality. The demands of completing Form E are such that in many cases, solicitors pace their clients in the completion of it, guiding their clients by telling them to complete certain sections at certain times and leaving others to be completed jointly in discussion with the solicitor.

While Form E is one example of an event in the environmental domain, the management of this environmental demand overlaps with the second domain relevant to understanding the impact of divorce and separation: the "preconscious normative domain". This domain lies in the realms of the preconscious and involves normative and predictable emotional responses associated with negotiating the transition out of a significant personal relationship. In so far as this transition involves accommodating losses, it is to be expected that partners will react in different ways. Some will be able to mourn their losses, which enables them to move on in their lives, valuing and not demeaning their past life and partner. Others may remain stuck in an attachment to previous relationships and ways of living, either because of a difficulty in relinquishing the past or because of anxiety and misgivings about embracing new relationships and ways of living. It is within the realm of the preconscious normative that models of grief such as Bowlby's (1980) four stage model (protest, yearning, despair, and reorganisation) or Kubler-Ross's (2008) five stage model (denial, anger, bargaining, depression, acceptance) may be thought to apply. These processes have their own pace for each individual but occur alongside and simultaneously to events in the environmental domain.

The third domain may be termed the "unconscious idiopathic domain" in which the workings of the unconscious projective cycle between the separating couple have an impact upon the unconscious functioning of each individual. It is the realm of individual psychopathology and has a powerful influence upon both the preconscious normative and the environmental realms. For example, Freud's (1917) distinction between mourning and melancholia noted how mourning was not possible when an individual could not bear an internal psychological separation from an internal object representing the person who had died. Melancholia was the result rather than any process of mourning. In this way, the unconscious idiopathic realm has significant influence on the other realms. A useful typology of divorces was suggested by Clulow and Vincent (1987) who conceptualised divorces according to the kind of projective system of the couple. They suggested three types of divorce:

i. The "shotgun divorce": the stereotypical image of divorce in which the marriage has allowed for the development of one partner and not the other. One partner therefore no longer requires the relationship in the same form, hence a process of reintrojection has occurred for one partner and not the other. The resulting tension is unsustainable and the partner who has developed leaves suddenly and to the complete surprise of the remaining partner. It can manifest in a number of ways, for instance, the woman who stops being a doormat and finds her voice may present too much of a challenge for her husband who then leaves.

ii. The "long lease divorce": the situation in which even after a couple has separated, one of them acts as if he/she has a proprietorial sense of ownership over the absent partner and gets offended if the partner's behaviour falls outside self-perceived accepted bounds, for example, when the absent partner has a new partner in his/her life or wants to get remarried. This could activate a court response, often an application over child care arrangements, designed to coerce the absent partner back into line. This behaviour suggests a lingering attachment long after the physical separation and divorce process have been completed.

iii. The "nominal divorce": a situation in which a couple is predominantly fused and enacts a divorce in an attempt to achieve a psychological separation, albeit in a highly ambivalent fashion.

This type of couple divorce in name only as they continue to live together and struggle with the possibility of some symptomatic improvement.

The three domains may be represented topographically, as shown in Figure 1. Doing so also allows the mapping of different agencies as they influence each of the post-divorce individuals and their families, given that, as Deutsch (2008) and Murch (Chapter Four) point out, courts now make decisions about how parenting is to be shared, which have significant clinical implications. The Children's Act 1989 embodies the principle that married parents continue to share parental responsibility after separation and divorce so that when parents cannot agree the terms of child care, the court will decide who will be the resident parent having day to day responsibility for child care, and the conditions under which the non-resident parent will have contact with their child(ren). Unless a parent is regarded as positively harmful to their child, the court will rarely suggest that parental responsibility is denied, concentrating instead on the day to day arrangements for child care assisted if necessary by reports and representations from parents, solicitors, and officers of the Child and Family Court Advisory and Support Service (CAFCASS).

In the three domains outlined, solicitors, mediators, and CAFCASS officers have a highly valid input into environmental and

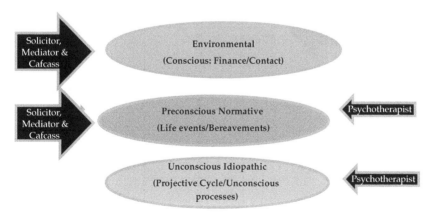

Figure 1. A topographical map of psychological domains.

preconscious normative domains while psychotherapists would apply themselves more so, but not exclusively, to the unconscious idiographic domain.

The stress of separation and divorce may therefore be understood as arising from change occurring simultaneously in all three domains. However, with couples who are separating in a highly conflictual way, my experience is that the unconscious idiopathic domain assumes greatest importance, as illustrated in Figure 2 below. This way of conceptualising conflict affords primacy to the importance of unconscious phantasy in shaping how events are subjectively perceived and influence behaviour.

In high conflict divorce, the unconscious idiopathic domain effectively becomes the lens through which all events are seen, and the individual concerned may develop a limited capacity to attend to the different aspects of the situation. The divorce process, in effect, grinds to a halt in the face of what on the surface appears to be an almost wilful misconception of events of which the individual him/herself is almost blind.

The high rating afforded to divorce by the Holmes and Rahe (1967) scale thus becomes more understandable given the extent and number of psychological changes to which a divorcing person has to adapt. These multiple changes will impact on a person's sense of their own identity, which was succinctly captured by Freud purportedly claiming

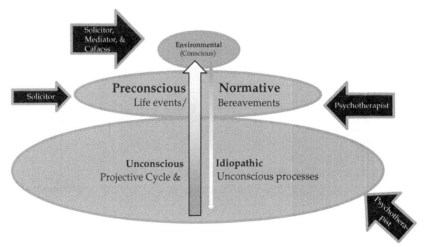

Figure 2. A map of psychological domains scaled for influence.

that the purpose of a fulfilled life is to help patients "to love and to work" (Erikson, 1950). Many divorces result in these twin pillars of personal identity being eroded or destroyed. Under these circumstances it is no surprise that individuals might fight to reclaim what is perceived to have been lost and to punish the person who is perceived to have been responsible for the loss. Divorce can easily be experienced as a life and death struggle.

Under these circumstances parenting offers an obvious conduit through which any fight can be pursued. The law reflects that the rights and the welfare of children are upheld by encouraging the continuing active engagement of both parents following family breakdown. Yet this encouragement to work cooperatively as parents may intersect and clash with the psychological processes involved in separating. Wallerstein, for example, noted in one study of disputing couples that in 50% of the cases couples were still disputing child care arrangements ten years after divorce (Wallerstein & Lewis, 2007). I have commented on the way that much of the literature attempts a false distinction between parenting and adult functioning in a post-divorce context. Where adult identity is so enmeshed with parenting this distinction is difficult to maintain (Shmueli, 2005).

Central casualties and central tasks in high conflict divorce

While divorce and separations are stressful as a result of the losses and changes encountered in the three domains outlined above, it is important to tease out what factors distinguish high conflict divorces from all others.

At presentation, couples in high conflict or entrenched divorce appear locked into a blaming pattern characterised by the claim that "I am right and you are wrong". The intensity of the experience is akin to a life and death struggle and a state of mind characterised by angry omnipotence and excitement that is far removed from the depression, confusion, and abject misery associated with staying with doubt and uncertainty. In psychoanalytic terms this behaviour is typical of Klein's (1946) paranoid/schizoid position which, in the context of high conflict divorce, has a number of recurring features.

First, there is a diminished capacity to reflect and to acknowledge the viewpoints of others. Differences of view cannot be accommodated if these depart from a personal script of blame and scapegoating.

This thick-skinned holding onto certainty can be described as narcissistic (Donner, 2006; Bateman, 1998) and may reflect personality traits, present when the relationship was intact, but now significantly exacerbated. It follows from this that therapeutic observations and interpretations may be hard to accept from professionals, while the experience of former partners may appear to come from another universe. A colleague working on the TCCR's 1980s study of the divorce court welfare service, when asked what would help to make sense of the differing accounts given by divorcing partners battling through the courts, replied, only half jokingly, that a "lie detector" would help to reconcile discrepant realities (Dearnley, personal communication). The fact that the two separate accounts are incompatible bears witness to the breakdown and relative weakness of secondary process thinking within each individual and enacted between the couple. Adult functioning yields to the pressures of more infantile impulses and fantasies. In other words, the fantasies that normally are held within the couple, and are more unconscious and subject to primary process functioning, now exert far greater influence on each of the individuals and effectively detract from each individual's capacity to think on a day to day basis.

The partners in one couple, who could hardly bear to be in the same room together, each described how they had resorted to videotaping the other's behaviour at handovers so as to provide evidence of the other's unsuitability as a parent. It was left to the therapist to realise that each must have been filming the other simultaneously.

In a session following the decision to divorce, the wife suddenly began talking about the fact that she was not mad, and not ill as had been consistently suggested by her husband over the past years. In talking, she seemed completely unaware of her husband's presence and continued talking to me while her husband quite spontaneously and suddenly began to describe how he could not be the terrifically powerful mal-intent portrayed by his wife. Both spoke suddenly and simultaneously and without any recourse to each other.

Second, couples in high conflict divorce rarely talk about either their former sexual relationship or their own individual sexuality. This avoidance seems to be more than a reflection of the fact that this side of the relationship has either died away or needs to be denied. For each individual in the relationship, the notion of the partner as a libidinal object, or as having once been such an object, is strikingly absent.

It is as if each individual's sexual functioning in relation to the other has not only become denied but become much more immature than would be expected under normal circumstances. There is a far greater sense of relating to an internal, asexual figure, possibly from childhood.

Third, and related to the above, it is well known that clinically significant traumatic states involve a difficulty in the perception of time as well as of person, this itself being very much a secondary process phenomenon.

> A mother had been involved in an extended battle through the courts to establish contact with her son. She remarked that the memories she had of seeing him felt so far away that they belonged to a different world. For this mother the all-consuming nature of the court battle had relegated her good memories of happy times with her son to a distant past. Her perception of time passing was discontinuous to the extent that she felt her past did not belong to her.

It is perhaps no coincidence that the observations made above bear a striking resemblance to what Anna Freud noted in her 1966 paper, *Normality and Pathology in Childhood*, in which she compares child and adult mental functioning. These areas relate to ego-centricity, the immaturity of the infantile sexual apparatus, the relative weakness of secondary-process thinking, and the different evaluation of time at various age levels. Her work on psychic development encompassed Sigmund Freud's earlier definition of the concept of regression first introduced in his seminal work, *The Interpretation of Dreams* (1900). In keeping with his early economic model, Freud first outlined a topographical regression in which excitation moves in a forward and backward direction, and as he described there, "from the motor end to the sensory end of the mental apparatus" until it reaches the perceptual system. This regressive process consequently produces hallucinatory wish fulfilment in the place of rational thinking.

We would describe it differently today but the experience for individuals of a subjective clear understanding emerging from a mass of painful confusion, and offering clarity and understanding to the individual even if to others the idea is incorrect, is an experience commonly encountered. It does not have the status of a formal delusion or hallucination but functions in such a fashion. Second, Freud then outlined a temporal regression as a harking back to older psychic structures, earlier styles of functioning, and then, third, a formal regression which causes primitive methods of expression and representation to take the place of contemporary ones. Anna Freud certainly emphasised the "normal" place of regression in "normal" development, and in her own inimitable style managed to encapsulate and illustrate these profound concepts in everyday colloquial sayings such as "two steps forward, one step back".

In my view what makes both separation and divorce traumatic is the way that it propels adults into a psychologically regressed state. While this chapter cannot do justice to the concept of regression, Kris (1956) usefully distinguished between pathological regression in which the ego is simply overwhelmed and under siege, and "regression in the service of the ego" which is an example of Freud's formal regression (Etchegoyen, 1999). The latter is essentially aimed at a reworking of past developmental problems in the context of the present crisis, through the individual's internal experience being enriched by "fresh" content from unconscious primary processes allowing for the development of new mental representations.

High conflict divorces may therefore be distinguished from others by the possibility that the regression that dominates either one or both of the partners is a pathological one. Whatever developmental hopes were present at the outset of the relationship, and could be identified in the joint unconscious phantasies that drew them together, have not borne fruit. A regression in which whatever unconscious aspects of each individual originally sought expression in the couple relationship now no longer have that possibility and by definition cannot have preconscious representation within the individual's own psyche. The dominating process in the divorce may therefore be one of regression where the main casualty is the capacity for mental representation and thought.

The difficulty of managing change at this level is compounded by the fact that these behaviours do not occur in the relatively stable safety of the consulting room of a couple psychotherapist but do so in the realm of the adversarial family justice system. Consequently, problems are easily displaced onto arguments about child care and ancillary financial disagreements and are not viewed as primarily located in the unconscious idiopathic domain. The regression of the partners, whether momentary or persistent, is effectively consolidated and then ignored through environmental reinforcement. It is also a measure of the strength of this phenomenon and of the trauma of divorce that therapists themselves seem to abandon the recognition of enactment between the couple and may also effectively encourage an enactment, under the guise of "support".

The psychoanalytically informed therapist, however, works predominantly with these domains but needs also to recognise that he/she is working with patients in a regressed state who are unable to have a representation of an internal state that was centrally important at the start of the relationship. In considering regression, Sandler and Joffe (1967) developed Freud's (1933) notion of persistence when they noted that:

> Structures are, in the normal course of events, never lost but rather that new and auxiliary structures of increasing complexity are created; the newer structures becoming superimposed on the old in the course of development. The more complex, emergent organisation must not only provide an effective means for discharge and control but must also include systems of inhibition directed against the utilisation of older structures. It is not that the new replaces the old but that the new builds upon the old, implicit in which is an in-built inhibition of the old structure.

Regression, therefore, in Sandler's view, is not the loss of a new structure, but a dis-inhibition with regard to older structures. It is not an actual reversal or backward movement to older structures but a weakening of the psychic forces limiting these structures. Sandler's contribution is therefore not only to emphasise the developmental and connected basis of a regressive process but also to place it more firmly in a dynamic unconscious. It becomes possible to understand the individual's functioning as the dis-inhibition of older, more primitive models of functioning which thereby make available a clearer and more in-depth potential access to both the unconscious phantasy of the individuals and the couple's shared phantasy.

Consequently, the central task of the therapist working in high conflict divorce becomes one of attempting to develop and then convey an understanding of those aspects of individual and couple functioning that could not find expression in the couple relationship itself and which led to the current breakdown. In doing so, the therapist provides not only a cognitive understanding of the shared problem but an emotional engagement with the very interaction the couple found difficult. It is this different type of engagement, which the couple find difficult to generate between them, in combination with an intellectual grasp of the problem, which is potentially therapeutic (Carpy, 1989). To do so, however, requires the therapist working clinically, as opposed to medico-legally, to work within a number of tensions. The task is to work with a pathological regression in the hope that it will become a regression that is actually in the service of the ego.

Functioning therapeutically in high conflict divorce

A psychoanalytically oriented therapist working in the context of divorce and separation and especially with high conflict divorce must be thoughtful in relation to a number of aspects which are different to "standard" psychoanalytic psychotherapy with a couple. These may be considered under the general headings of the setting for the work and aspects of technique. What follows is by no means an exhaustive list but a highlighting of some significant aspects of clinical work in this context.

i. Considerations on the setting of the therapy
The meaning of the term "setting" in this context requires considering both the physical and pragmatic aspects of how, when and where the patient(s) is seen and also the therapist's internal mental approach.

First, couples or individuals seen in this context have not presented from the baseline of an intact and relatively stable couple relationship. Often referral to the service has been directed by the solicitor, in some cases the courts themselves, while the couple are in the midst of the intense pressures resulting from ongoing conflict and tensions between and within their respective environmental, preconscious normative, and unconscious idiopathic domains. Given the referral route, long-term therapy is not often envisaged or welcomed, and almost by definition those referred will be more oriented towards concerns in the environmental domain. The therapist needs to have an internal recognition of this while simultaneously maintaining the boundaries of the session in both the arrangement of the consultations and in their conduct. The structure of the setting therefore offers a metaphorical lens through which to view the couple in particular circumstances. The current service of the Tavistock Centre for Couple Relationships'

Divorce and Separation Unit encapsulates this in being a service that offers short interventions which run parallel to the legal service and are not a substitute for it. The frequency and number of consultations are negotiated but weekly long-term work is eschewed in favour of specific brief interventions at specific times. To aid in this, it is often very useful if the therapist has at least a rudimentary knowledge of the different steps in the divorce process.

Second, in high conflict divorce the identified "patient" may be differ from the "patient" that attends consultations. That is to say, in high conflict divorce it is often the case that only one partner attends, and if both partners wish to be seen, they are often seen individually rather than as a couple. While the "patient" remains the couple relationship, their presentation highlights the very important distinction between the concrete couple in the process of divorcing, and the internal psychological couple present within each of the respective partners. Whilst each partner may freely discuss their own situation and the actions of their former partners, the therapist needs to maintain the view that first and foremost their statements are also disguised and symbolic descriptions of their own internal worlds. This becomes especially difficult when discussion turns to the interests of children in the divorce. Current advice to couples with children who are divorcing, for example, *Separation and Divorce: Helping Parents to Help Children* (Resolution, 2008), is based on highly rational and conscious perspectives but does not recognise either preconscious normative or unconscious idiopathic dimensions. On the other hand, research findings are ambiguous. Current outcome research regarding the impact of divorce on children ranges from pessimistic clinical case studies (Wallerstein & Lewis, 2004) to more rigorous designs which are beset by conceptual, methodological (i.e., mediating versus moderating factors), and measurement issues. Overall conclusions are therefore inevitably general:

> There is no simple or direct relationship between parental separation and children's adjustment, and poor outcomes are far from inevitable. As a rule of thumb, many adverse outcomes are roughly twice as prevalent among children from divorced families compared with children from intact families. However, the disadvantages identified by research typically apply to only a minority of those whose parents have separated during childhood. (Rodgers & Pryor, 1998)

Furthermore, Kelly's (2000) review of ten years of research on children's subsequent post-divorce adjustment highlighted that many of the psychological symptoms presented in children of divorce could be accounted for in the years prior to the divorce. Kelly concluded that the primary focus needed to be the couple relationship: "The view that divorce, per se, is the major cause of these symptoms must be reconsidered in light of newer research documenting the negative effects of troubled marriages on children" (p. 963).

Third, and relatedly, whilst it is of course true that the children of any divorcing couple need to be thought about in terms of the impact of residence and contact upon them, the therapist working with high conflict divorcing couples must maintain his/her internal setting so that descriptions of the children are heard as descriptions of aspects of the internal psychological world of the individual and couple as well as a purportedly accurate description of external reality. The difficulty in doing so is testament to the pressures operating on both individuals at the time, although the therapist should also bear in mind that in high conflict divorce, it is likely that arguments about children have been run and re-run many times in the lead-up to the couple or individual being seen in a psychotherapeutic context. This serves to further underline the symbolic importance of children rather than the children being considered as only separate entities caught up and affected by the divorce process.

ii. Considerations of therapeutic technique
Given the chronic breakdown in the projective cycle between the couple, and dependant on the specifics of the conflict, so each partner tends to draw the therapist into a particular "role-responsivity" (Sandler, 1976). A particularly useful typology of roles was put forward by Vincent (1995, 1997) who noted how the patient may wish the therapist to be either a magician, judge, or a servant in relation to the couple's situation. Alongside this, the therapist must struggle to maintain a meta position from which it is possible to observe who is trying to do what to whom (Etchegoyen, 1999). That is, the therapist must maintain an internal setting for him/herself to the same extent that the external setting of the consultation is maintained.

As a consequence of the above, countertransference reactions are likely to be in keeping with the intensity of each partner's struggle. It is often the case that the therapist is powerfully invited to join in with or even be assaulted by a partner's phantasies and projections, and as a consequence experience important countertransference reactions which are also very informative about the partner's own mental state. However, given the setting of the consultations, and unless he/she is very certain of the ground, the therapist should refrain from making therapist oriented interpretations and generally make "patient oriented" interpretations as defined by Steiner (1994). Whilst it would be important to be able to consider all that the patient communicates as part of a transference, the therapist must find his/her way to talk from within the perspective of reduced ego functioning if there is any hope of a beneficial interaction.

The consequences of these efforts may be surprising and unexpected as both the therapist and the couple learn from their immediate experiences with each other:

> Jo and Ted found it extremely difficult to attend any sessions. Joint couple sessions were offered, and after much telephone contact with a skilled receptionist, the situation evolved into one in which only one partner would arrive for the session, the other having been delayed at the "last minute". In this way they had managed unwittingly and unintentionally to provide each other with a number of individual sessions with their therapist. At the first jointly attended session, Jo had to be escorted by the therapist from the lift in the building to the consulting room for fear of being attacked by Ted, who was waiting peacefully in the room itself. Joint couple sessions were difficult for all concerned. Infrequently occurring, they nevertheless had a predictable pattern of pleadings, accusations, counter-accusations, and unresolved arguments which created sessions dominated by an emptiness that left little room for anything else. Eventually the therapist lost heart, feeling totally deskilled and defeated, and slumped into a silence which the couple joined him in, the silence ensuing for the next ten minutes. In that time, the therapist "suddenly" had a thought. Reflecting on what he was made to feel most powerfully he was able to comment on the couple's tremendous difficulty in talking about the disappointment each had in the relationship given their initial hopes, these themselves being based on prior unresolved losses. Each of them was therefore understandably powerfully taken by surprise by their own reaction to the loss of the relationship and

the separation. In allowing a deeper countertransference to be experienced, the therapist's "thought" had linked the predominant affect of each partner's past, that is, from the unconscious idiopathic domain, to the struggle with the current losses for both related to separation and contact with their child: issues related to the normative and environmental domains. Further silence ensued and after a while Jo told Ted that he could have as much contact with their daughter as he wished. She would no longer stand in his way. He in turn was able to acknowledge her capacities as a mother and recognise the quality of her child care. Over a few further sessions, each was able to acknowledge the central role of losses in their lives and the degree to which little psychological work had been done. Both obviously needed much by way of psychotherapeutic help but repeated court applications appeared to be a thing of the past.

For all the complexity of working with divorcing couples, the changes that do occur and developments that can be made are testament to the workings and resilience of the human mind.

References

Bannister, K., Lyons, A., Pincus, L., Robb, J., Shooter, A. & Stephens, J. (1955). *Social Casework in Marital Problems*. London: Tavistock.

Bateman, A. (1998). Thick and thin-skinned organisations and enactment in borderline andnarcissistic disorders. *International Journal of Psychoanalysis, 79*: 13–26.

Bowlby, J. (1980). *Attachment and Loss III: Loss, Sadness and Depression*. International Psychoanalytical Library, No. 109. London: Hogarth and the Institute of Psycho-Analysis.

Carpy, D. (1989). Tolerating the countertransference: a mutative process. *International Journal of Psychoanalysis, 70*: 287–294.

Clulow, C. & Vincent, C. (1987). *In The Child's Best Interests: Divorce Court Welfare and the Search for a Settlement*. London: Tavistock.

Deutsch, R. (2008). Divorce in the 21st century: Multidisciplinary family interventions. *The Journal of Psychiatry and Law, 36*: 41–66.

Donner, M. (2006). Tearing the child apart: the contribution of narcissism, envy, and perverse modes of thought to child custody wars. *Psychoanalytic Psychology, 23*(3).

Erikson, E. H. (1950). *Childhood and Society*. New York: W. W. Norton.

Etchegoyen, R. H. (1999). *Fundamentals of Psychoanalytic Technique*. London: Karnac.

Freud, A. (1966). *Normality and Pathology in Childhood*. London: Hogarth.

Freud, S. (1900). *The Interpretation of Dreams*. *S. E.*, *4*. London: Hogarth.

Freud, S. (1917). *Mourning and Melancholia*. *S. E. 14*, p. 239. London: Hogarth.

Freud, S. (1933). New introductory lectures on psychoanalysis. *S. E.*, *22*, pp. 1–182. London: Hogarth.

Holmes, T. & Rahe, R. (1967). The social readjustment rating scale. *Journal of Psychosomatic Research*, *11*(2): 213–218.

Johnston, J. (1994). High-conflict divorce. *The Future of Children*, 4: 164–182.

Johnston, J. & Campbell, E. (1988). *Impasses of Divorce: The Dynamics and Resolution of Family Conflict*. New York: The Free Press.

Kelly, J. B. (2000). Children's adjustment in conflicted marriage and divorce: A decadereview of research. *Journal of the American Academy of Child & Adolescent Psychiatry*, *39*(8): 963–973.

Klein, M. (1946). Notes on some schizoid mechanisms. *International Journal of Psychoanalysis*, *27*: 99–110.

Kressel, K., Jaffee, N., Tuchman, B., Watson C. & Deutsch, M. (1980). A typology of divorcing couples: Implications for mediation and the divorce process. *Family Process*, *19*(2): 101–116.

Kris, E. (1956). On some vicissitudes of insight in psychoanalysis. *International Journal of Psychoanalysis*, *37*: 445–455.

Kubler-Ross, E. (2008). *Death and Dying*. London: Routledge.

Lauter, J. S. (2009). *Treatment with Parents in High-conflict Divorce: An Integrative Literature Review*. Berkeley, CA: The Wright Institute.

Mattinson, J. & Sinclair, I. (1979). *Mate and Stalemate*. Oxford: Blackwell.

Rahe, R. H., Mahan, J. L. & Arthur R. J. (1970). Prediction of near-future health change from subjects' preceding life changes. *Journal of Psychosomatic Research*, *14*(4): 401–406.

Resolution, (2008). *Separation and Divorce: Helping Parents to Help Children*. Orpington, UK: Resolution.

Rodgers, B. & Pryor, J. (1998). *Divorce and Separation: the Outcomes for Children*. York, UK: Joseph Rowntree Foundation.

Ruszczynski, S. (1994). *Psychotherapy with Couples*. London: Karnac.

Sandler, J. (1976). Countertransference and role responsiveness. *International Review of Psycho-Analysis*, *3*: 43–47.

Sandler, J. (1983). Reflections on some relations between psychoanalytic concepts and psychoanalytic practice. *International Journal of Psychoanalysis*, *64*: 35–45.

Sandler, J. & Joffe, G. W. (1967). The tendency to persistence in psychological function and development, with special reference to fixation and regression. *Bulletin of the Menninger Clinic*, *31*: 257–271.

Sherick, I. (1983). Anna Freud's views on the role of the mother in early child development and psychopathology. *Bulletin of the Anna Freud Centre*, 6(3).

Shmueli, A. (2005). On thinking of parents as adults in divorce and separation. *Sexual and Relationship Therapy*, 20(3): 350–357.

Steiner, J. (1994). Patient-centred and analyst-centred interpretations: Some implications of containment and countertransference. *Psychoanalytic Inquiry*, 14: 406–422.

Stewart, R. (2001). *The Early Identification and Streaming of Cases of High-Conflict Separation and Divorce: A Review*. Department of Justice, Canada.

Vincent, C. (1995). Consulting to divorcing couples. *Family Law*, Dec., 25: 678–681.

Vincent, C. (1997). The impact of the client's emotional state. *Newsletter of the National Council for Family Proceedings*, 11: 11–14.

Wallerstein, J. (1994). The early psychological tasks of marriage: Part 1. *American Journal of Orthopsychiatry*, 64(4): 641–650.

Wallerstein, J. & Lewis, J. (2004). The unexpected legacy of divorce. Report of a 25-year study. *Psychoanalytic Psychology*, 21(3): 353–370.

Wallerstein, J. & Lewis, J. (2007). Sibling outcomes and disparate parenting and stepparenting after divorce: Report from a 10-year longitudinal study. *Psychoanalytic Psychology*, 24(3): 445–458.

Winnicott, D. W. (1975). *Through Paediatrics to Psycho-Analysis*. International Psychoanalytical Library. London: Hogarth and the Institute of Psycho-Analysis.

COMMENTARY ON CHAPTER FIVE

Christopher Vincent

In the opening paragraphs of our book about the divorce court welfare service (the branch of the Probation Service that, in 2001, became absorbed into the new Children and Family Court Advisory and Support Service, CAFCASS), Clulow wrote:

> War is not too strong a metaphor to apply to the experiences of some who divorce. They fight for what they believe to be right, to protect their territory and security, and against forces that sometimes seem to threaten life itself. And there are social pressures to treat partners as adversaries once marriage ends. Divorcing men and women snipe at each other from their trenches partly through fear, mistrust, and a sense of injury, and partly because those who define the "rules of engagement" are understood to encourage such behaviour. (Clulow & Vincent, 1987, p. 1)

Avi Shmueli's chapter provides one way of understanding how some couples seen in the Divorce and Separation Unit (DSU) at the TCCR arrive at being in a warlike state and to provide some therapeutic ways of helping them relinquish the fight and to mediate their differences in the process of separating. He takes as his clinical example a couple, Jo and

Ted, whom we understand to be representative of other couples seen in the unit. This couple had been helped to gain a breathing space in their protracted battle over care of their only child by the court insisting that they seek therapeutic help. This pressure resulted in them coming to the DSU. Progress with this couple was hard won. Sessions were infrequent, and separate sessions were offered to help Jo manage her fear of being physically intimidated by Ted until eventually they could tolerate being in the same room together. Even then conversation was difficult and the therapist had to accept their stubborn reluctance to participate. Reflecting on his resulting countertransference experience of being a failure and disappointment as their therapist, he was able to formulate a comment that addressed their long-held sense of disappointment with each other. This intervention resonated with them both in a way that previous attempts had not managed to achieve. It was a turning point that freed them to become more reflective about other losses in their lives and, in due course, to relinquish a need to fight over care of their daughter and to denigrate each other through court proceedings.

This brief clinical example provides an illustration of a complex interpersonal theory about couple engagement and disengagement which forms the central thrust of the chapter. The TCCR model of developmental and defensive fit captures and explains the aspirational and creative potential in forming an intimate adult relationship. It is suggested that divorce may arise for some couples when those developmental hopes are not achieved. This failure is a great loss which needs to be mourned appropriately yet, paradoxically, high conflict divorcing couples seem unable to mourn what they have failed to achieve together, and instead seem stuck in a cycle of mutual blame and recrimination. This avoidance of normative grief is seen as a consequence of deep-seated unconscious problems that requires a psychotherapeutic response. As a way of illustrating this depth of disturbance a hierarchical topographical model is put forward which is, in part, a model of mental functioning but which also connects with professional roles within the family justice system.

As a way of commentating on these ideas I will follow the ordering of the chapter by first reflecting on some distinctive characteristics of families engaged in high conflict divorce. In doing so I hope to identify some of the factors that explain why many high conflict couples find it difficult to engage with therapeutic services. I will then add an attachment theory perspective to the main theoretical ideas put forward in Shmueli's chapter. The ideas drawn from an attachment theory perspective provide an additional dimension in understanding the function of high conflict in a divorcing context and carry some implications for how professionals then respond.

As Murch points out in Chapter Four, cases coming before the family courts may be the result of so-called private law proceedings involving disputes over residence and contact with children consequent to divorce, or they may be the result of public law proceedings where social services have intervened to make a child subject to care proceedings. Some of the couples turning to the courts to help resolve difficulties over child care arrangements following divorce will be locked into the sort of entrenched disputes described by Shmueli and some of these couples find their way to the DSU. Those who do will be a subset of the wider group of high conflict couples going through the courts in at least two ways.

First, as Jo and Ted's circumstances reveal, they, and others who come to the DSU, have managed an important transition in voluntarily entering an agency that, however it is perceived by its clients, stands for an approach to problems that is non-adversarial. In my experience this engagement of high conflict couples with a non-adversarial process is often hard to achieve but this commitment is essential if the type of therapeutic work described in the chapter is to have any chance of success. It may be that some couples will respond favourably to the exhortations of professionals within the court system to seek outside help from whatever quarter this is provided—mediation services, counselling and psychotherapy services, anger management programmes, etc. However, many couples reveal great resistance to taking up these recommendations for which many reasons are given. Some resistance is linked to fears of confronting an abusive partner or, at least, a partner who is alleged to be abusive. In helping Jo and Ted, worries about violence had to be managed by the DSU receptionist, skilfully negotiating separate interviews for them both. In a study based on families seen by CAFCASS (hereafter I shall refer to this work as the Oxford Study), the research staff were surprised to find a high incidence of violent, abusive, and intimidating relationships, where in 78% of cases at least one parent reported fear of their ex–partner, and in 56% of cases reported actual physical violence when living together (Buchanan, Hunt, Bretherton & Bream, 2001). This study noted that the proportion of women reporting violence or fear of violence dropped once legal proceedings began. This should not, however, be taken to mean that violence drops at the point of separation. In fact there is considerable evidence to suggest that for some couples, violence becomes heightened at the point of separation (Bartholomew, Henderson & Dutton, 2001; Feeney & Monin, 2008). This possibility has implications for couple therapists engaging with clients who are struggling to separate. Do therapists routinely ask about domestic violence in all its forms and, if they do, what implications does it have for whether and how the work is conducted?

Beyond concerns about violence, some clients are anxious that engagement with services involving both partners talking together will involve being exposed to pressures to reinstate the marriage rather than to help with the process of disengagement. This anxiety heightens the importance of services accurately describing the values that underpin their approaches to offering help. This clarity will assist fellow professionals in the family justice system make clear to couples whom they refer for help that services exist to enable couples to work out their own problems rather than have solutions imposed upon them. In some circumstances, when one party has engaged with therapy in parallel with a divorce process, it has been my experience that individual help has been harnessed to support an adversarial position rather than to change it. It may be that support from individual therapy for an adversarial stance is warranted where victims of abuse lack the confidence to seek legal protection. However, in some situations individual therapy can be used to buttress an unjustifiable stubbornness not to conciliate at any level.

Second, Jo and Ted were able to pay for their therapy, unlike many of the clients seen by CAFCASS who are on low incomes. While it is true that the families seen by CAFCASS represent a diverse range of occupational groups with a correspondingly wide range of household incomes, in the Oxford Study one third of families were in receipt of income support and, in 60% of cases, one or both parents were legally aided (Buchanan, Hunt, Bretherton & Bream, 2001, p. 11). The relationships between income, employment, social class, and divorce are complex and patterns of cause and effect are difficult to disentangle. While some studies have suggested that the risk of divorce is higher among lower social class groupings, particularly when the husband is in an unskilled manual occupation (Haskey, 1984) other studies have concluded that, when other demographic characteristics like age at marriage and childbearing experience are taken into account, the significance of social class differentials in the propensity to divorce is relatively small (Clarke & Berrington, 1999; McAllister, 1999). By contrast, in our study we were struck by how some men attributed becoming unemployed to the stresses of divorce. In our core sample, six out of the thirty fathers saw their job losses resulting directly from the stress of divorce. For these men, unemployment was one of a cluster of losses (loss of marriage, loss of home, loss of contact with children) which seemed to produce a downward depressive spiral from which recovery was slow and difficult. We also know that, whether or not job losses follow on from divorce, the process and its aftermath can make families poorer. Increased or extra charges to the family budget are now generated by having to find separate accommodation, to finance transport, and other costs associated with contact visits and to pay for legal services.

One outcome of the latest government spending review is the proposal that legal aid be withdrawn from litigants in private law proceedings unless it can be shown that there may be serious adverse consequences to adults and children (Ministry of Justice, 2010). At the same time the government has also announced that extra funds are to be granted to mediation services. These policy changes raise important questions about their impact on high conflict divorces. Will some families be denied access to legal services they cannot afford? Might some families find a creative outcome to their difficulties through recourse to an expanded network of mediation services which they would not otherwise have approached, or might some families exaggerate the extent of the harm being experienced by adults and children in order to gain legal aid?

Individuals who are in conflict and seeking to defend their positions against what they perceive as the destabilising potential of conciliation, not surprisingly, register significant levels of dissatisfaction with court processes designed to help them. In large part this arises from the impossibility of providing solutions that please both sides. In our study the ratio of complaint to appreciation was in the region of two to one (Clulow & Vincent, 1987, p. 163), and this level of dissatisfaction was echoed in the later Oxford Study. The problem of forming a cooperative and satisfying working alliance may also be compounded by gender, racial, and ethnic differences working in a complex interaction. This is important to think about because cases coming before the courts reflect the increasing diversity of racial and ethnic groups in the population at large. In 2007, for example, of the 57,000 private law cases worked by CAFCASS staff, 80% were of white British background while the other 20% came from a range of different ethnic and religious backgrounds of which the single largest grouping was of Asian origin (Brown & Davies, 2007). In 40% of the families seen in the Oxford Study at least one parent came from a non-white ethnic group and it is reasonable to assume that different cultural assumptions about the respective roles of men and women as partners and as parents inevitably come up against the implicit assumptions, real and imagined, of professionals and the courts in these same matters. This was brought home to me when supervising two white women social workers who were helping an Iraqi man, who had been in this country eight years, and his English wife of Pakistani descent. As a result of domestic violence their baby was taken into care and I supervised the two workers who were helping this couple resolve their difficulties so that the baby's return home might be considered. This man's sense of pride and honour had been severely dented by having his child taken into care, and helping him come to terms with his anger about this narcissistic wound was not made easy by having help from a professional pairing of two white women. Talking openly about these problems and their connections to background culture was necessary for him to accept the help that was on offer.

In this brief overview an attempt has been made to identify some of the characteristics that may be particularly salient when working with high conflict couples. But they also share in common with other divorcing couples the experience of losing a significant attachment figure in their lives. An examination of this process from an attachment theory perspective can help us understand the place of anger as a normal and predictable emotion when significant separations occur. Anger has functional value in helping adults come to terms with the loss of a significant relationship, but may also help in restoring a significant relationship which is threatened to end. The suggestion in this commentary is that what characterises the anger demonstrated in high conflict divorces is an unresolved dilemma for one or both of the partners as to whether they want the relationship to end or to continue. Caught up in this uncertainty the relationship continues on its destructive path neither giving satisfaction and pleasure nor being properly grieved as a lost cause.

Bowlby and Robertson, in their studies of young children separated from their mothers, were able to identify three stages that children typically passed through, each stage characterised by a particular attitude towards the missing mother figure. These stages were labelled "protest", "despair", and "detachment". During the first of these stages the child communicated his distress in a variety of ways, such as crying loudly, showing anger, and being preoccupied with searching activities. At this early stage of the separation the dominant hope was that the mother might return and, during this period of uncertainty, the dominant emotions were fear, anger, and distress. Fear and distress indicated a child's appraisal of danger at being separated from a primary attachment figure. Anger served to mobilise the child's efforts to re-establish contact with the mother (Kobak & Madsen, 2008). The second stage of despair, which succeeded protest, was marked by behaviour that suggested increased hopelessness about the mother's return, as the child withdrew from engagement with others. Bowlby thought of this phase as one of mourning the absent parent, as the child could appear sad and depressed. Children who reached the third stage of detachment made little show of affection or anger on their mother's return. In Heinicke and Westheimer's study (1966), some of the mothers reported their detached children as treating them like strangers. This progression identified by Bowlby and confirmed by subsequent studies helps us understand the two dimensions when faced with a significant separation. At one end of the spectrum the attachment response may be hyperactivated. Attachment behaviours become heightened and intense, as anxious clinging, pursuit, and even aggressive attempts to obtain a response from a loved one escalate. At the other end of the spectrum is the bid to deactivate the attachment system, especially when hope for any satisfying future relationship is lost. Emotional investment is withdrawn from the previously significant loved person and possibly from involvement in other risky personal attachments. Relationships with children may be the exception to this rule, particularly if they are young, needy, and dependent.

In our classification of divorcing patterns encountered in the family courts the category of what we termed "shotgun" divorces were those that exhibited the highest degrees of overt conflict. They also happened to constitute the largest category, representing 70% of the core sample. These were essentially divorces where the decision to leave was seemingly one-sided, the news of the separation being communicated without warning: a situation very well portrayed in the film, *Kramer versus Kramer* (Benton, 1979). The shocked reaction of those who were left resulted in behaviour that was significantly different for men and women. Men tended to react with anger, abuse, and sometimes physical violence, and they were more likely to seek out, engage, and pursue their partners or others who threatened their position. Women, on the other hand, tended to try for a clean break, often extending this bid by refusing contact between father and children. This denial of all contact could be experienced as violent by both parties. Direct communication between parents in these circumstances broke down, sometimes reinforced by non-molestation orders and ouster injunctions, and took place only indirectly through solicitors and court hearings concerned with residence and contact arrangements.

It is possible to see in this pattern of behaviour the hyper-activation, or up-regulation, of the attachment system, particularly in men who felt rejected and wished to regain what they felt they had lost. In fact, in the research team we often speculated about the ambiguity in the meaning of the angry and protesting partner's behaviour. Was he trying to *get back at* or trying to *get back to* his former partner? Matching this response one can see the behaviour of the partner who seeks to cut off all contact as striving to deactivate, or down-regulate, the attachment system; to present an emotionally avoidant, dismissing response. The tragedy was that care of children became the conduits through which these diametrically opposed attachment strategies were enacted. The deactivated, cut-off response was often allied with a wish to terminate contact with the non-resident parent who, in contrast, would seek to re-establish contact with the former partner through applications in the courts for residence or contact.

This pattern of interaction may be transient as each partner comes to terms with the reality of post-divorce life, but it may become entrenched and become a "self-maintaining pattern of social interaction and emotion regulation" (Shaver & Clark, 1994). The angry bid for proximity reinforces the angry and fearful rejection, which in turn feeds the initial and unsatisfied bid for closeness.

An attachment perspective helps advance our understanding of how to help couples caught up in these destructive cycles in a number of ways. First, it helps to understand the importance of providing continuity of personnel in the provision of services to such clients. At the heart of these destructive and avoidant patterns of behaviour is a wariness and mistrust of getting close to another person. This mistrust is compounded if helping services have a high staff turnover that prevents practitioners sticking with families over the period of their separation.

Second, an attachment perspective helps practitioners understand the meaning of behaviour whether this surfaces in the solicitor's office, the consulting rooms of mediators, children and family reporters, guardians ad litem, and centres offering anger management programmes. It, therefore, contributes to programmes of interdisciplinary training.

Third, attachment theory helps practitioners understand the ambiguities and contradictions in the behaviours of parents. In doing so it also helps tease out how, in complex ways, the separate functions of partnering and parenting overlap with each other. This may help guide not only what practitioners take up in the consulting room, but may help pitch interventions at the level of primary prevention (Cowan & Cowan, Chapter One) when, hopefully, the patterns described in this commentary and in Avi Shmueli's chapter are less well entrenched.

References

Bartholomew, K., Henderson, A. & Dutton, D. (2001). Insecure attachment and abusive intimate relationships. In: C. Clulow (Ed.), *Adult Attachment and Couple Psychotherapy*. London: Brunner-Routledge.

Benton, R. (1979). *Kramer versus Kramer*. Columbia Picture Industries.

Brown, P. & Davies, A. (2007). *Race Equality Scheme and Equality and Diversity Strategy*. CAFCASS Annual Report 2007, available online at www.cafcass.gov.uk

Buchanan, A., Hunt, J., Bretherton, H. & Bream, V. (2001). *Families in Conflict: Perspectives of Children and Parents on the Family Welfare Service*. Bristol, UK: Policy Press.

Clarke, L. & Berrington, A. (1999). *Socio-Demographic Prediction of Divorce, Paper 1, Vol. 1, Research Series*. London: Lord Chancellor's Department.

Clulow, C. & Vincent, C. (1987). *In the Child's Best Interests: Divorce Court Welfare and The Search for a Settlement*. London: Tavistock.

Feeney, B. C. & Monin, J. K. (2008). An attachment-theoretical perspective on divorce In: J. Cassidy & P. R. Shaver (Eds.), *Handbook of Attachment: Theory, Research and linical Applications*, 2nd edition. New York: The Guilford Press.

Haskey, J. (1984). Social class and socio-economic differentials in divorce in England and Wales. *Population Studies, 38*: 419–438.

Heinicke, C. & Westheimer, I. (1966). *Brief Separations.* New York: International Universities Press.

Kobak, R. & Madsen, S. (2008). Disruption in attachment bonds: Implications for theory, and clinical intervention. In: J. Cassidy & P. R. Shaver (Eds.), *Handbook of Attachment: Theory, Research and Clinical Applications, 2nd edition.* New York:

McAllister, F. (1999). *Effects of Changing Material Circumstances on the Incidence of Marital Breakdown, Paper 2, Vol. 1, Research Series.* London: Lord Chancellor's Department.

Ministry of Justice, (2010). *Proposals for the Reform of Legal Aid in England and Wales, Consultation Paper CP12/10.* London: HMSO.

Shaver, P. R. & Clark, C. L. (1994). Couple and family therapy. In: *Handbook of Attachment: Theory, Research and Clinical Applications, 2nd edition.* New York: The Guilford Press.

CHAPTER SIX

Depression, couple therapy, research, and government policy

Julian Leff, Eia Asen, and Felix Schwarzenbach

Global prevalence of depression

Depression is one of the commonest psychiatric disorders, affecting one in four women and one in seven men at some point in their life in high-income countries. A recent cross-sectional survey in eastern Europe found rates in women of between 34% and 44%. Some particularly vulnerable populations suffer very high rates: 35% of women in Kayalitsha, a South African township, were found to be clinically depressed at a two-month postnatal examination (Tomlinson, Cooper, Stein, Swartz & Molteno, 2006). Mathers and Loncar (2006) predicted that by 2030 depression will be responsible for the second highest burden of ill health globally. A number of different modalities of treatment exist and have been shown to be effective, including antidepressant medication, interpersonal therapy, cognitive behavioural therapy (CBT), and couple therapy. However, depression often goes untreated, due to failure of medical practitioners to detect it in high-income countries and lack of psychiatric expertise and/or antidepressant drugs in primary care clinics in middle- and low-income countries. A study by the WHO of psychiatric disorders in primary care services in fifteen countries found that the proportion of cases of depression that were correctly detected ranged from 19.3% in Nagasaki to 74.0% in Santiago, Chile (Üstün & Sartorius, 1995). The WHO urged the incorporation of psychiatry into primary care in the Alma Ata Declaration of 1978, but as slow progress was made over the next thirty years, it launched a new exhortative document in November 2008 drawing attention to some innovative services that had been established in a variety of countries, including some classified as low-income such as India and Uganda. The decision concerning the treatment of choice for depression has to take into account the feasibility of providing that treatment to all who need it. Treatments which are judged to be optimal in high-income countries may be undeliverable in middle- and low-income countries due to lack of financial resources, trained personnel, and/or an inadequate infrastructure.

Involving the partner in therapy

The importance of the partner for the outcome and treatment of depression has been recognised for many years. A number of therapeutic interventions involving the partner have been evaluated in controlled trials, but rarely have these been based on empirical research. Rather they have been engendered by clinical observations and intuitions. At the time we were considering mounting a trial of couple therapy we reviewed the relevant existing literature. Five randomised controlled trials (RCTs) of marital therapy for depressed patients were identified (Emanuels-Zuurveen & Emmelkamp, 1996; Friedman, 1975; Jacobson, Dobson, Fruzetti, Schmaling & Salusky, 1991; O'Leary & Beach, 1990; Waring et al., 1988). The duration of these trials varied between ten and twenty weeks and none included a follow-up period after treatment to assess any prophylactic effect. There was a consistent finding that marital therapy and individual cognitive therapy were equally effective in reducing depressive symptoms, but only marital therapy improved the marital relationship. Since publication of our trial a number of other RCTs on this topic have appeared in print (see Balfour & Lanman, 2011 for a review).

Partner's expressed emotion and the course of depression

Our own trial of intervention grew out of a series of research studies on the emotional response of the partner to the depressed patient.

All of these utilised the expressed emotion (EE) measure. Originally developed to study schizophrenia (Brown & Rutter, 1966) it was applied to patients with depression by Vaughn and Leff (1976). Whereas many of the patients with schizophrenia in these two studies lived with parents, none of those with depression in the later study did so: instead they all resided with a partner. Over-involvement was commonly detected in the parents of people with schizophrenia, but was rare in the partners of those with depression. However, critical comments were as frequently expressed by partners of depressed patients as by the parents of people with schizophrenia. A difference between these two diagnostic groups appeared when the outcome of each over nine months was compared. Whereas a cut-off point of six critical comments predicted relapse of schizophrenia, for depressed patients the cut-off point needed to be lowered to two to achieve a significant difference between the relapse rates in high and low criticism relationships. This indicated that depressed patients are more sensitive to criticism from their partners than are those with schizophrenia. Our finding was then replicated by two further studies, one in Oxford (Hooley, Orley & Teasdale, 1986) and the other in Cairo (Okasha et al., 1994). This confirmatory evidence gave us the impetus to design and implement an intervention study for depressed patients living with a partner.

We had already conducted two studies of family work for schizophrenia based on the EE measure (Leff, Kuipers, Berkowitz, Eberlein-Fries & Sturgeon, 1982; Leff, Kuipers, Berkowitz & Sturgeon, 1985; Leff et al., 1989; Leff et al., 1990). These involved all patients being maintained on antipsychotic medication, as a basis on which work with the families was built. The studies on couple therapy reviewed above convinced us that, in contrast to schizophrenia, psychosocial interventions were effective in treating depression without the sheet anchor of medication. Consequently we designed our study as a comparison between antidepressant medication and two forms of psychosocial intervention.

The London depression intervention trial

The aim of this trial was to compare the efficacy of couple therapy, antidepressant medication, and CBT in treating depression and in preventing further relapses. Depression is known to respond to a number of different treatments but has a strong propensity to recur, which was the reason for including in the trial a prolonged follow-up period.

The design was a randomised controlled trial in which patients and their partners were assigned to one of the three treatments for one year, following which all treatments would be discontinued and subjects followed up for a further year. The inclusion criteria for the trial were that the subjects should score at least fourteen on the Hamilton Depression Rating Scale (HDRS), a standard requirement for trials of treatment for depression, and should be living with a heterosexual partner who expressed two or more critical comments during the Camberwell Family Interview. The stipulated age range was eighteen to sixty-five years. An economic analysis was included in order to assess the cost-effectiveness of the treatments being studied, and was conducted by Daniel Chisholm, a health economist.

It was deemed essential for each of the treatments to be delivered by acknowledged experts in their fields, so that the trial could not be criticised on the grounds of employing inadequate or inexperienced therapists. Before the trial proper began, a pilot phase of one year was instituted during which the recruitment and assessment procedures were tested and the CBT and couple therapists treated at least ten subjects. Both CBT therapists had been trained by Beck; both systemic couple therapists, Eia Asen and Elsa Jones, had international reputations, and the pharmacotherapist was a very experienced psychiatrist. The antidepressant regime was established through consultation with an expert in this treatment, and comprised stabilisation on Desipramine, a tricyclic antidepressant, followed by a treatment period of six weeks, during which the subject's score on the Beck Depression Inventory (BDI) was monitored weekly. If the subject failed to respond, Fluoxetine, an SSRI, was substituted for the initial treatment. At the end of the first year of the trial all these patients were gradually weaned off their medication. However, three patients relapsed within a short time and their medication had to be resumed.

Crafting a manual

While antidepressant treatment regimes have been standardised through experience over many years, and CBT for depression is manualised, this is not the case for couple therapy. It was considered essential for the two couple therapists to construct a manual so that, if successful, the therapy could be tested in further trials and taught to those interested. So Asen and Jones collaborated in developing a manual.

After several months and a number of drafts they produced a 100 page document in which the interventions in each session of the course of treatment and their sequence were precisely described. On reading this it was evident that the level of detail prescribed would stifle initiative and creativity, both of which are essential for good therapy. After discussing this together we agreed that a much more flexible manual was required which allowed each therapist to express their individual style, while delineating the aims of the successive stages of the therapy. After more drafting this was successfully achieved and was later published (Jones & Asen, 2000). Asen (personal communication) has recently written:

> Re-viewing the manual now, some ten years later, we are intensely aware of the many compromises that were made, between our different perspectives and systemic orientations, and especially in order to comply with the requirements of a manual that could be used by researchers. Somewhat to our surprise, the manual proved expansive enough to allow us to work in ways not unlike our normal practice, and to show "protocol compliance" according to the researchers, even though there were times when the constraints bit deep. There is a cliché in the dialogue between researchers and clinicians that suggests that, "in the swampy lowlands of everyday practice", an approach such as that described in the manual is quite impracticable, if not undesirable. Whether this is valid or not could be debated, but, as we hoped to make clear, the manual was written for a particular purpose and at a particular time, and was always meant to be a document in process, with an open invitation to each user to change it and adapt it to their respective work setting(s).

The stages of therapy described in the manual are: 1. Defining problems and trying new solutions. 2. Examining long-term relationship patterns. 3. Preventing relapse by anticipating likely crisis points. The therapists agreed to limit themselves to between twelve and twenty sessions for each couple during the first year of the trial. In the event few couples exceeded the lower number.

The tribulations of a trial

When the pilot phase ended we were faced with a serious dilemma: the two CBT therapists refused to continue with the definitive trial.

The reason they gave was that the patients they had been asked to treat in the pilot phase were, in their opinion, not suffering from depression but from personality disorders, despite the fact that they had passed the selection criteria for the trial including an HDRS score above thirteen. It was true that their depressive symptoms were of long standing, some persisting for over ten years, but the couple therapists had no reservations about taking on patients with this length of history. With hindsight, as we shall see, the CBT therapists' decision should have alerted us to a problem that emerged in the course of the trial and almost scuppered it. In order to make up for the loss of the Beck-trained therapists, we approached a psychologist in my research unit and asked him if he was willing to go to Philadelphia for the four month training course run by Beck. He jumped at the opportunity and off he went. This delayed the start of the trial a little but we still had plenty of preparatory work to do.

When the psychologist returned from his training the trial started. Power analysis indicated that we needed to recruit at least 150 subjects and we had expected to obtain these from the outpatient clinics of our colleagues at the Maudsley Hospital. It was soon apparent that the recruitment rate was far too slow, so we tried other sources. Eventually we found that advertisements in local newspapers brought in large numbers of volunteers for the trial, not all of whom were suitable, but in due course we made up the numbers we needed. But not before we hit another crisis. All trials, including pharmacological ones, suffer from high drop-out rates and ours was no exception, but the drop-outs were very uneven from the three treatment groups. The worst was the CBT arm: of the first eleven patients randomised to this treatment, eight dropped out before completing the course. Given that the therapist had successfully completed the training in CBT, we needed to look for another explanation. This took us back to the complaint of the CBT therapists in the pilot phase. We concluded that CBT is designed for depressed patients with a recent onset who can be expected to recover in a relatively short period of time, which was not the case with the subjects we were recruiting for our trial. The high drop-out rate from this arm of the trial meant that it was not sustainable and we took the hard decision to eliminate it from the trial. There was a compensatory benefit from this in that we were then aiming for fewer subjects than the original estimate of 150.

The drop-out rates from the other two arms were also dramatically different: 57% from the antidepressant group compared with only 15%

from couple therapy, a highly significant difference. This tells us that although subjects were willing to take a chance on being assigned to either of these treatments, there was far more satisfaction with couple therapy than with pharmacotherapy. This was no surprise since several surveys in different countries of public attitudes towards psychiatric illnesses and their treatment have shown that the public believe the main cause of these conditions to be stress and that they prefer talking therapies to medication and other physical treatments.

Adherence to the treatment modalities

It is obviously important in a trial comparing three different treatment modalities that what the patients receive is distinctive within each modality and that there is little or no overlap between the treatments. In our trial there was a clear protocol for each treatment to ensure minimal overlap, but the question remains of how strictly the therapists adhered to their protocols. Treatment integrity varies with "level of therapist training, therapist commitment to the research requirement of integrity, therapist commitment to the treatment under investigation, therapist exposure to and comfort with other treatment models and procedures, and the degree of supervision" (Shaw & Dobson, 1988). In the trials of marital therapy published up to that time, only O'Leary and Beach (1990) and Jacobson, Dobson, Fruzetti, Schmaling, and Salusky (1991) controlled for adherence to the specifications for each therapy.

To test the degree of treatment adherence in our trial, every session within each treatment was intended to be videotaped. From the bank of tapes, fifteen sessions with a total time of 1026 minutes for CBT, thirty-eight sessions with a total of 1971 minutes for couple therapy, and forty-seven sessions with a total of 1445 minutes for pharmacotherapy were available. For each patient a first session was chosen at random and then all the following sessions with the same patient were included. All tapes of less than ten minutes were excluded from analysis, which was conducted by an independent researcher, Felix Schwarzenbach. He derived a set of six specific interventions from each protocol and the relevant literature, and in addition made up a list of shared techniques. He then rated the tapes using the list of specific and general interventions he had compiled.

Purity indices were calculated according to the rules formulated by Luborsky, McLellan, Woody, O'Brien, and Auerbach (1985). The purity indices in the sample examined by Luborsky and colleagues ranged from 0.49 to 1.00. We found a much narrower range in our sample: 0.70 to 0.85. When the indices were calculated without the interventions shared across the three therapies, the indices ranged from 0.75 to 0.93, approaching the maximum of 1.00. Two of the techniques identified as specific were in fact shared by two or three therapies. "Therapist sets agenda" was shared by CBT and pharmacotherapy but not by couple therapy, although the differences between the therapies in the use of this technique were not significant. The same was true of "Questions about use of alcohol, coffee, medication, nicotine, or street drugs" which were used in all three therapies.

The CBT therapist used two techniques classified as specific to couple therapy: "circular interviewing" in 40% of sessions and "challenging techniques" in 20%. From the pharmacotherapy manual he used "reassurance" in 27% of the sessions. The couple therapists used "identification of negative thoughts/depressogenic assumptions" from CBT in 21% of sessions. The pharmacotherapist used "reattribution" from CBT in 23% of sessions.

The CBT and pharmacotherapists were allowed by the study protocol up to two joint sessions including the partner. Six pharmacotherapy sessions with one patient included her husband. The manual for couple therapy allowed individual and separate sessions, so that the five individual sessions with one patient are within the protocol. Differences between therapies in the average time of sessions were surprisingly large. Whereas couple therapy was well within the stipulated bounds, the CBT therapist exceeded by far the recommended duration of fifty minutes. Pharmacotherapy sessions were close to the target duration of twenty to thirty minutes. The differences in frequency counts of shared techniques were minimal between the three therapies. One noteworthy difference is that the couple therapists focused on "strengths and assets of the patient and couple" significantly more often (84%) than the CBT therapist (60%) and the pharmacotherapist (55%).

We can conclude from this analysis that any difference between the therapies in outcome for patients and their partners is most unlikely to be explained by low therapist adherence to their protocols. The surprisingly excessive length of the CBT sessions does prompt the question of whether this was a contributory factor to the high drop-out rate from this modality.

Results of the trial

Clinical outcome

A total of thirty-seven couples were assigned to the antidepressant arm and forty to the couple therapy arm. The BDI was used to assess the initial level of depression and any changes over the course of the trial. At entry into the trial the patients in the antidepressant arm had a slightly but significantly higher BDI score than those in the couple therapy arm. This was adjusted for in the statistical analysis conducted by Brian Everitt (1998), who also used a likelihood approach to allow for the drop-outs from each group. As shown in Figure 1, both groups experienced a significant reduction in the BDI score during the first year (Leff et al., 2000). However the improvement in depression was significantly greater in the couple therapy arm than in the antidepressant arm. Following the cessation of treatment at the end of the first year (except for the three patients who had to resume their medication) the improvement in depression was maintained at a steady level for both groups, with those who had received couple therapy continuing to be significantly less depressed than those in the medication arm.

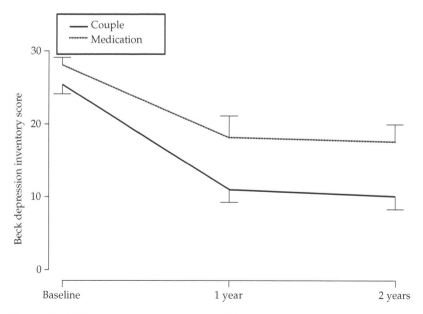

Figure 1. BDI scores over the course of the trial.

Economic analysis

Regrettably, costing of the services was incomplete as the collection of data on service use did not form part of the original battery of instruments, with the result that data were missing for the first twenty-seven out of the eighty-eight randomised patients. Drop-outs during the treatment phase who failed to return for the two-year follow-up, and other failures of compliance, further reduced the sample available for economic analysis. Therefore the findings on costs must be treated cautiously. Not surprisingly, the pharmacotherapy was less costly than the couple therapy since the psychiatrist prescribing the medication spent considerably less time with each patient than the therapists did with each couple, and the cost of the drugs was trivial compared with the cost of the therapists' time. Over the treatment period of the trial the mean monthly cost of couple therapy was £106, compared with £48 for the pharmacotherapy. However, patients receiving medication used far more additional clinical services than those in couple therapy. When the costs of these are added in, couple therapy cost on average £5 per month more than drug therapy, a non-significant difference. We can conclude that couple therapy is more effective in containing the patients' need for care than medication, and that the overall cost of couple therapy is consequently no more than the cost of pharmacotherapy. Costs were also monitored over the follow-up period, which included drop-outs from the treatment phase who agreed to be interviewed. It is noteworthy that the monthly service use costs of the ten patients who did not engage in either couple therapy or pharmacotherapy (£111) were three times as great as for the thirty-eight patients who did (£38). Thus there is an additional cost benefit for couple therapy due to its much greater effectiveness than pharmacotherapy in retaining patients in treatment.

The effect of couple therapy on the partner

In the initial assessment of the couples, the HDRS was administered to the partner as well as the patient. One third of the partners scored above the threshold of thirteen, meaning that they could just as well have been included as patients in the trial. This is consonant with the observation that a high proportion of carers of a person with any long-term illness suffer from depression. We were interested to follow up the partners' HDRS scores as they would constitute a test of the "see-saw" hypothesis, namely that if one individual in a relationship improves, the other will get worse to maintain homeostasis in the system. In fact the partners' scores reduced significantly by the end of the second year, paralleling the patients' improvement. This supports the view that the stress involved in the caring role leads to the carer becoming depressed, and that as the need for care reduces, the carer experiences relief.

Understanding the efficacy of couple therapy

The spur to this trial was twofold: the success of family interventions for schizophrenia in lowering relatives' EE, and the consequent dramatic reduction in the patients' relapse rate. Therefore we were curious to discover whether the advantage of couple therapy over pharmacotherapy was related to an amelioration in the partner's critical attitude towards the patient. The assessment of EE includes two different ratings of the carer's anger towards the patient: critical comments and hostility. Hostility is an extension of criticism and takes the form of a string of critical comments about different aspects of the patient's behaviour, or criticism directed at the patient's personality. Remarks such as "You are lazy and selfish" are particularly painful for the patient to hear, and amount to rejection of the person.

In contrast to our family intervention in schizophrenia, couple therapy employed in this trial did not include a specific focus on reducing critical comments. Nevertheless it was conceivable that improving the relationship between the partners had this effect. Therefore we compared the changes in critical comments over time between the couple therapy and pharmacotherapy groups. It is evident from Table 1 that partners in both groups showed a marked

Table 1. Changes in partners' critical comments over the course of the trial.

	Couple therapy		Drug treatment	
	n	Mean critical comments	n	Mean critical comments
Baseline	40	8.30	37	8.75
One-year follow-up	26	4.69	13	3.92
Two-year follow-up	26	3.46	23	3.57

and equivalent reduction in critical comments. Therefore this change could not account for the superiority of couple therapy in reducing the patients' depression.

A different picture emerged when we examined hostility. Patients would no longer be exposed to hostility if the partner desisted from expressing it or if the couple separated. During the course of the study, nine of the forty couples in the couple therapy group separated compared with five of the thirty-seven in the pharmacotherapy group, a non-significant difference. In the couple therapy group all eight partners who were hostile initially had either lost their hostility by the two-year follow-up or separated from the patient. However, two partners who were not hostile at baseline had developed hostility by the follow-up. In the pharmacotherapy group the number of partners expressing hostility reduced from ten at baseline to seven at follow-up. The reduction in exposure to hostility of patients in the couple therapy group was significant (exact p = 0.033), whereas that for patients in the drug therapy group was not. This difference raises the question of whether the advantage for couple therapy in effecting a greater reduction in BDI scores can be accounted for by the effect of the therapy on the patients' exposure to hostility. To answer this question, the mean change in BDI scores over the two years of the trial was compared for patients who were exposed to a hostile partner at the two-year follow-up and those who were no longer in a hostile relationship (Leff et al., 2003). Although the reduction in mean BDI score for those patients no longer in a hostile relationship was twice that for those still living with a hostile partner, 14.69 *vs.* 7.44, this difference failed to reach significance (p = 0.149). This may be because of the small number of subjects involved.

Table 2. Mean change in BDI scores for patients with and without a hostile partner at two-year follow-up.

n Mean change in BDI score		
Partner hostile at baseline and/or two years	9	−7.44
Partner hostile at baseline not at two years	13	−14.69

Conclusions from the trial

This study has demonstrated the superiority of couple therapy over an approved antidepressant regime both in reducing the symptoms of depression and in maintaining the improvement. The differential drop-out rates reaffirmed the negative views of the public on medication for psychological conditions (Paykel, Hart & Priest, 1998). When the costs of therapy were added to the costs of other service use, couple therapy was not more expensive than pharmacotherapy. Although the couple therapy did not specifically target critical comments, one of the aims was to help the patient and partner experiment with new ways of relating to one another. It was presumed that if the couple changed their interaction, the depressive symptoms might change (Jones & Asen, 2000). It was found that couple therapy achieved a significant reduction in the number of patients in a hostile relationship compared with pharmacotherapy. However, although there was suggestive data that this was linked to a reduction in depression, larger numbers of subjects are necessary to test this proposition further.

Incorporating couple therapy into standard clinical practice

The accumulation of evidence on the impact of the partner's emotional response on the patient's depression, and the completion of the London Depression Intervention Trial took many years. Difficult as these endeavours were, they feel like child's play when compared with the problems of incorporating couple therapy into everyday clinical practice. There are many obstacles to be overcome. Firstly we have entered the age of evidence-based medicine which requires that a unique trial be replicated several times before it is given any weight. Meta-analysis of a series of trials on the same issue has become the touchstone of admissible evidence. The criteria for inclusion of a trial in surveys of evidence can be quite rigid. Systemic couple therapy had been recommended in the 2004 National Institute for Health and Clinical Excellence guidelines on the basis of the London trial, but was then excluded in 2009 from a listing of studies on psychotherapeutic interventions for depression because of the overall drop-out rate of 40%. However, as we have seen, the low drop-out rate from couple therapy (15%) is informative about the acceptability of this therapy compared to the high drop-out from the antidepressant group. Furthermore, a highly regarded RCT of

CBT and pharmacotherapy for depression also had an overall drop-out rate of 40% (Hollon et al., 1992).

Couple therapy shares with other psychosocial interventions the problem of not having financial backing for its implementation. New drugs are launched on the market with massive and sustained advertising campaigns, often costing millions of pounds. There are no profits to be made from couple therapy so it can only become known through word of mouth or by therapists reading the relevant scientific literature. Furthermore, learning to prescribe a new drug requires little effort since the pharmaceutical companies and their representatives are eager to give doctors instruction in prescribing and to flood them with promotional literature. Acquiring the skills needed for couple therapy is a lengthy procedure and demands commitment. Inertia is common in many practitioners, who would prefer to continue doing what they are used to rather than having their assumptions challenged, and being confronted with a steep learning curve. For these reasons it is crucial for the government to give strong backing to a new therapy and to make available resources for the necessary training. It is informative at this juncture to review the government's policy on psychological therapies for depression.

Government policy

A survey of general practices in six health authorities in 1991 found that 17% had links with a counsellor. Ten years later approximately half the 9,000 general practices in England employed a counsellor. This dramatic change was probably facilitated by the Department of Health's white paper of 1996 entitled *Choice and Opportunity*, which allowed primary care in England to pilot new forms of organisation. However, the main impetus must have come from the public's demand to have more than the average seven minutes with their general practitioner to talk about their emotional problems. The rapid expansion of counselling in general practice prompted a review of the evidence for its efficacy by the Cochrane Collaboration (Fletcher et al., 2007). This meta-analysis found that in a six month follow-up counselling for depression in primary care gave a significant reduction in anxiety and depression compared with usual care by the general practitioner.

There are a number of possible strategies to improve the detection and management of depression in primary care. Training of primary care staff is usually undertaken in academic psychiatric departments and has received a great deal of input and evaluation from David Goldberg and his team in Manchester. Consultation-liaison involves the attendance at general practices of mental health specialists, who educate general practitioners by discussion of individual cases with them. Collaborative care refers to the addition of new quasi-specialists to the primary care team. Counsellors would come under this rubric. Finally, problematic patients can be referred to secondary or tertiary care. These four models have been carefully evaluated by Bower and Gilbody (2005). From a review of the literature they concluded that training staff by dissemination of guidelines and short courses failed to improve patients' outcome, while more intensive training in psychosocial interventions showed more consistent benefit. Collaborative care, such as that given by counsellors, produces small to medium effects on symptoms, patient satisfaction, and compliance, but is relatively costly. Referral to secondary or tertiary care is clinically effective, at least in the short term, but of course is at variance with the WHO policy of integrating mental health care into primary care. Bower and Gilbody end by pointing out a paradox: what is feasible is not effective, and while collaborative care is effective, it is not feasible. Given the rapid expansion of counsellors attached to general practices, we must contest the second half of their paradox.

Perhaps the government was influenced by the last statement of Bower and Gilbody's review, because rather than considering options for collaborative care they have gone overboard for a completely different strategy, namely computerised psychological therapies. The Department of Health has issued guidelines on the use of computerised CBT, citing two programs, *Beating the Blues* for mild and moderate depression, and *Fear Fighter* for phobias and panic. The primary care trusts were expected to offer these to their patients by 31 March 2007. They were advised to do the groundwork to achieve this, including undertaking a local needs assessment, purchasing software licences, ensuring the availability of suitable hardware, ensuring that suitably trained staff are available to supervise delivery, and developing referral protocols. This grandiose scheme may have been somewhat premature as an editorial in the *British Journal of Psychiatry* in 2008 concluded that "The published evidence regarding on-line CBT for depression without therapist support is extremely weak and drop-out rates are unacceptably high" (Andersson & Cuijpers, 2008). While evidence-based medicine has become a current mantra and is promoted by the government, it does not necessarily inform policy. For example, deinstitutionalisation was endorsed by successive governments of the right and left long before any evidence for its effect on patients was available (Leff, Trieman, Knapp & Hallam, 2000).

It is evident that counselling in general practice is feasible, and though it is seen as costly, half the primary care trusts in England are prepared to meet the costs. Obviously counsellors are able to treat depressed patients without partners, while these are excluded from couple therapy, so the question is: which is more cost-effective for depressed patients with partners, counselling or couple therapy? A convincing answer can only be produced by a randomised controlled trial of these two therapies, and this clearly needs to be undertaken. However, there exist many different forms of training for counsellors and it would be important to select counsellors representative of those working in general practices and to conduct the trial in these settings.

Training for couple therapy

Jones and Asen's manual has been published but a training course has yet to be developed using it as a basis. We did not start training psychiatric nurses in the family work for schizophrenia until we had the confirmatory results of our second trial of this intervention. It would be sensible to delay the development of a training course for couple therapy for depression until another trial of this approach confirms the outcome of the London trial. A trial of a similar approach to treating depression has been completed (Lemmens, Eisler, Buysse, Heene & Demyttenaere, 2009), evaluating a multi-family approach for depression. The three phases in this therapy are very similar to those described by Jones & Asen (2000), and the intervention includes some elements of their therapeutic work, but in addition the aims and management of the multi-family group have much in common with the carers' group which was a crucial part of our interventions for schizophrenia (Leff et al., 1989). Lemmens and colleagues' results favour their approach, giving some support to the London trial. However, we would still need a more direct replication to provide a rationale for establishing a training course based on Jones and Asen's manual.

References

Andersson, G. & Cuijpers, P. (2008). Editorial. *British Journal of Psychiatry, 193*: 270–271.

Balfour, A. & Lanman, M. (2011). An evaluation of time-limited psychodynamic psychotherapy for couples: A pilot study. *Psychology and Psychotherapy: Theory, Research and Practice.* doi: 10.1111/j.2044–8341.2011.02030.x.

Bower, P. & Gilbody, S. (2005). Managing common health disorders in primary care: conceptual models and evidence base. *British Medical Journal, 330*: 839–842.

Brown, G. W. & Rutter, M. (1966). The measurement of family activities and relationships: a methodological study. *Human Relations, 19*: 241–263.

Emanuels-Zuurveen, L. & Emmelkamp, P. M. (1996). Individual behavioural cognitive therapy v. marital therapy for depression in maritally distressed couples. *British Journal of Psychiatry, 169*: 181–188.

Everitt, B. S. (1998). The analysis of repeated measures: a practical review with examples. *Statistician, 44*: 113–135.

Fletcher, J., Bower, P. J., Gilbody, S., Lovell, K., Richards, D. & Gask, L. (2007). Collaborative care for depression and anxiety problems in primary care (Protocol). *Cochrane Database of Systematic Reviews 2007,* issue 2.

Friedman, A. S. (1975). Interaction of drug therapy with marital therapy in depressive patients. *Archives of General Psychiatry, 32*: 619–637.

Hollon, S. D., DeRubeis, R. J., Evans, M. D., Wiener, M. J., Garvey, M. J., Grove, W. M. & Tuason, V. B. (1992). Cognitive therapy and pharmacotherapy for depression: singly and in combination. *Archives of General Psychiatry, 49*: 774–781.

Hooley, M., Orley, J. & Teasdale, J. D. (1986). Levels of expressed emotion and relapse in depressed patients. *British Journal of Psychiatry, 148*: 642–647.

Jacobson, N. S., Dobson, K., Fruzzetti, A. E., Schmaling, K. B. & Salusky, S. (1991). Marital therapy as a treatment for depression. *Journal of Consulting and Clinical Psychology, 59*: 547–557.

Jones, E. & Asen, E. (2000). *Couple Therapy for Depression.* London: Karnac.

Leff, J., Alexander, B., Asen, E., Brewin, C. R., Dayson, D., Vearnals, S. & Wolff, G. (2003). Modes of action of family interventions in depression and schizophrenia: the same or different? *Journal of Family Therapy, 25*: 357–370.

Leff, J., Berkowitz, R., Shavit, N., Strachan, A., Glass, I. & Vaughn, C. (1989). A trial of family therapy v. a relatives group for schizophrenia. *British Journal of Psychiatry, 154*: 58–66.

Leff, J., Berkowitz, R., Shavit, N., Strachan, A., Glass, I. & Vaughn, C. (1990). A trial of family therapy versus a relatives' group for schizophrenia, two year follow-up. *British Journal of Psychiatry, 157*: 571–577.

Leff, J., Kuipers, L., Berkowitz, R., Eberlein-Fries, R. & Sturgeon, D. (1982). A controlled trial of social intervention in the families of schizophrenic patients. *British Journal of Psychiatry, 141*: 121–134.

Leff, J., Kuipers, L., Berkowitz, R. & Sturgeon, D. (1985). A controlled trial of social intervention in the families of schizophrenic patients: two year follow-up. *British Journal of Psychiatry, 146*: 594–600.

Leff, J., Trieman, N., Knapp, M. & Hallam, A. (2000). The TAPS Project: a report on 13 years of research, 1985–1998. *Psychiatric Bulletin, 24*: 165–168.

Leff, J., Vearnals, S., Brewin, C. R., Wolff, G., Alexander, B., Asen, E., Dayson, D., Jones, E., Chisholm, D. & Everitt, B. (2000). The London Depression Intervention Trial: Randomised controlled trial of antidepressants versus couple therapy in the treatment and maintenance of people with depression living with a partner: clinical outcome and costs. *British Journal of Psychiatry, 177*: 95–100.

Lemmens, G. M. D., Eisler, I., Buysse, A., Heene, E. & Demyttenaere, K. (2009). The effects of adjunctive single-family and multifamily group therapy in the treatment of hospitalized patients with major depression: A 15 month follow-up study. *Psychotherapy and Psychosomatics, 78*: 98–105.

Lemmens, G. M. D., Eisler, I., Migerode, L., Heiremann, M. & Demyttenaere, K. (2007). Family discussion group therapy for major depression: a brief systemic multi-family group intervention for hospitalised patients and their family members. *Journal of Family Therapy, 29*: 49–68.

Luborsky, L., McLellan, A. T., Woody, G. E., O'Brien, C. P. & Auerbach, A. (1985). Therapist success and its determinants. *Archives of General Psychiatry, 42*: 602–611.

Mathers, C. D. & Loncar, D. (2006). Projections of global mortality and burden of disease from 2002 to 2030. *PloS Medicine, 3*(11): e442.

NICE (2009). *Guideline on Depression in Adults.* www.nice.org.uk

Okasha, A., el Akabawi, K. S., Snyder, K. S., Wilson, A. K., Youssef, I. & el Dawla, A. S.(1994). Expressed emotion, perceived criticism, and relapse in depression: a replication in an Egyptian community. *American Journal of Psychiatry, 151*: 1001–1005.

O'Leary, K. D. & Beach S. R. H. (1990). Marital therapy: a viable treatment for depression and marital discord. *American Journal of Psychiatry, 147*: 183–186.

Paykel, E. S., Hart, D. & Priest, R. G. (1998). Changes in public attitudes to depression during the Defeat Depression Campaign. *British Journal of Psychiatry*, *172*: 519–522.

Shaw, B. F. & Dobson, K. S. (1988). Competency judgements in the training and evaluation of psychotherapists. *Journal of Consulting and Clinical Psychology*, *56*: 666–672.

Tomlinson, M., Cooper, P. J., Stein, A., Swartz, L. & Molteno, C. (2006). Post-partum depression and infant growth in a South African peri-urban settlement. *Child: Care, Health and Development*, *32*: 81–86.

Üstün, T. B. & Sartorius, N. (Eds.) (1995). *Mental Illness in General Health Care, an International Study*. Chichester, UK: Wiley.

Vaughn, C. & Leff, J. P. (1976). The influence of family and social factors on the course of psychiatric illness: a comparison of schizophrenic and depressed neurotic patients. *British Journal of Psychiatry*, *129*: 125–137.

Waring, E. M., Chamberlaine, C. H., McCrank, E. W., Stalker, C. A., Carver, C., Fry, R. & Barnes, S. (1988). Dysthymia: a randomised study of cognitive marital therapy and antidepressants. *Canadian Journal of Psychiatry*, *33*: 96–99.

World Health Organization & Wonca (2008). *Integrating Mental Health into Primary Care A Global Perspective*. Geneva, Switzerland: World Health Organization.

COMMENTARY ON CHAPTER SIX

Christopher Clulow

In their chapter, Leff, Asen, and Schwarzenbach paint a vivid picture of the trials and tribulations of psychotherapy research. The fantasy that there is such a thing as clean-cut empiricism is quickly dispelled by this authentic account of how the London Depression Intervention Trial was carried out. The real world is messy and not easily shoehorned into pre-planned designs, so why should we expect psychotherapy research to be any different? And when government funding of services depends on there being an evidence base we should not be surprised (although we should be concerned) that politics have a bearing on which outcome studies are taken seriously.

I want to pick up on four questions in responding to this chapter: What is depression, and how do we understand it? What counts as evidence? What aspects of couple therapy account for change? Where do we go from here?

The most recent report on depression published by the UK's National Institute for Health and Clinical Excellence (NICE) (2009) suggests we are facing an epidemic of depressive illness that could be costing the country £9 billion per annum. Yet forty years ago depression did not feature as a mental illness. So are we witnessing the emergence of a new illness, or the repackaging of old conditions that used to come under catch-all categories such as "nervous breakdown"?

Psychiatrists are likely to turn to the American Psychiatric Association's *Diagnostic and Statistics Manual of Mental Disorders* (DSM) for a description of the symptoms associated with depression (for example, absence of positive affect, anxiety, physical ailments, cognitive and behavioural changes) when making a diagnosis, distinguishing between major and minor depressive disorders in terms of the severity, range, and persistence of symptoms. But this does not help us much in understanding what can be a whole range of debilitating and distressing conditions. By classifying the symptoms of depression as a mental disorder the *Manual* gathers depression into the medical domain. The advantage of this is that it destigmatises those suffering from depressive symptoms and opens up possibilities for medicine to relieve if not cure them. The risk lies in its potential to medicalise emotional states, transforming them into a set of illnesses requiring treatment—note, for example, that the 2013 edition of the DSM will include shyness as "social phobia" and anger as "temper disregulation disorder" (Kenny, 2010). For the pharmaceutical companies there is money to be made from peddling unhappiness as disease (Greenberg, 2010), so maybe psychotherapists need to exercise caution before jumping onto the same bandwagon.

While we know that genetic endowment and a family history of depression are risk factors when assessing depression, so too are social/environmental factors such as being a woman, poor, isolated, the victim of adverse childhood experiences, and subjected to stressful life events. James (2007) asserts that environment is of greater aetiological significance than genetic endowment in precipitating mental illness (if we allow ourselves to disconnect the two), and argues that the depression "epidemic" in countries with developed economies is a product of a materialistic culture that drives us unrelentingly to compete and consume. So, we might suppose, an effective response to depression, in all its various presentations, will require us to adopt a multi-pronged treatment approach if we are to do justice to the range of factors that are relevant to its ontogenesis.

The National Institute for Health and Clinical Excellence decides what constitutes an adequate evidence base for health services in the UK, and this body has affirmed that such a thing exists for the treatment of depression not only by pharmacotherapy and cognitive behavioural therapy but also by couple therapy. This body excluded from its evidence base the London Depression Intervention Trial (Leff et al., 2000), the only controlled trial of manualised couple therapy for depression in this country, on the basis that the drop-out rate in the control group receiving pharmacotherapy was too high Despite their having included it in an earlier edition this body .... So the publically approved evidence base for treating depression through couple therapy is restricted to six studies, stretching back over thirty years, all but one of which relates to behavioural couple therapy.

This raises important questions about the nature of evidence in psychotherapy research. Scientific methods are there to help researchers maximise objectivity in designing research, whittling the relevant variables down to the minimum possible in comparing their impact on outcomes. So what is usually considered to be the ideal outcome design compares, in quantitative terms, the impact of a repeatable intervention on a large group of subjects (sufficient to give the figures statistical power) against the impact of no intervention on an identical group, both groups being protected as far as possible from other variables (including the research design) that might distort the results. These are the grounds on which randomised controlled trials (RCTs), which NICE uses in identifying its evidence base, have become the gold standard for scientific research.

In contrast to the blinkered approach essential to such a research design, clinicians must take into account as much information as possible that sheds light on a condition and what might change it (Bowlby, 1988). While researchers may acknowledge the complexity of the systems they are studying, their methods will privilege the simple and objective over the complex and subjective. This can be anathema to clinicians. Within the Tavistock Centre for Couple Relationships (TCCR) there has, over the years, been considerable tension resulting from trying to integrate research and clinical practice. Only recently has empiricism become a virtue rather than a threat, and this followed a growing acquaintanceship with and discovery of methods that are compatible with clinical values (Clulow, Shmueli, Vincent & Evans, 2002; Lanman, Grier & Evans, 2003). As a practice-led organisation we have adopted process research, qualitative methods, and single case study designs in preference to undertaking RCTs (although such an evaluation is currently under way in connection with its Parenting Together service). In terms of therapeutic outcomes we know that it is not only what works for whom, but what gets created (or not) between therapists and those they see. People do not simply act *on* each other, they interact *with* each other. Mutual influence is the order of the day when considering relationships, whether of the research or therapeutic kind. This kind of practice-based evidence, complementing evidence-based practice, needs bringing into the frame (Barkham & Margison, 2007).

But we must also take into account our bias as trained and committed clinicians: our belief in what we do gives us an investment in showing that it works (which is the criticism often levelled at practitioners by researchers). So even when TCCR can show in quantitative terms that relationship counselling significantly reduces depression in a vulnerable group of users, as it has done (Clulow & Donaghy, 2010), such comparisons of pre- and post-intervention scores are not sufficiently rigorous to provide an evidence base in NICE terms.

Developments since the completion of the earliest of the studies included in the NICE evidence base (Jacobson, Dobson, Fruzetti, Schmaling & Salusky, 1991; Jacobson, Fruzetti, Dobson, Whitman & Hope, 1993) are instructive in terms of what research can conceal as well as reveal. Having completed the studies that demonstrated behavioural marital therapy worked as a treatment for depression, the principal researcher and therapist (Neil Jacobson) was unhappy with the results. In effect, he had no conviction that one of the main techniques used in the study, reciprocal behaviour exchange ("Do this for me and I'll do that for you"), worked for any couples who were not well-motivated to change in the first place. While his research had established an association between intervention and outcome, he did not believe it was the technique that accounted for the change. This courage to be self-critical and reflective led him to a central question that taxes all therapists of whatever persuasion: what is it about the therapeutic process that is mutative? Other researchers have commented on the fact that most couple interventions, whatever their orientation (behavioural, psychodynamic, systemic, integrative), show positive results (Gurman & Fraenkel, 2002), supporting the "Dodo hypothesis" that Shmueli and I have commented on (Shmueli & Clulow, 1997). Jacobson's journey prompted him to reconsider what was mutative in behavioural couple therapy, and to refocus on the potential gains from enabling partners to accept each other, and to accept what cannot be changed in their relationship (Jacobson & Christensen, 1998). His doubts clearly resonated with others in his field, since reciprocal behavioural exchange is nowadays low on the ladder of techniques used in behavioural couple therapy (Crowe & Ridley, 2000).

When identifying the competences therapists would need to treat depression (Clulow, 2010a), two things struck me from reviewing the manuals used in the research. First, most of the studies employed therapies that focused simply on improving the relationship between partners, and used no methods that were tailored to the needs of one or both partners being depressed. Only two of the manuals focused specifically on techniques for managing depression in the couple, and even these directed most of their attention towards improving the relationship overall (Beach, Sandeen & O'Leary, 1990; Rounsaville, Weissman, Klerman & Chevron, 1986). This opened up the possibility that there might be a much larger pool of evidence for the effectiveness of couple therapy for improving relationships that met the stringent conditions of NICE but were overlooked because they had not recorded depression scores in the partners. The exclusion of such studies was an important omission if relationship quality is a key variable in preventing and reducing depressive symptoms. Taking this point seriously provided the rationale for increasing the range of studies with manualised treatments from which the competences for couple therapy for depression might be drawn.

The second thing that struck me was a sense that there has been a convergence of therapeutic approaches over the past thirty years, and what unites us in our methods is greater than what divides us. This is not to deny that there remain important differences in working philosophies, theories, and techniques, but to comment on the increasing areas of overlap. In much the same way that Jacobson came to see that couple therapy involved taking account of what psychoanalytic therapists might describe as resistance to change, or the couple's investment in maintaining their problem, most therapists, whatever their persuasion, know about the importance of maintaining balance between partners in their work, the potential for working with relationship boundaries, and the relevance of firmly held beliefs and assumptions about relationships to scripting couple conflict. Indeed, a recent meta-analysis of the efficacy of psychodynamic therapies suggests that non-psychodynamic therapies may be effective in part because their more skilled practitioners use psychodynamic techniques (Shedler, 2010).

So it came to be that the competences model that resulted from reviewing therapeutic procedures and methods used in the enlarged evidence base turned out to be more eclectic and, hopefully, integrative than some partisans might have wished. Certainly by including the London Depression Intervention Trial, and thereby the manual of systemic therapy used in the study (Jones & Asen, 2000), we could enlarge and enrich the pool of competences, approaches, and techniques that will be of real value to clinicians working with depressed couples.

So where do we go from here? I want to conclude with a proposal. It is one that will take clinicians out of their comfort zone and possibly incur some risk. But in terms of potential learning and outcomes it could make a huge contribution to developing the field of couple therapy. From the review of the relevant research (Hewison, 2010a) has come a method and outcome for establishing competences for couple therapy for depression (Clulow, 2010a; 2010b) and a training syllabus (Hewison, 2010b). What remains is for the competences and syllabus to be converted into a therapy manual, and for the therapy to be trialled according to the stringent conditions laid down by NICE. My contention is that the reason valuable approaches to couple therapy have not been broadly recognised is that, apart from the behavioural therapies, we have been slow not only to submit ourselves to research scrutiny but also to influence the nature of the research from what we know through our experience as practitioners. Things are changing, so perhaps now is the moment to seize the challenge of demonstrating the potential of what we couple therapists do in terms that are accepted by the fiercest of our critics.

References

Barkham, M. & Margison, F. (2007). Practice-based evidence as a complement to evidence-based practice: from dichotomy to chiasmus. In: C. Freeman & M. Power (Eds.), *Handbook of Evidence-Based Psychotherapies: a Guide for Research and Practice* (pp. 443–476). Chichester, UK: Wiley.

Beach, S., Sandeen, E. & O'Leary, K. (1990). *Depression in Marriage: A Model for Etiology and Treatment*. New York: Guilford.

Bowlby, J. (1988). Psychoanalysis as art and science. In: *A Secure Base: Clinical Applications of Attachment Theory* (pp. 39–57). London: Routledge.

Clulow, C. (2010a). Couple therapy for depression: competences framework http://www.ucl.ac.uk/clinical-psychology/CORE/Couple-Therapy-for-Depression_framework.htm

Clulow, C. (2010b). Couple therapy for depression: information for clinicians and commissioners. http://www.ucl.ac.uk/clinical-psychology/CORE/Couple-Therapy-for-Depression_framework.htm

Clulow, C. & Donaghy, M. (2010). Developing the couple perspective in parenting support: evaluation of a service initiative for vulnerable families. *Journal of Family Therapy, 32*(2): 142–168.

Clulow, C., Shmueli, A., Vincent, C. & Evans, C. (2002). Is empirical research compatible with clinical practice? *British Journal of Psychotherapy, 19*(1): 33–44.

Crowe, M. & Ridley, J. (2000). *Therapy with Couples. A Behavioural-Systems Approach to Couple Relationship and Sexual Problems* (2nd edn.). Oxford: Blackwell.

Greenberg, G. (2010). *Manufacturing Depression. The Secret History of a Modern Disease.* New York: Simon & Schuster.

Gurman, A. & Fraenkel, P. (2002). The history of couple therapy: A millennial review. *Family Process, 41*: 199–260.

Hewison, D. (2010a). *Survey of Research Cited in NICE Guidelines.* London: TCCR (unpublished).

Hewison, D. (2010b). *Couple Therapy for Depression Modality.* London: TCCR (unpublished).

Jacobson, N. & Christensen, A. (1998). *Acceptance and Change in Couple Therapy. A Therapist's Guide to Transforming Relationships.* New York: W.W. Norton.

Jacobson, N., Dobson, K., Fruzetti, A., Schmaling, K. & Salusky, S. (1991). Marital therapy as a treatment for depression I. *Journal of Consulting & Clinical Psychology, 59*(4): 547–557.

Jacobson, N., Fruzetti, A., Dobson, K., Whitman, M. & Hope, H. (1993). Marital therapy as a treatment for depression II. The effects of relationship quality and therapy on depressive relapse. *Journal of Consulting & Clinical Psychology, 61*: 516–519 .

James, O. (2007). *Affluenza.* London: Vermilion.

Jones, E. & Asen, E. (2000). *Systemic Couple Therapy and Depression.* London: Karnac.

Kenny, M. (2010). Medicalising depression. BBC Radio 4 broadcast on 29 October.

Lanman, M., Grier, F. & Evans, C. (2003). Objectivity in psychoanalytic assessments of couple relationships. *British Journal of Psychiatry, 182*: 255–260.

Leff, J., Vearnals, S., Brewin, C., Wolff, G., Alexander, B., Assen, E., Drayton, D., Jones, E., Chisholm, D. & Everitt, B. (2000). The London Depression Intervention trial. Randomised controlled trial of antidepressants vs. couple therapy in the treatment and maintenance of people with depression living with a partner: Clinical outcomes and costs. *British Journal of Psychiatry*, *177*: 95–100.

NICE (2009). *Depression in Adults (update). Depression: the Treatment and Management of Depression in Adults*. National Clinical Practice Guideline 90. http://guidance.nice.org.uk/CG90/guidance/pdf/(English).

Rounsaville, B., Weissman, M., Klerman, G. & Chevron, E. (1986). *Manual for Conjoint Marital Interpersonal Psychotherapy for Depressed Patients with Marital Disputes (IPT-CM)*. New Haven, CT: Yale University School of Medicine (unpublished).

Shedler, J. (2010). The efficacy of psychodynamic psychotherapy. *American Psychologist*, *65*(2): 98–109.

Shmueli, A. & Clulow, C. (1997). Marital therapy: definition and development. *Current Opinions in Psychiatry*, *10*(3): 247–250.

CHAPTER SEVEN

Approaches to researching the evidence: an exploration of TCCR's research into couple relationships and couple therapy, past and present

David Hewison

The Tavistock Centre for Couple Relationships (TCCR)[1] began life as a mixed practice and research organisation looking to find effective ways of intervening in family distress after the Second World War (see Bannister et al., 1955; Menzies, 1949; Wilson, 1947a, 1947b, 1949; Wilson, Menzies & Eichholtz, 1949). It has been engaged in this project ever since in one form or another (see Woodhouse, 1990 for a review of its history and development up to 1990, and Haldane, 1991 for a review of its publications). As such it has used a variety of approaches to researching couple relationships and the ways in which workers and the couples they work with affect each other, whether this is in socially-based casework, in the intimate privacy of an ongoing psychotherapy, or in the ways that agencies and organisations work with and against each other. In this variety it is a proud (and productive) member of the Tavistock family of organisations and shares with them an interest in the application of psychoanalytic ideas to social and psychological

---

[1] Note: for ease of reading, the various names and name-changes of the Tavistock Centre for Couple Relationships over the past 60 years have been omitted in favour of the current title. Details of TCCR's publications since 1948 are available on its website: www.tccr.ac.uk

matters (see Dicks, 1970; Trist & Murray, 1990). As a centre of advanced study into the couple relationship and its therapeutic treatment TCCR has a particular perspective on both research and evidence in the field of couple relationships, and is well qualified to enter into contemporary debates about this complex area.

In the psychological therapies, currently at least, there appears to be an assertion of a hierarchy of evidence, with that based on randomised controlled trials (RCTs) being given priority over other forms of evidence (see the guidelines of the UK's National Institute for Health and Clinical Excellence (NICE) for an example of the value of this approach across medical treatments generally: www.nice.org.uk). The specialist research technology of RCTs was developed to test the impact of particular chemical compounds on specific physical conditions so as to enable the production of effective medication while minimising harm. It is a technology that relies on a high degree of control over the elements being tested, so that the experiments can lead to a clear and logical conclusion that medication X is better than medication Y (or better than a placebo, or better than nothing) for the treatment of the specific condition Z. More than this, the methodology utilised means that the experiment can be repeated to ensure that the result was not simply the effect of chance or accident, and the randomised element means that the impact of the personal qualities of the subjects being tested is similarly minimised. RCTs have proved their effectiveness in the pharmaceutical industry—as in the experimental sciences—and they are an essential part of our culture and quality of life. There is, however, still considerable debate about how their findings can be transferred to non-experimental settings, particularly those involving human psychological states and interactions rather than chemicals and their effects. As early as 1981, objections to the claims being put forward for this form of evidence-testing for the psychotherapies pointed out the basic problem of trying to control the idiosyncrasies of human beings sufficiently to say that the experiments actually *proved* anything as to which therapy is suitable for which condition: assuming there are 250 different forms of psychologically based therapy and 150 discrete diagnostic mental disorders in the DSM-III, as was the case in 1981, a full comparison would need approximately 4.7 million experiments; a more limited one would need nearly 7,000 (Parloff, 1982). The problem is more complex thirty years later as the number of different therapies has proliferated to 400 or more, and each test would still need to be confirmed (at least once).

This, however, is not the only difficulty in relying on RCTs in psychological therapies. Because they claim to show the efficacy of a *specific* therapy for a *specific* diagnosis, they cannot automatically be applied to cases where the diagnosis is mixed: where there is not just anxiety, for example, but anxiety mixed with depression, or with a physical condition, or with a serious life-stressor such as sudden unemployment or divorce or even the birth of a child. Unfortunately, many, if not most, conditions are mixed ("co-morbid"); similarly, not all patients are identical to those who volunteer to take part in RCTs and neither are all therapists the same even when working with a manualised therapy that attempts to ensure uniformity of treatment. The complex mix of ingredients outside the laboratory can mean that a treatment which has proved its worth in a trial does not work outside it. In the language of research, it has proven its *efficacy* but not necessarily proven its *effectiveness*. Nonetheless, it is this form of assessment of therapy that has now been given the role of arbiter as to whether a *particular treatment* should be available or not in the NHS, or paid for by insurance companies, and indeed has been given the function of determining whether a particular therapy is to be considered "evidence-based" or not. There is now a false but widely held assumption that RCT-evidenced psychotherapy helps people whereas a treatment which has not been subject to an RCT does not (Smith & Pell, 2003). Evidence, in fact, comes in many forms (see, e.g., Barkham, Stiles, Lambert & Mellor-Clark, 2010 for a review of the pros and cons of different types of evidence, including RCTs).

The complications of this approach have been highlighted in the recent development of couple therapy as a treatment for adult depression in the NHS through the Improving Access to Psychological Therapies (IAPT) initiative (Department of Health, 2007). A behavioural form of couple therapy was endorsed by NICE (2009) as having the approved RCT evidence base for its efficacy as a treatment for depression. A process of expert review of this evidence, followed by national and international consultation, took place in 2010 led by the Tavistock Centre for Couple Relationships in partnership with Relate. This process of RCT-based endorsement and definition is a familiar one in the moves to find cost-effective and appropriate forms of treatment for severe and debilitating conditions requiring the expenditure of public monies. The review discovered that the behavioural RCT evidence was old and had been superseded by subsequent developments and refutations in the models of therapy used in the original trials; the evidence was also thin, contradictory, and not based on any therapy practised to any substantial degree in the UK. This meant that the contemporary competences defining "Couple Therapy for Depression", as it is now called, could not simply be lifted from the original manuals of behavioural treatment and updated, but instead careful integration of competences from other models of therapy had to be done. The result is an elegant mix of different clinically proven therapeutic interventions that can be used on the basis of clinical need (Clulow, 2010; Hewison, 2011). It is not solely limited to the research evidence cited by NICE, yet it is still rigorous and pragmatic and is now the base for training and delivery of couple therapy in IAPT services in the NHS.

This process of assessing the evidence has been endorsed by the chair of NICE, Sir Michael Rawlins. Addressing the need to abandon the hierarchy of evidence that puts RCTs at the top, he said:

> Hierarchies attempt to replace judgement with an oversimplistic, pseudo-quantitative, assessment of the quality of the available evidence. Decision makers have to incorporate judgements, as part of their appraisal of the evidence in reaching their conclusions. Such judgements relate to the extent to which each of the components of the evidence base is "fit for purpose". Is it reliable? Does it appear to be generalizable? Do the intervention's benefits outweigh its harms? And so on. Decision makers have to be teleoanalysts. Although techniques such as Bayesian statistics will undoubtedly assist, they will not be a substitute for judgement. As William Blake (1757–1827) observed "God forbid that truth should be confined to mathematical demonstration". (Rawlins, 2008, p. 34)

In Rawlins's call for teleoanalysis (for a *pluralistic* evidence base that takes account of different forms of evidence (Wald & Morris, 2003)) there is a wish to go beyond the RCT-based results of individual tests of specific therapies for specific diagnoses, and beyond even the results of meta-analyses that have attempted to recover some useful information within and across the plethora of such research papers (all with slight differences and quirks that prevent them being easily compared and aligned with each other). Barkham and colleagues in the UK and beyond have responded to the limitations of evidence-based practice (or empirically supported therapies as it is called in the United States) by calling for the systematic gathering of *practice-based evidence* (Barkham,

Hardy & Mellor-Clark, 2010). This focuses on the ways in which practitioner and client can both contribute to the generation of pragmatic evidence of the outcomes of therapy; on dissemination to others; and on the establishment of a substantial "bottom-up" flow of knowledge that can become the counterpart of the "top-down" evidence-based practice directives (Duncan, Miller & Sparks, 2004). Their work is a brilliant example of the rigour and care that exists in contemporary attempts to research and improve outcomes for users of psychological therapies; it does raise a question, however: other than the delight that comes from seeing excellence, why should TCCR pay any particular attention to it?

One of the things that TCCR has stood for is not just the discovery of what works, but also the finding-out of what *kind of a thing* a couple relationship is, in all its forms. This means that outcome-based research is only one part of a strand of inquiry in our clinical and clinically derived practice; we are also interested in the relationship between researchers and researched, between couples and therapists, and between organisations, the people they employ, and the people they aim to help. This task requires a variety of research activities and perspectives.

Varieties of researcher and research evidence

One of the curious things about discussions of research and evidence in psychotherapy is the frequent polarisation that occurs: a division happens between those who see research as antithetical to psychotherapy (psychotherapy as an art) and those who see it as an essential part (psychotherapy as a science) (Joyce, Wolfaardt, Sribney & Aylwin, 2006). Each reads the other's position as dismaying at best and incendiary at worst. Freud's line that the two were indivisibly linked—the "Junctim" argument (Freud, 1926e)—has not endeared him to everyone, not least because it suggests a model psychoanalyst that few of us can live up to, and is contradicted by his own attachment to his theory in the face of evidence to the contrary (Hewison, 2007). Where this polarisation is more nuanced, it is clear that there are overlaps between the professional integrities of the psychotherapist and the researcher, and indeed the Tavistock model has long had the slogan "No therapy without research; no research without therapy". Taken narrowly, this would mean that little work of either therapy or research was possible, because of the conflicts between the two positions, especially where psychoanalytic work is concerned. Fortunately, it has given rise to a tradition of inquiry that has been fruitful and valuable in exploring relationships between adults in a variety of different forms: the intimate adult relationship in its struggles with both ordinary and extraordinary life events; the mutually entwined well-being of parents and children; and the unconsciously influenced relationships between colleagues and across organisations.

We can identify three main clusters of research identity that work *within*, *between* and *across* relationships and can be associated, crudely, with a psychoanalytic, a psychological and a social science point of view respectively:

> *Within*—the individual psychoanalytic clinician or small group of clinicians trying to understand how psychoanalytic theories illuminate and are themselves illuminated by work in the consulting room: this group focuses on a specific couple as the object of its research and uses case studies as its medium;
>
> *Between*—the psychologist trying to understand the relationship between types of clinical service delivery and outcomes of therapy: this group focuses on aggregations of couples and uses comparisons of scores on validated measures as its medium;
>
> *Across*—the social scientist trying to understand the lived experience of groups of people in their conscious and unconscious interactions with each other: this group shifts back and forth between the individual couple case study and a particular aggregation of case studies in an iterative process that uses narrative and meaning as its medium.

TCCR traditionally has done the two types of research that focus on the case study, and has tended to try to discover meaning and process rather than test "what works for whom" (Roth & Fonagy, 2004). For fifty-five years, this matched the task of TCCR as an advanced research and training institute rather than a deliverer of clinical services, as the clinical work that was done at TCCR was to inform its other functions. It was the nature of the adult couple relationship that was the subject of interest, rather than the effectiveness of the therapy used as a tool to explore this. With the incorporation of the clinical service previously supplied by London Marriage Guidance in 2005, this situation changed radically. TCCR found itself delivering five times as much clinical work, and research interest has necessarily turned towards this aspect of organisational life as a result. Finding ways of meaningfully exploring the evidence available in 10,000 clinical sessions a year (2010 figures) is an exciting challenge to the research life of the organisation.

Case study evidence

Casework in a local authority

In the 1970s the organisation undertook a three-year action research project in conjunction with an inner London social services department into work with married couples. These couples formed a small part of the department's overall case load, but took up a disproportionate amount of staff time and resources: emotional as well as practical. The project was characterised by its three-way functions: to engage with couples as social workers working (part-time) in the service; to study the dynamics of the couple interaction and the interaction between them and their workers and the wider setting of the service itself; and finally, to engage with the managers of the department as to the most effective ways of dealing with the demands and tensions of such difficult work, given the range of feelings and the conscious and unconscious dynamics it gave rise to. The written account of the work, *Mate and Stalemate* (Mattinson & Sinclair, 1979), gives a vivid picture of the complex and troubling lives and relationships brought to the social services department and the ways in which the social workers dealt with them, with other agencies engaged with them, and with the anxiety ricocheting between all of them—sometimes acknowledged and worked-with, and sometimes denied and acted-out. The project is iterative with the researchers' and caseworkers' experience informing their developing conceptualisation of the work, and this in turn enhancing their practice, and so on. Mattinson and Sinclair make the important point that they did not attempt to set up a representative sample of couple cases, but simply took those that were allocated to them and those that were brought to their weekly workshop; neither did they set up a control group to allow them to identify which specific variable could be discovered as the "key" to enabling change. Instead, they relied on working as usual, making the point that some key dynamics are to be found in the individual case, but are invisible across cases, and that the accretion and investigation of a number of single case studies discussed in a workshop can reveal patterns which can themselves be investigated subsequently but which cannot be discovered through an RCT technology. They point to a case in which the key findings of research into the causes of depression in women (that they are less likely than non-depressed women to have a supportive partner, to be in satisfactory accommodation, or to be in work, and that they are more likely to have three or more children under the age of fourteen (Brown, Bhrolchain & Harris, 1975)) were systematically tackled in an attempt to alleviate the depression. Attempts to improve all these led to an unexpected result:

> A temporary improvement in the marriage led to a further pregnancy which, in its turn, led to more stress; apparent improved housing led to rent arrears and increased anxiety; and the placement of a child in day nursery, far from enabling the wife to go out to work, increased her sense of inadequacy as a mother and hence her depression. (Mattinson & Sinclair, 1979, p. 22)

They go on to say, in words remarkably similar to those of contemporary research commentators on evidence-based practice, "We believe that a clinical approach has a respectable logic of its own and that, as in this case, it can supplement control studies and deepen the understanding they provide" (Mattinson & Sinclair, 1979, p. 22). This is teleoanalysis many years before it was coined (Rawlins, 2008; Wald & Morris, 2003).

Unemployment

In the 1980s the organisation undertook a study of the impact of unemployment on the couple relationship, published in 1988 as *Work, Love and Marriage* (Mattinson, 1988). It was the classic mix of research and therapy in which the work influences the theory and vice versa, and it was conducted as a multi-agency project with three sites: the London base of the organisation; the University of Exeter in Devon; and the Northumbria Probation Service in Tyneside. As mass unemployment built during the 1980s as a result of the Thatcher government's economic policies, the organisation put on a series of workshops to explore the experience of unemployment on the adult couple. Workshops are tellingly defined by Mattinson as different from training courses in that in the latter the organisation has knowledge or expertise it wants to sell to others, and in the former the assumption is that the organisation will also be gaining from the knowledge of others while simultaneously offering an understanding of that knowledge from a psychoanalytic perspective (Mattinson, 1988, p. 9).

The workshops were aimed at a multidisciplinary membership of marriage guidance, social services, probation, health visiting, general practice, and the Church, and had a particular design: part I was the structured sharing in small groups of detailed clinical material of couples in which unemployment figured, and hypotheses developed about the subsequent impact on the couple dynamic explored in large plenary groups; part II was the return to the casework setting for three months to "try out" the ideas generated in part I; part III was the coming back-together of the workshops to explore their experiences and subsequent conclusions. *Work, Love and Marriage* is characterised by its attention to stories rather than to numbers; measures are not used, neither does the book rely on experimental psychology. Instead it is full of *narrative*: the words of the men and women experiencing or dealing with unemployment appear alongside fragments of poetry, fiction, and plays, as well as psychoanalysis, sociology, and political science; Marx, Byron, Turkel, and Ilich are interspersed with Freud, Jung, Klein, and Skynner. What is remarkable about the book is evident from this list: its richness and connectedness to the lived experience of the people it is writing about—which, deliberately, includes the people working with those who are unemployed and seeking help (psychologically and sociologically the "not-yet-unemployed"). Together with this is the clear voice of its principal author, Janet Mattinson, who was herself wrestling with the unemployment that comes with retirement, and reflecting on the meaning of work in her life too.

Over and above opening up an area of clinical inquiry, the project also addressed itself to the emotional impact of unemployment more generally: one of its most striking findings was that unemployment was invisible (despite being prevalent)—no one wanted to acknowledge it. Indeed, one worker accused the workshop of "inventing unemployment" (Mattinson, 1988, p. 160): on returning to her work after part I of the project, newly sensitised to unemployment as a reality, Mattinson was shocked to realise that the majority of her case load involved families with one or more unemployed member—a knowledge that, despite her interest in this area, she had previously unconsciously wiped-out. The book concludes that the struggle to keep in mind what is otherwise split-off and denied has to be maintained in the face of considerable internal and external pressures. This links with a suggested redefinition of welfare as the necessary means to enable people to adapt to a changing social world so that individual and societal development can go along hand-in-hand.

TCCR has recently revised and re-released the training and video materials related to understanding the impact of unemployment as the country has again entered a period of increasing stress on families due to unemployment, underlining the value of the earlier study (Thompson & Buss Twachtmann, 2009).

Telephone helpline for child abusers

Again in the 1980s the organisation was engaged in another workshop form of research: the work of a volunteer telephone helpline set up for parents who felt themselves to be at risk of, or who actually were, harming their children physically or sexually. TCCR has never run a telephone helpline and so was not in a position, as it was with the unemployment study, to bring its direct experience to the work; it was however, as with all its applied work, able to apply its understanding of the nature of the dynamic interactions within couples to the kinds of interactions that occurred between workers and clients (or indeed between agencies (see Woodhouse & Pengelly, 1991)). In this study, spanning two and a half years, a time-limited weekly workshop was set up so that telephone helpline workers at Parents Anonymous in London, concerned about the increasing complexity and difficulty of the calls they were receiving, could be better trained in how to deal with them. The subsequent monograph, *On Call* (Colman, 1989), explores the emotional experience of receiving calls from parents and from children as well as from hoaxers who were using the fact of a listener to engage in their own form of abuse: getting excited at provoking anxiety and distress in the workers (at length and apparently across agencies). The monograph explores the gradual semi-professionalisation of the agency, the use of boundaries and authority, as well as the development of listening skills that focus on the dynamic meaning of what is being presented. Like the *Work, Love and Marriage* text, this too goes beyond the immediate subject matter to explore emergent areas of interest; in this case, the ambivalent feelings that such helplines generate in society, and the fine line between professionalisation and volunteer skills.

The model of casework/clinical investigation combined with a joint training/reflection workshop has been a highly successful one for discovery and for the development of knowledge at TCCR. It has been used in areas as far apart as:

- Marriages between partners who both have learning difficulties (Mattinson, 1970)
- The parental relationship and its effects on illness in their children (Mainprice, 1974)
- The development of training programmes for probation and social work (Mattinson, 1975)
- Group work preparations for parenthood (Clulow, 1982)
- Prison social work (Vincent & Evans, 1983)
- The emotional dynamics of "struck" separations and divorces and their impact on legal professionals in the family justice system and on the children caught in the middle, and on clinicians trying to work with them (Clulow & Vincent, 1987, 2003; Shmueli, 2005; Vincent 1995, 1997, 2001)
- Inter-agency conflict and collaboration in difficult cases (Woodhouse & Pengelly, 1991)
- The impact of infertility (Cudmore, 1992, 1997; Pengelly, Inglis & Cudmore, 1995)
- The impact of the death of a child (Judd & Cudmore, 1997, 1999)
- The development of a model of effective staff supervision and its application in a social services department (Hughes & Pengelly, 1997; Olney, 2001; Olney & Wheeler, 1999) (see also Olney and Hughes's chapter in this volume for a fuller account).

Empirical study evidence

TCCR has also used the "between" clinical outcome methods of the psychologist to find ways of understanding and measuring couple dynamics in more "objective" ways than the "within" and "across" case studies allow. It has also used this approach to explore the effectiveness of its project-based clinical services. A repeating difficulty has been in finding couple measures that take a view of the couple *as a whole* rather than as two individuals—see table 1.

Table 1. Measures used at TCCR (past and present).

Name	Type
Adult attachment interview (George, Kaplan & Main, 1985)	Individual measure of attachment status
CORE (BPS CORE, 1997; Abidin & Konold, 1999)	Individual measure of mental health (work is going on to make a couple version for psychosexual therapy and for families)
Couple attachment joint interview (Fisher & Crandell, 2001)	Couple measure of shared attachment status
Personal relatedness profile (Hobson, Patrick & Valentine, 1998), as adapted for couples (Lanman, Grier & Evans, 2003)	Psychodynamic measure of state of mind in relation to another
Dyadic adjustment scale (Spanier, 1976)	Individual measure of adjustment to a couple relationship
Edinburgh Postnatal Depression Scale (Cox, Holden & Sagovasky, 1987)	Individual measure of depression
Golombok Rust Inventory of Marital Satisfaction (Rust, Bennun, Crowe & Golombok, 1986)	Individual measure of experience of the couple relationship
Locke-Wallace Marital Adjustment Scale (Freeston & Plechaty, 1997)	Individual measure of adjustment to a couple relationship
Malan Global Rating Scale (Malan, 1976)	Individual measure of mental health
Parenting alliance measure (Abidin & Konold, 1999)	Individual measure of capacities to share parenting
The relationship dynamics scale (Simons, Morison, Reynolds & Mannion, 2003; Stanley & Markman, 1997)	Individual measure of experience of the couple relationship
The relationship questionnaire (Bartholomew & Horowitz, 1991)	Individual measure of experience of relating to another

Early empirical studies included a review study of a year's intake to the clinical service where sexual problems were the presenting issue (Clulow, 1984). An examination of the cases showed a contrast between the views of the couples and of the therapists about the ways in which the problems were understood. Were they best seen as specific disorders needing treatment or were they ways in which the couple could manage closeness and distance—between themselves as well as between them and the therapist in the consulting room? Another review study looked at factors predicting engagement in couple therapy (Cohen, Fisher & Clulow, 1993)—couples seemed to engage better where there had been a delay in returning application forms; where couples had been married/ living together for a long time; where men described their emotional state as part of the application rather than argued a case; where couples engaged those reading their applications in a similar way; where the couple had an interactive view of the problem between them; and where space for reflection rather than problem solving or emotional crisis management was expected in terms of help.

Brief psychotherapy

In 1986, a pair of papers based around a case study of a six-session therapy with "Mr and Mrs Frazer" was published (Balfour, Clulow & Dearnley, 1986; Clulow, Dearnley & Balfour, 1986). The first paper was an account of the clinical work with the couple, outlining their difficulties, their individual and shared histories, and the nature of the very brief work that was done with them. The second paper was an account of an assessment review of the couple relationship eighteen months after the short-term intervention had ended. The assessment of the outcome of the work was based on Malan's work assessing individual patients with the Malan Global Rating Scale (1976) and used a modification of his procedure in that the treating therapists were involved in rating the improvement, and the different nature of couple dynamics had to be accommodated. The outcome assessment required the therapists, Clulow and Dearnley (joined by F. Balfour), to identify the main issues which the couple had been facing that had brought them to therapy. Once these were identified, a hypothesis was drawn up about the nature of their unconscious dynamic, based around their shared unconscious phantasy of their relationship—the deep, hidden conviction of what a relationship *is like* and *is for*; using this hypothesis, four criteria were drawn up that, taken together, would constitute the criteria by which change would be assessed.

The four criteria were:

a. Each has a conviction that what they have chosen to do is right, is accepted, and allows each to flourish.
b. They must feel themselves to be appropriately separate persons.
c. In their relationship with each other and/or others, they must show a capacity to be sensitive to the whole range of feelings which maintain healthy relationships without fear of breakdown or other catastrophe. Certainly there should be an absence of idealisation and denial in the maintenance of their relationships.
d. They should be free of all symptoms and disturbances. (Balfour, Clulow & Dearnley, 1986, p. 138)

The therapists were asked to score the achievement of these criteria on a range from "0—Completely unchanged" to "4—Complete psychodynamic and symptomatic change" in 0.5 increments. The scale, in other words, was a range of nine. After shared discussion, the therapists rated the couple as "1.5—Substantial symptomatic improvement", but with no psychodynamic change. Although the follow-up study is unique in TCCR's publications to date, there are methodological limitations with the approach because the definitions and ratings of outcome are made by the therapists who did the clinical work. Interestingly, the couple themselves appear to have done well, despite the raters' reluctance to grade their change highly. Although part of this reluctance is based on the way the couple put their problems "aside and then forgot about them" (Balfour, Clulow & Dearnley, 1986, p. 143), perhaps another part stems from the ambitious criteria for change used. Curiously, despite the suggestion that Malan's method could be used as a model for assessing outcome, it has not been taken up in this way at TCCR since this work ended.

In 2001, Lanman and Grier reported on the results of a study into the impact of a brief psychotherapy consisting of up to six sessions (Lanman & Grier, 2001). This report was a mix of literature review and account of the work in classic case study format. The work itself is thoughtfully described, particularly the ways in which the six-session frame was used by couples (some of whom had their six sessions over an extended period of time, thus making the therapy longer that might have been expected). In this particular write-up of the work, there is no systematic analysis of the types of couples or presenting problems, the conclusions of the assessment and its relationship to the course of the work, or the numbers of outcome questionnaires returned and their results. What there is instead is a conversation addressed to fellow clinicians about the experience of the work: the pull and push of the unconscious dynamics, and the pros and cons of psychoanalytic brief work; and the paper ends with an extended clinical description of the development of the therapy with "Catherine and Guy", and their struggles with dependency and development. The description allows the reader into the session and into the therapist's understanding of what was going on, in a classic "within" psychoanalytic case study.

In 2003 a key paper was published in the *British Journal of Psychiatry*, which continued the attempt to find a robust measure of the couple relationship that was also clinically meaningful to the psychoanalytically-oriented therapist (Lanman, Grier & Evans, 2003). The paper reported the development of an existing measure used to study individuals—the personal relatedness profile (PRP) (Hobson, Patrick & Valentine, 1998), which was being amended and applied to the couple as part of a three-year project to explore the efficacy of brief psychoanalytic therapy with couples (Lanman & Grier, 2003), a follow-up to the 2001 report. The couple version of the measure was used by a series of raters who examined different segments of video recordings of ongoing couple therapies. The raters were all trained couple psychoanalytic psychotherapists who were asked to use their clinical intuition to assess the degree to which the couple *as a couple* were displaying either paranoid-schizoid or depressive position phenomena (Klein, 1935, 1946). The paper showed that independent raters assessing couples in this way could agree significantly about what they saw; it showed, in a sense, the objectivity of these raters' apparently "subjective" judgements of the couples' psychodynamic functioning. In other words, when used with couples, as with individuals (Hobson, Patrick & Valentine, 1998), the measure showed excellent inter-rater reliability as well as evidence that the two states of mind being assessed, paranoid-schizoid and depressive, were inversely related, showing that the conceptualisation of the measure was sound. Furthermore, since they are conceptualised as alternative states of mind along a continuum, with the latter associated with greater psychological maturity and capacity to relate to oneself and to another, they could be used also as a measure of the effectiveness of psychoanalytic therapy that aims at increasing such capacities.

The measure was therefore used in a second study (see below) looking at the outcome of couple psychotherapy (Balfour & Lanman, 2011).

A limitation of the PRP is that it can only be used by highly trained psychotherapists as it attempts to discover something going on beneath the awareness of the couple themselves. It is not a measure that can be used in a cooperative way with the couple to assess the effectiveness of the therapy, though it could be used as an adjunct to a rich case study. The second study that it was used in at TCCR was a forty-session time limited couple psychotherapy (Balfour & Lanman, 2011).

This study took eighteen couples into weekly treatment, and looked at the outcome of the therapy as measured using the PRP (Hobson, Patrick & Valentine, 1998) adapted for couples (Lanman, Grier & Evans, 2003), alongside two individual self report measures. Although there was not a control group, these measures were also taken three weeks before the treatment commenced, as well as at the start, the mid-point, and the end of the therapy. This baseline period before treatment commenced indicated no significant change in couples' scores without the intervention, whereas from the mid-point in the therapy results showed statistically significant change in the couples' scores of individual psychological state (as shown by CORE), which continued to improve significantly at the end of therapy. At this point there were also statistically significant improvements in the psychological development of the couple, as determined in the observer rating of videotapes of the therapy sessions using the personal relatedness profile. On a standard measure of impact of therapy the "effect size" of the treatment was comparable or greater than that shown in other, non-psychodynamic studies (Christensen et al., 2004; Shadish et al., 1993). What was particularly interesting about this study was that the positive changes in the couples only became significant after twenty sessions on the CORE measure of psychological state and after forty sessions on the PRP observer-rated assessment of couple functioning, suggesting that time is an important factor in measuring outcome in psychodynamic work.

Attachment and the couple

In 2001 the organisation attempted to develop a rating system that captured the shared attachment relationship of the couple: their "complex attachment" (Fisher & Crandell, 2001). The hope was to move beyond the measures of individual attachment status that the adult attachment interview (George, Kaplan & Main, 1985) captured so as to get a snapshot of the complex world of the couple *as a couple* by developing a "couple attachment joint interview". The attempt drew also on the organisation's clinical understanding of the relationship that developed between two people in an intimate committed partnership and drew on post-Kleinian thinking about triangular space in the mind (Britton, 1989), pointing out that there is always a third element at play in a relationship: the ways that each partner keeps the relationship in mind as well as the other partner. The work was able to reach the conceptual stage but it proved too complex to manualise in a way that could make it into a reliable instrument and work on it has currently ceased.

As late as 2002, however, despite all the research activity itemised above, the organisation was still debating the role that "empirical" research could have in a psychoanalytic setting as it continued to systematically investigate adult attachment in couple relationships and, at this point, the links with tactics used to manage conflict between the couple (Clulow, Evans, Shmueli & Vincent, 2002). This paper asked the question, "Is empirical research a toxic introject, an idealized object and/or a real cultural, developmental experience for a clinical service?" It noted that the development away from case study based clinical research to more quantitative research required action to effect a shift in culture through convergence of clinical and research interests; that this involved both leadership and trust; and could only really be done in a supportive environment that could allow the development without being overly threatened and so defensive. It is clear that the organisation was in a process of change in relation to empirical research, more open to its methods and approaches. This shift of culture, towards encouraging quantitative empirical research alongside TCCR's traditional focus on qualitative and case study methods, is exemplified in the outcome research conducted over the past few years and referred to above (Balfour & Lanman, 2011), and in the fact that a RCT of the work of the Parenting Together Service at TCCR commenced in 2011.

Postnatal depression

After all these attempts at developing its own measures, latterly and pragmatically TCCR has moved to more off-the-shelf tools. A recent example is in a project run in the London Borough of Greenwich that compared three different interventions providing support for parents: postnatal support groups; parenting workshops; and relationship counselling (Clulow & Donaghy, 2010). The project was set-up as a workforce development programme for Greenwich MIND and its aims were to develop a couple focus in its work with parents. The premise was a well-founded one that better relationships between parents as a couple directly influence better outcomes for children (Cowan & Cowan, 2000, 2009; Cox, Paley & Harter, 2001; Davies, Cummings & Winter, 2004; Emery, 1999; Harold, Aitken & Shelton, 2007; Schultz, Cowan & Cowan, 2006; Walker, 2008). The project used standard before and after tests of postnatal depression (Edinburgh Postnatal Depression Scale (Cox, Holden & Sagovasky, 1987)), relationship satisfaction (Relationship Dynamics Scale (Simons, Morison, Reynolds & Mannion, 2003; Stanley & Markman, 1997)) and attachment (relatedness questionnaire (Bartholomew & Horowitz, 1991)), as well as project-specific satisfaction questionnaires that allowed for a mix of quantitative and qualitative data. It found that all three interventions improved the levels of depression in the women using the services, but that only the relationship counselling also improved relationship satisfaction; attachment status, unsurprisingly, was unchanged. All participants in the project (parents and workers) rated the experience highly.

The relationship counselling was the only intervention that consistently reached the male partners/fathers of the children (very few attended the parenting workshops, for example), suggesting that it is a useful tool in the attempts to improve outcomes for children through accessing *both* parents rather than just the mother as most parenting services do. The project demonstrated that there is a demand for accessible relationship counselling that focuses on postnatal depression and can be delivered from locally accessible centres that cover generic adult mental health difficulties, as well as from centres that attempt to engage parents per se. In addition, in line with the Tavistock ethos of cascading applied knowledge and skills, the programme of workforce development was aimed at developing skills and confidence in addressing relationship and attachment issues across the range of services that workers might find themselves engaged in. It followed a mixed model of full and half-day seminars and ongoing consultancy to practice delivery (Clulow, 2008), and enabled changes in individual practice as well as agency development.

One of the particularly important things about this project is that subsequent funding and changes in MIND in Greenwich's circumstances have allowed the work to be repeated, allowing for a test of the robustness of the original project. The full results are expected in 2011–12.

In conclusion

Research at TCCR is still continuing and finding new areas of interest: a project has recently begun to develop and test a couple-based intervention for Alzheimer's disease; the randomised controlled trial of its "Parenting Together" services to separated parents in conflict over contact with their children (Hertzmann & Abse, 2010) is due to report in 2014–15; and TCCR is part of a comparative evaluation of couple counselling commissioned by the Department for Education, reporting in 2013.

One of the things that is very clear from this survey of the different approaches to researching the evidence is that the Tavistock Centre for Couple Relationships has been consistent in its interest in the unconscious, dynamic relationship between people, especially those in an intimate adult relationship, and has sought different ways of making sense of what it has found there. To its existing strengths in the "within" of the psychoanalyst and the "across" of the social scientist, it has added the interest in the "between" of the psychologist, and has gradually focused its attention on practice-based research in its clinical services. It is also clear that in doing so it has had a number of false starts, exploring the evidence using complex, idiosyncratic measures that were not able to be developed further, or in ways that lacked sufficient evidential rigour to be convincing to anyone outside the field. This has been the inevitable result of attempting to explore something that cannot be captured consciously and is not the property of either partner: the relationship between them. Nonetheless, the commitment to discovering and explicating "what is there" has led to a very rich, emotionally engaging, and convincing picture of the ways in which we all receive and simultaneously create our relational world, at times for ill and at times for good. For TCCR to build on its growing strengths, it needs to look not to the past or the present, but to the future. The following *Manifesto for the Future* is an aid to this vision.

A Manifesto for the Future

- TCCR will become more robust in its understanding and use of routine clinical outcome measures, taking part in the ongoing and developing debates about the nature of therapeutic change and the role of theory, model, therapist, and couple/client within it. It will need to attend more to ways that the couple/client can be given a lead in this (Duncan, Miller & Sparks, 2004). There may be an opportunity in the development of Couple Therapy for Depression (CTD) for involvement in outcome and effectiveness research of this specific short-term clinical treatment across England and Wales.

- TCCR will continue to write and publish case study oriented research, paying attention to the need to be part of a psychoanalytic debate about concept-building and testing (Dreher, 2000; Leuzinger-Bohleber, Dreher & Canestri, 2003; Tuckett et al., 2008), as well as addressing the increasingly sophisticated demands of qualitative research and writing (Mays & Pope, 1995; Pistrang & Barker, 2010). (As indicated, above, in a way this will be a return to a pre-existing strength.)

- TCCR will publish quantitative research in ways that meet the standards increasingly expected within the field—for example the Consolidated Standards of Reporting Trials (CONSORT) for RCTs, and the Transparent Reporting of Evaluations with Nonexperimental Designs (TREND) standard outlined by the American Psychological Association (APA Publications and Communications Board Working Group on Journal Article Reporting Standards, 2008). TCCR will always seek to include sufficient qualitative material to give something of the lived experience of the participants in the research, without which the meaning of the research is diminished.

- TCCR will continue to use the practice/workshop model to explore key issues in the lives of couples, parents, and the people who work with them in a variety of settings.

- TCCR will continue to keep research awareness as a core part of its clinical trainings and academic programmes, and will continue research training to national standards in its doctoral programme in couple psychotherapy.

References

Abidin, R. R. & Konold, T. R. (1999). *Parenting Alliance Measure*. Odessa, FL: Psychological Assessment Resources.

APA Publications and Communications Board Working Group on Journal Article Reporting Standards (2008). Reporting standards for research in psychology. Why do we need them? What might they be? *American Psychologist, 63*(9): 839–851.

Balfour, A. & Lanman, M. (2011). An evaluation of time-limited psychodynamic psychotherapy for couples: A pilot study. *Psychology and Psychotherapy: Theory, Research and Practice.* doi: 10.1111/j.2044–8341.2011.02030.x

Balfour, F., Clulow, C. & Dearnley, B. (1986). The outcome of maritally focused psychotherapy offered as a possible model for marital psychotherapy outcome studies. *British Journal of Psychotherapy*, 3(2): 133–143.

Bannister, K., Lyons, A., Pincus, L., Robb, J., Shooter, A. & Stephens, J. (1955). *Social Casework in Marital Problems*. London: Tavistock.

Barkham, M., Hardy, G. E. & Mellor-Clark, J. (Eds.) (2010). *Developing and Delivering Practice-Based Evidence. A Guide for the Psychological Therapies*. Chichester, UK: Wiley-Blackwell.

Barkham, M., Stiles, W. B., Lambert, M. J. & Mellor-Clark, J. (2010). Building a rigorous and relevant knowledge base for the psychological therapies. In: M. Barkham, G. E. Hardy & J. Mellor-Clark (Eds.), *Developing and Delivering Practice-Based Evidence. A Guide for the Psychological Therapies* (pp. 21–61). Chichester, UK: Wiley-Blackwell.

Bartholomew, K. & Horowitz, L. (1991). Attachment styles among Young adults. A test of a four category model. *Journal of Personality and Social Psychology*, 61: 226–244.

BPS CORE (1997). *Development of a Clinical Guideline for the Psychological Therapies*. London: BPS Centre for Clinical Outcomes Research and Effectiveness.

Britton, R. (1989). The missing link: parental sexuality in the Oedipus Complex. In: J. Steiner (Ed.), *The Oedipus Complex Today: Clinical Implications* (pp. 83–101). London: Karnac.

Brown, G. W., Bhrolchain, M. N. & Harris, T. (1975). Social class and psychiatric disturbance among women in an urban population. *Sociology*, 9: 225–254.

Christensen, A., Atkins, D. C., Berns, S., Wheeler, J., Baucom, D. H. & Simpson, J. (2004). Traditional versus integrative behavioral couple therapy for significantly and chronically depressed couples. *Journal of Consulting and Clinical Psychology*, 72(2): 176–191.

Clulow, C. (1982). *To Have and to Hold: the First Baby and Preparing Couples for Parenthood*. London: Aberdeen University Press.

Clulow, C. (1984). Sexual dysfunction and interpersonal stress: the significance of the presenting complaint in seeking and engaging help. *British Journal of Medical Psychology*, 57: 371–380.

Clulow, C. (2008). *Couples and Parents. Working with Attachment in Family Relationships*. (Unpublished training programme.) London: Tavistock Centre for Couple Relationships.

Clulow, C. (2010). *The Competencies required to deliver effective couple therapy for partners with depression. Background document for clinicians and commissioners*. London: TCCR & DoH. http://www.ucl.ac.uk/clinical-psychology/CORE/couples_therapy_competences/Couple%20Therapy%20clinician%20guide.pdf

Clulow, C., Dearnley, B. & Balfour, F. (1986). Shared phantasy and therapeutic structure in a brief marital psychotherapy. *British Journal of Psychotherapy, 3*(2): 124–132.

Clulow, C. & Donaghy, M. (2010). Developing the couple perspective in parenting support: evaluation of a service initiative for vulnerable families. *Journal of Family Therapy, 32*: 142–168.

Clulow, C. & Vincent, C. (1987). *In the Child's Best Interests? Divorce Court Welfare and the Search for a Settlement.* London: Tavistock/Sweet and Maxwell.

Clulow, C. & Vincent, C. (2003). Working with divorcing partners. In: M. Bell & K. Wilson (Eds.), *The Practitioner's Guide to Working with Families.* Basingstoke, UK: Palgrave Macmillan.

Clulow, C., Evans, C., Shmueli, A. & Vincent, C. (2002). Is empirical research compatible with clinical practice? *British Journal of Psychotherapy, 19*(1): 33–44.

Cohen, N., Fisher, J. & Clulow, C. (1993). Predicting engagement with psychoanalytical couple psychotherapy. *Sexual and Marital Therapy, 8*(3): 217–230.

Colman, W. (1989). *On Call: the Work of a Telephone Helpline for Child Abusers.* Aberdeen, UK: Aberdeen University Press.

Cowan, C. P. & Cowan, P. A. (2000). *When Partners Become Parents: the Big Life Change for Couples.* Mahwah, NJ: Lawrence Erlbaum.

Cowan, C. P. & Cowan, P. A. (2009). Couple relationships: a missing link between adult attachment and children's outcomes. *Attachment and Human Development, 11.*

Cox, J., Holden, J. & Sagovasky, R. (1987). Detection of postnatal depression. Development of the 10-item Edinburgh Depression Scale. *British Journal of Psychiatry, 150*: 782–786.

Cox, M. J., Paley, B. & Harter, K. (2001). Interparental conflict and parent-child relationships. In: J. H. Grych & F. D. Fincham (Eds.), *Interparental Conflict and Child Development: Theory, Research, and Applications* (pp. 249–272). New York: Cambridge University Press.

Cudmore, L. (1992). The impact of infertility on the couple relationship. In: D. Reich & A. Burnell (Eds.), *Infertility and Adoption.* London: Post-Adoption Centre.

Cudmore, L. (1997). The loss of the fantasy baby. *Journal of Fertility Counselling, 4*(3): 16–18.

Davies, P. T., Cummings, E. M. & Winter, M. (2004). Pathways between profiles of family functioning, child security in the interparental subsystem, and child psychological problems. *Development and Psychopathology, 16*: 525–550.

Department of Health (2007). *Commissioning a Brighter Future: Improving Access to Psychological Therapies.*London: Department of Health.

Dicks, H. V. (1970). *Fifty Years of the Tavistock Clinic*. London: Routledge & Kegan Paul.

Dreher, A. U. (2000). *Foundations for Conceptual Research in Psychoanalysis*. Madison, CT: International Universities Press.

Duncan, B., Miller, S. & Sparks, J. (2004). *The Heroic Client: A Revolutionary Way to Improve Effectiveness Through Client-Directed, Client-Informed Therapy*. New York: Jossey-Bass.

Emery, R. E. (1999). *Marriage, Divorce, and Children"s Adjustment*. Thousand Oaks, CA: Sage.

Fisher, J. & Crandell, L. (2001). Patterns of relating in the couple. In: C. Clulow (Ed.), *Adult Attachment and Couple Psychotherapy. The "Secure Base" in Practice and Research* (pp. 15–27). London: Brunner Routledge.

Freeston, M. H. & Plechaty, M. (1997). Reconsideration of the Locke-Wallace Marital Adjustment Test: is it still relevant for the 1990s? *Psychological Reports, 81*: 419–434.

Freud, S. (1926e). The question of lay analysis. In: *S. E., 20* (pp. 179–258). London: Hogarth.

George, C., Kaplan, N. & Main, M. (1985). *The Adult Attachment Interview*. (Unpublished manuscript.) Berkeley, CA: University of California.

Haldane, D. (1991). Holding hope in trust: a review of the publications of the Tavistock Institute of Marital Studies, 1955–1991. *Journal of Social Work Practice, 5*: 199–204.

Harold, G. T., Aitken, J. J. & Shelton, K. H. (2007). Inter-parental conflict and children's academic attainment: a longitudinal analysis. *Journal of Child Psychology and Psychiatry, 48*(12): 1223–1232.

Hertzmann, L. & Abse, S. (2010). Parenting together—from conflict to collaboration. *The Review, Resolution Journal, 144*, January/February: 48–49.

Hewison, D. (2007). The power of our attraction to theory—or Oedipus meets Ganesh. In: M. Ludlam & V. Nyberg (Eds.), *Couple Attachments. Theoretical and Clinical Perspectives* (pp. 171–188). London: Karnac.

Hewison, D. (2011). A brief guide to couple therapy for depression. *Healthcare Counselling and Psychotherapy Journal*, April: 32–33.

Hobson, P., Patrick, M. & Valentine, J. (1998). Objectivity in psychoanalytic judgements. *British Journal of Psychiatry, 173*: 172–177.

Hughes, L. & Pengelly, P. (1997). *Staff Supervision in a Turbulent Environment. Managing Process and Task in Front-line Services*. London: Jessica Kingsley.

Joyce, A. S., Wolfaardt, U., Sribney, C. & Aylwin, A. S. (2006). Psychotherapy research at the start of the 21st century: The persistence of the art versus science controversy. *Canadian Journal of Psychiatry, 51*(13): 797–809.

Judd, D. & Cudmore, L. (1997). The impact of a child's death on the parent's relationship. *A Portrait of Family Grief: Babies, Children,*

Trauma, Grief and Crisis. Conference proceedings. London: Child Bereavement Trust.

Judd, D. & Cudmore, L. (1999). Thoughts about the couple relationship following the death of a child. In: F. Grier (Ed.), *Brief Encounters with Couples: Some Analytic Perspectives* (pp. 33–53). London: Karnac.

Klein, M. (1935). A contribution to the psychogenesis of manic-depressive states. *International Journal of Psychoanalysis, 16*: 145–174.

Klein, M. (1946). Notes on some schizoid mechanisms. In: *Love, Guilt and Reparation* (pp. 1–24). London: Hogarth.

Lanman, M. & Grier, F. (2001). A psychoanalytic approach to brief marital psychotherapy. In: F. Grier (Ed.), *Brief Encounters with Couples: Some Analytic Perspectives* (pp. 113–133). London: Karnac.

Lanman, M. & Grier, F. (2003). Evaluating change in couple functioning: a psychoanalytic perspective. *Sexual and Relationship Therapy, 18*(1): 13–24.

Lanman, M., Grier, F. & Evans, C. (2003). Objectivity in psychoanalytic assessment of couple relationships. *British Journal of Psychiatry, 182*, March: 255–260.

Leuzinger-Bohleber, M., Dreher, A. U. & Canestri, J. (Eds.) (2003). *Pluralism and Unity? Methods of Research in Psychoanalysis*. London: International Psychoanalytic Association.

Mainprice, J. (1974). *Marital Interaction and Some Illnesses in Children*. London: Institute of Marital Studies.

Malan, D. (1976). *The Frontier of Brief Psychotherapy: an Example of the Convergence of Research and Clinical Practice*. London: Plenum.

Mattinson, J. (1970). *Marriage and Mental Handicap*. London: Duckworth.

Mattinson, J. (1975). *The Reflection Process in Casework Supervision*. London: Institute of Marital Studies.

Mattinson, J. (1988). *Work, Love and Marriage. The Impact of Unemployment*. London: Duckworth.

Mattinson, J. & Sinclair, I. (1979). *Mate and Stalemate. Working with Marital Problems in a Social Services Department*. Oxford: Blackwell.

Mays, N. & Pope, C. (1995). Rigour and qualitative research. *British Medical Journal, 311*: 109–112.

Menzies, I. (1949). Factors affecting family breakdown in urban communities. *Human Relations, 11*(4): 363–374.

NICE (2009). *Depression in Adults (update). Depression: the Treatment and Management of Depression in Adults*. National Clinical Practice Guideline 90. http://guidance.nice.org.uk/CG90/guidance/pdf/(English).

Olney, F. (2001). Management, supervision and practice. *Professional Social Work*: 10–11.

Olney, F. & Wheeler, J. (1999). Supervision within a creative partnership. *Professional Social Work*: 10–11.

Parloff, M. B. (1982). Psychotherapy research evidence and reimbursement decisions: Bambi meets Godzilla. *American Journal of Psychiatry, 13*: 718–727.

Pengelly, P., Inglis, M. & Cudmore, L. (1995). Infertility: couples' experience and the use of counselling in treatment centres. *Psychodynamic Counselling, 1*(4): 507–524.

Pistrang, N. & Barker, C. (2010). Scientific, practical, and personal decisions in selecting qualitiative methods. In: M. Barkham, G. E. Hardy & J. Mellor-Clark (Eds.), *Developing and Delivering Practice-Based Evidence. A Guide for the Psychological Therapies* (pp. 65–89). Chichester, UK: Wiley-Blackwell.

Rawlins, M. D. (2008). *De Testimonio*: On the evidence for decisions about the use of therapeutic interventions. Reprinted in *The Lancet, 372*: 2152–2161.

Roth, A. D. & Fonagy, P. (2004). *What Works for Whom? A Critical Review of Psychotherapy Research*. London: Guilford.

Rust, J., Bennun, I., Crowe, M. & Golombok, S. (1986). The Golombok Rust Inventory of Marital State (GRIMS). *Sexual & Relationship Therapy, 1*(1): 55–60.

Schulz, M. S., Cowan, C. P. & Cowan, P. A. (2006). Promoting healthy beginnings: a randomized controlled trial of a preventative intervention to preserve marital quality during the transition to parenthood. *Journal of Consulting & Clinical Psychology, 74*: 20–31.

Shadish, W. R., Montgomery, L. M., Wilson, P., Wilson, M. R., Bright, I. & Okwumabua, T. (1993). Effects of family and marital psychotherapies: A meta-analysis. *Journal of Consulting and Clinical Psychology, 61*: 992–1002.

Shmueli, A. (2005). On thinking of parents as adults in divorce and separation. *Sexual and Relationship Therapy, 20*(3): 349–357.

Simons, J., Morison, L., Reynolds, J. & Mannion, J. (2003). How the health visitor can help with postnatal stress. *Journal of Advanced Nursing, 44*(4): 400–411.

Smith, G. C. S. & Pell, J. P. (2003). Parachute use to prevent death and major trauma related to gravitational challenge: systematic review of randomised controlled trials. *British Medical Journal, 327*: 1459–1461.

Spanier, G. B. (1976). Measuring dyadic adjustment: New scales for assessing the quality of marriage and similar dyads. *Journal of Marriage and the Family, 38*: 15–28.

Stanley, S. & Markman, H. (1997). *Marriage in the 1990s: A Nationwide Random Phone Survey*. Denver, CO: PREP.

Thompson, K. & Buss Twachtmann, C. (2009). *The Impact of Unemployment on The Couple and The Family: Training Workbook*. London: Tavistock Centre for Couple Relationships.

Trist, E. & Murray, H. (Eds.) (1990). *The Social Engagement of Social Science. Volume 1: The Social-Psychological Perspective*. London: Free Association.

Tuckett, D., Basile, R., Birkstead-Breen, D., Böhm, T., Denis, P., Ferro, A., Hinz, H., Jenstedt, A., Mariotti, P. & Schubert, J. (Eds.) (2008). *Psychoanalysis Comparable & Incomparable. The Evolution of a Method to Describe and Compare Psychoanalytic Approaches*. London: Routledge.

Vincent, C. (1995). Consulting to divorcing couples. *Family Law, 25*: 678–681.

Vincent, C. (1997). The impact of the client's emotional state. *Newsletter of the National Council for Family Proceedings, 11*: 11–14.

Vincent, C. (2001). Giving advice during consultations: unconscious enactment or thoughtful containment? In: F. Grier (Ed.), *Brief Encounters with Couples: Some Analytical Perspectives* (pp. 85–97). London: Karnac.

Vincent, C. & Evans, G. (1983). Chains, drains and welfare—where next for prison social work? *Probation Journal, 30*(1): 22–28.

Wald, N. J. & Morris, J. K. (2003). Teleoanalysis: combining data from different types of study. *British Medical Journal, 327*: 616–618.

Walker, J. (2008). Partnership and parenting. In: M. Davies (Ed.), *The Blackwell Companion to Social Work*. Oxford: Blackwell.

Wilson, A. T. M. (1947a). The development of a scientific basis in family casework. *Social Work, 4*: 62–69.

Wilson, A. T. M. (1947b). Some implications of medical practice and social casework for action research. *Journal of Social Issues, 3*: 11–28.

Wilson, A. T. M. (1949). Some reflections and suggestions on the prevention and treatment of marital problems. *Human Relations, 2*: 233–251.

Wilson, A. T. M., Menzies, I. & Eichholtz, E. (1949). Report of the marriage welfare sub-committee of the Family Welfare Association. *Social Work, 6*: 258–262.

Woodhouse, D. (1990). Non-medical marital therapy. The growth of the Institute of Marital Studies. In: E. Trist & H. Murray (Eds.), *The Social Engagement of Social Science. Volume 1: The Socio-Psychological Perspective* (pp. 299–322). London: Free Association.

Woodhouse, D. & Pengelly, P. (1991). *Anxiety and the Dynamics of Collaboration*. Aberdeen: Aberdeen University Press.

COMMENTARY ON CHAPTER SEVEN

Michael Rustin

Whit counts as "research" in the field of couple relationships, and what is at stake in whether (clinical) work is accorded the status of research or not? This is a framing issue for David Hewison's chapter, which begins by indicating the contemporary pressures upon couple therapy, and indeed all psychoanalytic therapy, to meet the need to demonstrate a scientific "evidence base" for its practices. The author refers to the established hierarchy of reputable research methods, with the randomised controlled trial at its apex, and goes on to explore the difficulties for couple therapy of conforming to these norms. Methodological standards which may be fully appropriate to the controlled trials of medical interventions do not seem readily applicable to the "talking therapies". Hewison's chapter seeks to find a way of negotiating these issues, which can both respond to the demand for outcome measures, yet also sustain the essential qualities of psycho-analytic couple therapy.

He provides a useful overview of research undertaken by members of TCCR during its history, and the wider influence which this has had. He distinguishes between three different genres of research. The first of these is psychoanalytic, based primarily on clinical case studies. The second he calls "psychological", mainly concerned with therapeutic outcomes. And the third is "social scientific" work which brings together interest in the internal dynamics of couple relationships with their wider social contexts. Some earlier TCCR research—for example, on couple relationships in troubled families, and on the impact of unemployment—comes into this category, as does current work on the impact of dementia on couple relationships. Although Hewison acknowledges that clinical case-based research has been the primary location of discovery in psychoanalysis, and perhaps in the psychoanalytic study of couple relationships too, the main emphasis of his chapter is on these two other genres.

Although one can certainly see the institutional logic of the research strategy which this chapter puts forward, and which is summarised in its concluding Manifesto, I think there are some risks in this approach. The principal limitation is the degree to which its agenda seems to be driven by "external" considerations, rather than by research purposes internal to the field of psychoanalytic couple therapy itself. Can or should one distinguish between the research topics and issues which couple therapists believe it would be intrinsically interesting and fruitful to investigate, and those which there are good *institutional* reasons to pursue? How would one characterise the essential "objects of study" within the field of the psychoanalytic study of couple relationships in the past? And what would one formulate as the research topics of most interest in the present?

Instead of seeking for a viable middle ground between the different methods of research which Hewison identifies, I want to set out a more "extreme" position. While in no way disputing the value of what Hewison calls the "psychological" and the "social scientific" modes of research (Rustin, 2010), I shall give most attention to the "psychoanalytic" genre of research, on the grounds that this has been foundational for the Tavistock approach. By a more extreme position, I mean one which faces up *both* to the inherent difficulties of research on couple relationships, and to the essential understandings which only a psychoanalytic perspective can give.

First, the difficulties. I identify three, in particular. The first arises from the frequent assumption that the main research that matters is research into the outcomes of treatment. The equation, which now pervades the psychoanalytical field, of research with the investigation of outcomes, has arisen for political reasons—the necessity to show that treatments "work" if anyone is to be persuaded to fund them, or indeed as some say if psychoanalysis is to survive. This approach detaches the understanding of "outcomes" from the psychological and relational processes which give rise to them. One can see how well such a separation might fit the testing of pharmaceutical compounds for their somatic effects—in that context, a full understanding of process might reasonably be left for later, until there is a "treatment effect" worth the trouble of explaining. But the separation of outcome from process does not work well for psychoanalysis, where the understanding of structure, process, and mechanism has always been the primary focus of investigation. Indeed, the link between process and outcome in this field is conceptually a deep one, since it is held that it is through patients' or clients' understanding of their own mental processes that personal change comes about.

There is a second more practical difficulty for couple therapy in a focus on treatment outcomes. This is the problem of scale. Quantitative measures of the outcomes of prescribed treatments require that treatments take place in sufficient numbers for comparisons and evaluations to be feasible. Only with difficulty is this requirement of scale now being met in individual psychotherapy with children and adults, for example in clinical trials on adolescent and adult depression in which the "other Tavistock"- the Tavistock and Portman NHS Trust—is now involved. The question is, can this requirement be met in the specialist field of couple relationships? It seems to me unlikely that it can be.

Where therapeutic work is taking place only on a small and intensive scale, it seems unavoidable that research findings will mainly belong in the "context of discovery"—the identification of new concepts, theories and techniques—rather than in the "context of verification", the formal testing of hypotheses with appropriate samples. It is in this "context of discovery" that most of the important findings of psychoanalysis have been obtained. A history of the elaboration of the conceptual field of the psychoanalytic study of the couple would surely also draw largely on clinical discoveries of this kind.

Hewison points out that the case load of TCCR has become enormously expanded through its merger with London Marriage Guidance in 2005. He refers to 10,000 clinical sessions being available for research. This increase of scale probably increases the external pressure to demonstrate effective outcomes, since larger resources are at stake. But whether it has become feasible now to design effective trials is a different question, since what may be offered at this larger scale of work may be at a lower level of clinical intensity than has been the clinical practice hitherto. This dilemma of how to balance quality and quantity has become a common one for mental health services at the present time (for example in the context of the Improved Access to Psychological Therapies initiative), where there is pressure to expand the availability of services, but also to provide them on a more generic and "manualised" basis.

A third problem for research in couple therapy lies in the conceptual difficulty in specifying desirable treatment outcomes. The question is, outcomes for whom? Couples consist of two persons, with very often children's well-being to be considered also. How does one assess overall benefit when some individuals may have been helped, or perceive that they have been helped, more than others, within a family relationship? These problems are noted in the research cited by Hewison, where "individual" rather than "couple" measures of outcome have more often been used. The "ideal outcome" in which an entire family are re-set on track for a happier life together can hardly be expected as a norm in this work. It seems that subtle balances of benefit and loss must have to be recognised in this form of therapy, defying straightforward comparison or summation. Indeed one can imagine that the form of evaluation which might be most appropriate, to therapists and clients alike, might be one which focuses on the quality of the interactive process itself, rather than on its outcome. The primary value of this kind of therapy might be in making it possible for couples to find new ways of working on their difficulties, rather than in achieving prescribed solutions to them.

Now to the positive side of the equation. I argue that psychoanalytic couple therapy, like psychoanalysis itself, has made its fundamental discoveries about the unconscious dimensions of relationships. Its primary form of "research" has been the achievement of new understandings of psychic structure and process. Its "research programme" over the whole history of psychoanalysis has been the development of this knowledge, primarily through the "empirical experience" of its clinical practice. Hewison acknowledges the historical importance of this area of study in the couple relationships field, while according it rather little emphasis in his outline of what is needed at the present time.

My view is that a central focus for research into couple relationships should remain the lexicon of fundamental concepts and theories which have been discovered by psychoanalytic couple therapists. It is a mistake to separate "research", in this or any other psychoanalytic field, from the structure of theories by which the discipline is constituted. Too great an emphasis on "treatment outcomes", or on research methodology, can be at the expense of attention to the core concepts and theories of the field itself. If one is not careful this can lead to a "year zero" approach to psychoanalytical knowledge, according to which any idea which has not been accredited by "empirical research" might as well not exist. In the guise of "saving" psychoanalysis, this approach threatens to undermine its foundations.

Rom Harré (2003) has argued that most major discoveries even in the natural sciences have depended on the use of "intensive" rather than "extensive" methods. That is, through the methods of the decisive laboratory experiment or observation, not through large-scale quantitative trials. Psychoanalysis has been an "intensive" method *par excellence*, in its focus on the consulting room and on giving theoretical meaning to the phenomena encountered there. The psychoanalytic study of couple relationships has been, at least in its "clinical" genre, of the same kind. This method is "intensive" in more than one sense of the term.

What have been the most fundamental and influential ideas of psychoanalytic couple therapy? For example, that partners are chosen for reasons of unconscious desire, and that relationships may be shaped by unconscious needs and phantasies which are unrecognised by the couple. That such unconscious predispositions are likely to have been shaped by adults' experiences in their infancy or childhood, and that there may therefore be "ghosts in the marital bed" as well as in Fraiberg's famous phrase, "in the nursery" (Fraiberg, Edelson & Shapiro, 1975). That unconscious anxieties about loss and separation may make change within a couple relationship unendurable, feared even as a threat of annihilation. That the Oedipus situation may be decisive in shaping couple relationships (Grier, 2005), for example in regard to the tolerance or intolerance of "threeness" (when infants appear), or of generational difference, as when parents are confronted with children's adolescence and the evidence of their own aging. Experienced couple therapists will have a rich lexicon of theories, concepts, and case examples to draw upon as they struggle to make sense of their work with a new couple in their consulting room. Thomas Kuhn (2000), in his later work, came to the view that the development of scientific ideas could be understood by the analogy of biological evolution, as a kind of "speciation". This may well be a useful metaphor by which to map the development of ideas concerning the psychodynamics of couple relationships. It is a surprising omission from Hewison's chapter that an outline of what specifically "clinical" research in this field has achieved is not provided.

The most important field of research in this and other psychoanalytic fields lies not in the study of "treatment outcomes", but rather in giving a more accountable and systematic basis to the fundamental understandings of psychic process. To do this the relatively informal procedures of clinical interpretation and inference which have supported psychoanalytic discovery hitherto need to be supplemented (as Hewison suggests) by more rigorous procedures of data gathering and data analysis, although still mainly located in the clinical setting. (The recent development of doctoral research programmes in various forms of psychotherapy, at the Tavistock Clinic and in TCCR, are making possible more research of this kind.) It should be possible, through obtaining more accurate records of clinical interactions (e.g., via audio or video recording), and through the use of systematic qualitative methods of analysis of clinical records (e.g., using an adapted version of the method of Grounded Theory), to make more transparent and public the grounds on which psychodynamic therapists assert the influence of unconscious mental processes on behaviours, and demonstrate how these can be changed through psychotherapeutic understanding (Anderson, 2006; Midgley, 2004, 2006; Rustin, 2001, 2007).

It seems to me that the more the concepts and theories which underpin couple therapy can be specified and made accountable through relevant clinical evidence, the more feasible it will then become to investigate both the outcomes of therapy, and the "couple relationship" dimension of other social phenomena. The clearer the understanding of a structure and process, the more possible it should be to explore interventions aimed to bring about changes to the states of mind and to the behaviours which are shaped by them.

It should be remembered that the primary "audiences" for research in psychotherapy are as much professional practitioners of various kinds as academics, policy makers, or managers. Psychoanalytic psychotherapy depends on what Clifford Geertz (1983) in an anthropological context has called "local knowledge", that is to say, understandings which are specific to their context of experience. In so far as one is able to set the understandings which underpin clinical practice onto a more transparent basis, clinicians should be able to do better work, whose strengths publics of various kinds will be more likely to recognise. Only if a field has intellectual confidence in itself is it likely to succeed in convincing those outside it of its value.

It seems to me that a research programme in the field of couple relationships and couple therapy needs not only the thorough attention to form, method, and context that it is given in David Hewison's chapter, but also a fuller specification of the substantive content of the research agenda.

References

Anderson, J. (2006). Well-suited partners: psychoanalytic research and grounded theory. *Journal of Child Psychotherapy, 32*(3): 329–348.

Fraiberg, S., Edelson, E. & Shapiro, V. (1975). Ghosts in the nursery: a psychoanalytic Approach to the problems of impaired infant-mother relationships. *Journal of the American Academy of Child Psychiatry, 14*: 387–421.

Geertz, C. (1983). From the native's point of view: on the nature of anthropological understanding. In: *Local Knowledge*. New York: Basic. Grier, F. (Ed.) (2005). *Oedipus and the Couple*. London: Karnac.

Harré, R. (1993). *Social Being* (2nd edn.). Oxford: Blackwell.

Kuhn, T. S. (2000). *The Road since Structure*. Chicago: Chicago University Press.

Midgley, N. (2004). Sailing between Scylla and Charybdis; incorporating qualitative approaches into child psychotherapy research. *Journal of Child Psychotherapy, 30*(1): 89–111.

Midgley, N. (2006). The inseparable bond between cure and research: clinical case study as a method of psychoanalytic inquiry. *Journal of Child Psychotherapy, 32*(2): 122–147.

Rustin, M. J. (2001). Give me a consulting room … the generation of knowledge in psychoanalysis. In: *Reason and Unreason*. London: Continuum.

Rustin, M. J. (2007). How do psychoanalysts know what they know? In: L. Braddock & M. Lacewing (Eds.), *The Academic Face of Psychoanalysis*. London: Routledge.

Rustin, M. J. (2010). Varieties of psychoanalytic research. *Psychoanalytic Psychotherapy, 24*(4) 380–397.

CHAPTER EIGHT

Couple therapy—social engineering or psychological treatment?

Andrew Balfour

Couple therapy is often seen as an outsider, without a natural place among the psychological therapies. It is not routinely offered in departments of psychological therapy, unlike other modalities such as individual, family, or group based interventions. In the UK, it has mostly developed outside the statutory services, chiefly in the voluntary sector. Although the situation is changing, historically, in the public domain, the debate around couple therapy has often been more political or moral than scientific, associated with negative connotations of social engineering.

Social engineering

Social engineering itself has tended to have a bad press, understandably perhaps, given that its most famous exponents have included Hitler, Stalin, and Pol Pot. But in a more ordinary way, social engineering refers to things like our laws, social mores, and even political lobbying—which aim to influence and change behaviour. One of the most important institutions responsible for developing couple psychotherapy in the UK since the Second World War, the Tavistock Centre for Couple Relationships, has the following strap line appearing on all its literature: "Supporting couples, strengthening families and safeguarding children". This reflects the values of the organisation, the sphere of social influence that it seeks to have, and so perhaps bears out the notion that there is a social engineering dimension in evidence. But there is a difference between the social mission, if you like, and how such institutions offering therapeutic help to couples work clinically. Yet there seems to be something about couple therapy that can lead to it being seen, not as a psychological therapy, but as linked to a socio-political agenda, of promoting marriage, or preventing divorce. There are historical reasons that may contribute to this. In the 1930s the Marriage Guidance Council was born from the British Social Hygiene Council (aimed at tackling venereal disease), and in earlier years couple therapy was more explicitly linked to social engineering than mental health. A Royal Commission on Marriage and Divorce in 1956 reported:

> It is our hope that a really marked extension in the work of … marriage guidance … would check the tendency … to resort too readily and lightly to divorce. Unless the tendency is checked there is a real danger that the conception of marriage as a life-long union of one man and one woman may be abandoned. This would be an irreparable loss to the community. (Wallace, 2000)

In more recent times, the family policy debates between politicians, as reported in the media, have often had a denuded quality with connotations of crude social engineering and moralising—phrases such as "family values" come to mind, begging the questions, which family, what kind of values?

What are we doing in couple therapy? Are we pushing family values, or indeed are we value free in our work? In the clinical setting, the focus is on the couple's relationship, creating a space to think about what emerges in the partners' internal worlds, trying to adopt a stance of openness—a therapeutic position that is not about manipulating a particular outcome, or "social engineering". We all bring our difficulties into our relationships and in that there may be the hope of development—that in rediscovering, or re-finding in the relationship, elements of earlier problems, there may now be a working-through, rather than simply a repetition of the difficulties. However, when things break down, what we often see is how, for each individual, the way in which they view their partner is so shaped by their own inner world, that there is a distortion, and imprisoning of both, in the fixed images of each other's perceptions. These can represent a kind of "bringing to life" of certain kinds of relationships with others which reverberate throughout the individuals' lives. The situation can be tragic: patients often describe marrying to escape a problem and then find it coming to life in a frustrating, maddening, or frightening contemporary version. What does this look like in the clinical situation?

Clinical material

I shall give an example from a two-session assessment, which made an impact on me at the time, which illustrates how anxieties, felt in the present between the couple and conveyed very powerfully in the therapeutic relationship, can be a contemporary manifestation of underlying patterns of experience that were coined in earlier times. These patterns one can see already being passed on as the psychological inheritance of the next generation.

> The husband came without his wife to the first session. Very quickly he presented me with a dilemma. Something very bad had happened, involving his wife and he felt she was ill and needed help. He couldn't tell me what had happened if there was a possibility that I might do something, "inform social services". His fear was that there might be a knock at the door, social services may come around, or some other uninvited intervention that his wife had not agreed to. That would be a disaster, catastrophic, and she would not recover from this. He went around this again and again, dropping hints that something was very wrong, and I became increasingly anxious, and full of fantasies about what it might be. Any minute, it seemed, he might walk out—and then what would I do? I thought he was bringing into the room, and giving me an experience of, his own internal situation, where I felt the anxiety of something alarming, which I was left with a burden of responsibility for, but felt impotent to do anything about, under pressure to do something, required to do nothing. I took this up with him, how he felt there was something very wrong, that he had come to me for help, but when he got here he felt that he had to be bound and gagged, that it was not safe to speak about it. He could only talk to me if I were similarly constrained. He seemed

to take something of this in. He spoke about the paranoia that his wife experienced. I pointed out that this was something he experienced in the room with me, that to talk was a betrayal; yet there was also a part of him that had come because he wanted help. Eventually, he made a decision to tell me what was in his mind. He told me about days and days of violent rows with his wife and conveyed how disturbing he found her irrational and depressed state of mind. It had become violent between them and it seemed that their young daughter was exposed to the parents' behaviour. On one occasion, he said, his wife had smashed things up in the flat in her rage and had destroyed a painting of his mother.

When describing how difficult he had found the experience, he mentioned that his wife had looked drunk, because of the sleeping tablets she had taken. I asked more about this, and then he said that his mother had been an alcoholic. He spoke of how as a child he had "been forced to watch his father beating up his mother". He had grown up in a large communal house with lots of artists. He said that he had always thought of his background as "cool" and colourful. I took up how, in fact, he was telling me about a disturbing situation that as a child he had not been protected from, which seemed to link to what was happening now, with his sense that there was something very disturbing happening which needed drastic intervention, but at the same time, he was terrified of this. He conveyed a very split world, with things feeling fine one minute and then very bad the next. I wondered if it became very hard for him to judge the situation, things seeming to be better and then very bad again, perhaps like the painting of his mother, which got destroyed and became, instead, a frightening picture, which I thought might have been his experience growing up; a picture which he had thought of as colourful, but which had at times been very disturbing.

This seemed to make some sense to him and he then told me the "sequel" to the episode of the previous week. A few days later, they had started to row again and she had called the police. This time, the potential for violence was more clearly seen as also being in him, and it was difficult for him to tell me about it—the knock on the door that had already happened so to speak, evidence too, I thought, of his wife this time being the one who showed concern for the impact on their child.

I arranged a second consultation and suggested that it would be helpful if his wife came too. Though he said that he did not think she would attend, in the event she did so. After the first consultation, I was left with a very disturbed picture of his wife. Couple therapists are used to this, waiting for the monster to appear who then turns out to be a more complex human being, a separate entity from the figure one has been positioned to expect and to imagine.

> When I saw them together, she looked very sad. She spoke of how cut off she could feel from him and from her daughter, in her depression, and how guilty this left her feeling. She described a strict upbringing, which she contrasted with his bohemian background. She had felt that she could not get through to her mother at all, and this was reminiscent of how she described her feeling of not being able to get through to her husband, and it was this feeling of being utterly cut off that she linked to her depression. She spoke of how she had thrown herself into his world for the first years of their marriage. She had found his bohemian way of life liberating and was pleased to be far away from the strict and confining relationships of her early years. As time went on, when she tried to reassert some of her different values, her own mind, she had felt stuck. This seemed to be expressed most of all in terms of her sense that he refused to take in her feelings, and her view of the difficulties, denying until recently his dependence on alcohol, refusing to recognise the difficulties in his own background and his contribution to the state of things. He found it very difficult to do this: and felt he was betraying his mother if he spoke about the problems in his earlier life, much as he had felt he was betraying his wife in the first meeting, and himself in a sense, if he allowed his own problems to be seen. Although I thought that he tried hard to be open in the session, there was a hint of his placating her, of having to be careful with her. I thought that he found himself looking after her in much the same way as he spoke of looking after his depressed mother. For her part, she felt she couldn't get through to him—and so I think experienced something much more familiar in terms of the difficulties with her own mother. The apparently open and libertarian lifestyle that initially attracted her to him, had nevertheless reproduced an experience of being confined and cut off, with no room for her own mind; an experience of not being able to get through to her

object and so she found herself back in the familiar psychic terrain that she thought she had escaped from.

For him, her depression and their disturbed rows, sometimes in front of their daughter, repeated his early experience of witnessing a violent and uncontained adult couple, bearing out the research evidence that shows that witnessing domestic violence as a child results in being more likely to engage in domestic violence as an adult (Whitfield, Anda, Dube & Felitti, 2003). In these different ways, they re-enacted disturbing experiences for each of them, and there was a tragedy for them that the difficulties were being enacted with their daughter now as the infantile witness to the disturbed adult coupling. Both of them could see this and found some common ground in their mutual wish not to pass on the damage intergenerationally any more. This vignette perhaps illustrates how useful it can be to see the couple. If I had only seen him, I would have been left with a very partial view of the situation, without the opportunity of trying to understand with them how they each replayed for the other frightening elements of their internal worlds. Although I have described how this dynamic could operate one way with them, emphasising how this re-capitulates something of their early experience, at other times these patterns could be reversed. When she withdrew into a very depressed state, unable to engage with herself as well as with him, she gave him the experience of being with a cut off and unavailable object. When working with couples we can see how there can be a repetitive replaying of relationships that can happen internally within either partner, and between the partners, and the direction can be reversed and switched around as different aspects of the self are projected.

We know from research about the ill effects of relationship problems, on adult partners, on families, on children, and we know too about the intergenerational transmission of mental health problems (See Chapters Two and Six, this volume, for further discussion of these issues). The research evidence for the intergenerational impact of difficulties in the parental couple relationship is reviewed by Harold and Leve in Chapter Two. What I am going to discuss now is not a comprehensive review of the research but the evidence of the importance of the couple relationship for child and adult mental health that is cited in one of the documents on family policy from the Cabinet Office, suggesting that this is the evidence that is being accepted by policy makers and informing their strategies. Or is it?

Relationships and mental health

The Cabinet Office document *Reaching Out: Think Family* (2007) cites the following evidence:

- The children of parents with mental ill health are twice as likely to experience a childhood psychiatric disorder. (Gopfert, Webster & Seeman, 2004)
- Around three million children have experienced the separation of their parents and at least one in three children will experience parental separation before the age of sixteen. (Rodgers & Pryor, 1998)
- Parental conflict and hostility both within and outside of marriage or a civil partnership can have significant social and psychological impacts on children, including risks of anxiety and depression. (Vandewater & Lansford, 1998)
- Children experiencing sustained family conflict also tend to have lower academic performance, independent of their socio-economic status. (Ellwood & Stolberg, 1993)
- However, a good relationship between both parents acts as a buffer from many of the negative impacts of parental separation and divorce. (McIntosh, 2003).

We also know of the value and importance of intervening clinically with couples in terms of the mental health of the adult partners. There are many relevant studies, but to pick out just a few—for example, as Leff, Asen, and Schwarzenbach describe in Chapter Six.

- The London Depression Intervention Trial (Leff et al., 2000) compared the effectiveness and cost of couple therapy with antidepressants for the treatment of people with depression. Couple therapy was found to be at least as effective and no more expensive overall.
- A recent outcome study of couple therapy at TCCR found highly significant improvements on self-reported psychological health, and observer ratings of couple functioning (Balfour & Lanman, 2011).
- Longitudinal research has demonstrated the powerful effect of couple intervention over the period of transition to parenthood, just before and after the birth of a baby, in reducing the

drop in marital satisfaction, preventing divorce, and improving parenting quality (Cowan & Cowan, 2000).

- A similar study compared an intervention focused on the couple relationship with one that focused on parenting and a control group, at the point that children were about to enter nursery school, and followed up the families for ten years. Results indicated that families receiving the couple relationship focused intervention demonstrated better parenting behaviour (as indicated by greater warmth, more direct engagement with the child, and more authoritative parenting behaviours), higher marital satisfaction, lower marital conflict, and improved child outcomes. Those who received the parenting focused intervention showed more effective parenting behaviour, but no improvements in the marital relationship (Cowan & Cowan, 2000, 2008).

This links to Harold and Leve's discussion (Chapter Two), and to the question of the effectiveness of interventions that target only parenting, rather than the relationship between the couple. They show that, while parenting itself is an important part of the pathway for the manner in which parental conflict affects the child, on its own, it is insufficient. By contrast, there is a direct impact on the child of, for example, witnessing parental conflict itself. One could say that the research cited by Harold and Leve is evidence for an internal impact of parental conflict upon the child—associated with anxiety, depression, aggression, and hostility, and also upon how the child perceives and experiences their relationships with others in their world. One could say that it is evidence of internalisation—that is, evidence of how the external atmosphere of the family, of the parents' relationship, becomes part of the inner lived world of the child, reproduced in their relationships with others.

We know that relationships can be protective against difficulty and we know that life events put relationships under pressure, for example, with the birth of a child, as the work of Cowan and Cowan (Chapter One) shows us. One in ten new mothers develops postnatal depression, and prolonged postnatal depression can have a negative effect on the child's cognitive development and ability to form social relationships (Social Exclusion Unit, 2004, Office of the Deputy Prime Minister). And from the other end of the lifespan, in older couples where one partner has dementia, researchers have found that poor quality of relating between the partners is predictive of hospitalisation and even mortality rates of the person with dementia, whereas closer couple relationships are associated with a slower rate of decline for the affected partner (Norton et al., 2009; Wright, 1991, 1994).

Given this evidence, why do we not make use of what we know?

At the Savoy Conference on psychological therapies in 2007, Lord Layard pointed out the misery caused by mental illness, singling out in particular the consequences of untreated depression and anxiety. He pointed out that 90% of people with physical ill health receive the appropriate treatment, but that this drops to 25% when it comes to mental illness—and that NICE guidelines for mental health problems, unlike those for physical ill health are often simply not implemented. This is true for couple therapy which, people may not realise, is actually featured in IAPT guidelines and yet is not consistently available as part of psychological therapy provision.

Couple therapy tends to fall between the two stools of adult and child mental health. A referral received from the courts of a separated couple describes this well. Initially, after leaving the family home, Mr Smith was having contact with his two sons. However, as the situation between the parents worsened, Mrs Smith reported to the courts that the children no longer wished to see their father, and were frightened of him; new allegations surfaced that had not been part of the picture before. But when attempting to intervene in the situation, and to make referrals for further investigation, there were difficulties for the courts. After some to-ing and fro-ing between different professionals, they tried a referral to a Child and Family Consultation Service, for family work, but the service only dealt with children and responded that they would not be dealing with adult issues. They suggested that a hospital based in a different town could deal with the adult issues. But when this service was contacted, they replied that they only dealt with adults suffering from mental illness, and generally wouldn't have anything to do with children. A third centre was then contacted, based in yet another city, that might be able to work with father and children on supervised contact. This was some distance away—and the hope was expressed that perhaps if this could get established, then it could be transferred to another centre, nearby. The solicitors' letter ends with the observation that there would need to be considerable co-ordination and liaison between the children's centre, adult services, and the centre supervising the contact: a comment reflecting the fragmentation of the services on the ground as they encountered them.

The policy context for this is reflected in the "Think Family" policy document from the Cabinet Office (2007) which conveys the broad thrust of strategic approaches in this field over the past years. The laudable government agenda has been to push for the integration of services around the family—so that, for example, adult and child services should be working closely together. This "... aims to show the dramatic impact that parent-based family circumstances have upon children—and it demands a more family-focused approach from agencies that work with adults and those that work with children, aiming to extend the Every Child Matters approach of joined up working around the child, to the whole family so that adults' and children's services work together" (Cabinet Office Social Exclusion Taskforce, 2007).

There is a powerful mix of forces that mitigate against the wishful injunction to "Think Family" in a way which includes thinking about the adult couple. Budgets are split—so that funding is attached to a child, or children—or to an adult patient. There is competition around funding between agencies and services, because, of course, there is a market place. It can be difficult for practitioners without specialist training to feel competent to intervene—not just because of a lack of technical skills. Anxieties about intervening with the adult couple often run very deep; it can be a daunting and difficult business to work with the couple in the room, facing the clinician with complex feelings, to do with our own experiences of couple relationships, and the internal legacy of negotiating the original parental relationship of our earliest years.

While successive governments emphasise the importance of supporting relationships, funding has tended to go to children's services and parenting support, and there has been too little recognition of the importance of therapeutic services for the adult couple. The work of researchers such as Cowan and Cowan (Chapter One) shows that the quality of the couple's relationship itself is an important indicator of how well they operate as parents—and parenting is improved by helping the couple with their relationship, not only by working on parenting issues. Often, at the TCCR, we get referrals from workers engaged in parenting work, who feel out of their depth if issues to do with the couple's relationship threaten to come into the therapy. This reluctance to attend to the couple relationship itself seems to be reflected at all levels: from the individual worker to the policy makers. This is important, because at the policy level, recognition of the importance of the parental couple relationship is easily lost. The literature in this area often begins with an outline of the profound impact of relationship conflict and breakdown and ends with a recommendation for "parenting support", not couple therapy (e.g., Hughes & Cooke, 2007). Yet in 2004, the Treasury estimated that relationship breakdown and its aftermath cost England and Wales £22 billion—and the budget given to organisations in the couple field, estimated at £7 million, is a tiny fraction of this. The Think Family document, despite the research evidence it cites that shows the ubiquity of these issues, targets "… the 2% of socially excluded families … who have not been lifted by the rising tide of living standards" (Cabinet Office, 2007). As the authors of this document themselves show, it is not only a question of socio-economic groupings but much wider than this, about emotional or psychological impoverishment, how we pass on intergenerationally our unhappiness and disturbance, and bring it to life in our intimate adult relationships. As the Think Family document says: parental and wider family problems, such as poverty and mental ill health "… can cast a shadow that spans whole lifetimes and indeed passes down the generations".

Couple therapy is the modality that historically has been vulnerable to being associated with promoting a particular socio-political agenda—"nuclear family values" one might say, but is often outside the mainstream, with no natural home in current service provision, most consistently found in the voluntary sector. The important message that our relationships are the crucible of our mental health—throughout life—and that interventions that help to address difficulties in the area are important, can be reduced to a political message, about the importance of "marriage", or "promoting relationships", to which banner some will nail their colours, and others oppose. As Hughes and Cooke (2007) put it: "… some on the right have suggested marriage matters for everything, with others on the left appearing to counter that it matters for nothing. This decades old dispute has invariably been more politically charged than child friendly." It seems to me that this reflects a struggle to maintain thinking in the domain as it is so close to home—we all have some kind of experience, which is central to who we are and how we think of ourselves, of couple and family relationships. The denuded debate, that we revisit in the media and in the political arena, of the importance of family values, which has hitherto gone alongside a neglect of real thinking about the importance of psychological work with couples, is testimony to how hard it is to maintain a creative, open state of mind—of enquiry—and the pull is instead into the social engineering argument—one that is traditionally associated with a polarisation between right and left. Perhaps it is a reflection at the political level of the kinds of conflicts and polarised, unthinking states of mind that couple therapists can be used to seeing in partners in couples, who may, outside the stress and difficulty of their relationship, be capable of considerable thoughtfulness.

Returning briefly to the couple I described earlier, towards the end of my meeting with them, he described how as a young child he had been left locked in a car while his mother and a friend went to the pub. He had been unwell, and a passer-by had noticed the state he was in, and intervened helpfully. For the couple, the paranoia and fear about revealing their situation that they had conveyed to me, enacted a neglect, like the two of them locked in the car, unwell and out of contact with any help. The image of the bystander who is able to take in the situation and respond, is perhaps a useful description of couple therapy—aimed at freeing couples from trapped and stuck states, through understanding, and helping them to face the reality of their inner situation. This is not through the wide-angle lens of the social engineer, focused on a social agenda, but a magnifying lens seeking to understand the unique situation of each couple. Now to widen the focus again—there is an opportunity, after more than sixty years of research and clinical practice at TCCR and other organisations like it, for an intergenerational transmission of what has been learnt, training for a new generation of couple therapists able to deliver services for couples right across the country, that are available locally, that people can access easily. It is time to acknowledge what we know, and to make use of what we know, in the service of psychological development, not social engineering.

References

Balfour, A. & Lanman, M. (2011). An evaluation of time-limited psychodynamic psychotherapy for couples: A pilot study. *Psychology and Psychotherapy: Theory, Research and Practice.* doi: 10.1111/j.2044-8341.2011.02030. xCabinet Office (2007). *Reaching Out: Think Family.* London: Cabinet Office Social Exclusion Taskforce.

Cowan, C. P. & Cowan, P. A. (2000). *When Partners Become Parents: The Big Life Change for Couples.* Mahwah, NJ.: Lawrence Erlbaum.

Cowan, P. A. & Cowan, C. P. (2008). Diverging family policies to promote children's well-being in the UK and US: Some data from family research and intervention studies. *Journal of Children's Services*, 3(4): 4–16.

Ellwood, M. & Stolberg, A. (1993). The effects of family composition, family health, parenting behaviour and environmental stress on children's divorce adjustment. *Journal of Family Studies, 9*(1): 63–80.

Gopfert, M., Webster, J. & Seeman, M. (2004). *Parental Psychiatric Disorder: Distressed Patents and Their Families.* Cambridge: Cambridge University Press.

Hughes, B. & Cooke, G. (2007). *Children, Parenting and Families: Renewing the Progressive Story (Politics for a New Generation).* London: The Institute for Public Policy Research.

Leff, J., Vearnals, S., Brewin, C. R., Wolff, G., Alexander, B., Asen, E., Dayson, D., Jones, E., Chisholm, D. & Everitt, B. (2000). The London Depression Intervention Trial: randomised controlled trial of antidepressants versus couple therapy in the treatment and maintenance of people with depression living with a partner: clinical outcome and costs. *British Journal of Psychiatry, 177*: 95–100.

McIntosh, J. (2003). Enduring conflict in parental separation: Pathways of impact on child development. *Journal of Family Studies, 9*(1): 63–80.

Norton, M. C., Piercy, K. W., Rabins, P. C., Green, R. C., Breitner, J. C. S., Ostbye, T., Corcoran, C., Welsh-Bohmer, K. M., Lykefsos, C. G. & Tschanz, J. T. (2009). Caregiver-recipient closeness and symptom progression in Alzheimer's disease. The Cache County Dementia.

O'Hara, M. W. & Swain, A. M. (1996). Rates and risks of postpartum depression: a meta-analysis. *International Review of Psychiatry, 8*: 37–54.

Progression Study. *Journal of Gerontology: Psychological Sciences, 64B*(5): 560–568.

Rodgers, B. & Pryor, J. (1998). *Divorce and Separation: the Outcomes for Children.* York, UK: Joseph Rowntree Foundation.

Social Exclusion Unit (2004). *Mental Health and Social Exclusion.* London: Office of the Deputy Prime Minister.

Vandewater, E. & Lansford, J. (1998). Influences of family structure and parental conflict on children's well-being. *Family Relations, 47*(4): 323–330.

Wallace, J. H. (2000). *Someone to Turn to: a Description of the Remedial Work of the National Marriage Guidance Council.* Chippenham, UK: Antony Rowe.

Whitfield, C., Anda, R., Dube, S. & Felitti, V. (2003). Violent childhood experiences and the risk of intimate partner violence as adults. *Journal of Interpersonal Violence, 18*(2): 166–185.

Wright, L. (1991). The impact of Alzheimer's disease on the marital relationship. *The Gerontologist, 31*: 224–326.

Wright, L. (1994). Alzheimer's isease afflicted spouses who remain at home: Can human dialectics explain the findings? *Social Sciences and Medicine, 3*(8): 1037–1046.

COMMENTARY ON CHAPTER EIGHT

Philip Stokoe

This is a very welcome paper in which Balfour points to both the vulnerability of families to political and social pressure and to the growing body of knowledge derived from psychotherapeutic work with couples that could prove powerful enough to have an impact on social policy in politics.

I would like to expand on three issues that arise from my reading of this chapter. First, the problem of perspective and being able to find a position that allows a clearer and deeper view. I shall link this to the problem of child protection. Second, the question of the task of the therapist, and I shall contrast the original IAPT (Improving Access to Psychological Therapies) method of choice, and CBT (cognitive behavioural therapy) with a psychoanalytic approach. Finally, I want to build on Balfour's descriptions of what affects the individuals in couples that arises in their separate pasts but gets played out in the couple relationship, and to consider Britton's concept of "unconscious beliefs" (1998), again in an attempt to link this to politics and social engineering.

In his clinical vignette, Andrew Balfour, amongst other things, demonstrates how easy it is to form a false view if one's perspective is limited; being able to meet both husband and wife enabled him to have a fuller picture of the true complexity of this relationship. I thought that, as well as providing a salutary warning about the dangers for a therapist in being led into a distorted view of a patient's external world, this worked as a symbol for how easy it is to apply a very limited perspective when considering social policy instead of being open to consider its full complexity. This is illustrated most vividly when Balfour refers to the area of parenting. In the specialist field of child protection there is something very depressing about the way responses to child fatalities unfold; each tragedy is followed by an inquiry, each inquiry draws the same conclusions that professionals have not communicated properly with one another, and each inquiry leads to the adoption of further structures designed to improve collaborative links. All that this does is to create more and more pressure on professionals to ensure that they have followed "procedure" properly. The "procedure" very quickly loses its meaning as social workers, police, paediatricians, health visitors, teachers, and other professionals make sure that they have informed everyone else about whatever intervention they have made in a particular family. The goal becomes one of "ticking a box" and, once again, no real communication takes place. Effective professional communication involves an exchange of thoughts, doubts, and suspicions based upon mutual interest and enquiry. It is only in the context of this sort of professional engagement that it is possible to identify a potential problem. For example, a bruise on a child noted by a social worker, but considered not sufficiently worrying to cause further investigation at the time, might be thought about more seriously when subsequent communication with the health visitor reveals that she had seen something very similar two weeks earlier. Two such bruises are more likely to initiate an investigation.

The political thinking and the "social engineering" resulting from these inquiries is extremely superficial. The assumption is often made that "communication" failed because a professional was incompetent. At its best there is sometimes a reference to the emotional and psychological pressure on (usually) a social worker, but the implication is that this failure would not have occurred had there been someone more experienced (meaning more competent) in role. A great deal of thinking goes into ensuring that this behaviour does not happen again but, without an understanding of the deeper factors that led to it happening in the first place, any strategy will be created from the *wrong perspective* and doomed to fail.

In the vignette we could all (including Balfour) have been forgiven for assuming that the wife was a very crazy woman, not really competent to take up an adult role as a partner or as a parent. Meeting her enabled us all to see something different: an adult woman potentially capable of being a good mother and partner but disabled by something outside her control that made her sad and depressed and left her cut off from her daughter, her husband, and her own "competent self". A similar phenomenon can occur in a professional context. It is my conviction, arising out of many years of consulting to teams of child care professionals, that where one member appears to be behaving "incompetently" or "unprofessionally" then something has happened during the work that has left him or her feeling emotionally "cut off" from their clients and which, in turn, has prevented them remaining in touch with their competent professional selves.

In his description of waiting for the appearance of the wife, Balfour says "… couple therapists are used to this, waiting for the monster to appear who then turns out to be a more complex human being …." It happens all the time. I would say that working in the most difficult areas of child protection has an impact on workers that cuts them off from their professional identity and makes them miss really important danger signs, and this "happens all the time". If, instead of condemning workers who get caught up in the unconscious dynamics of their clients (because that is what I am describing), we accepted that it is ubiquitous, we might take a different approach to the question of how to reduce the instances of severe and fatal child abuse. Instead of creating more rules for how professionals should behave, we might make mandatory a particular approach to supervision of individuals and teams: an approach designed to identify unconscious factors affecting the individuals and their teams. The task would be to identify these dynamics and to understand them as key information about the relevant case.

Balfour's reference to IAPT raises a question about the role of a therapist. The government focus on psychological therapies has been a very important development for mental health services because IAPT has created new money. This has happened because Lord Layard, who is an economist, was able to show that adult patients suffering from mild to moderate depression or anxiety cost the state an enormous amount of money in invalidity and other benefits; he showed that a comparatively small investment used to train people in CBT would get sufficient patients back to work, with the result that the reduction in demand for unemployment benefits would more than pay for the original investment. This was an argument that appealed to politicians for two reasons: the first was an argument presented purely in economic terms but the second was that its effectiveness could be demonstrated in less than four years; politicians tend only to think in four-year periods between elections.

I think that it is fair to say that CBT helps patients to take conscious control of their symptoms by helping them recognise false cognitions, or mistaken views that lead to feelings of anxiety or depression. It seems to me that a therapist working in this way stands in the place of a friend, challenging the patient's ideas about himself in a way that the patient can accept, so that he can take conscious control of his life. The best outcome measures for CBT with this population of patients indicate that it works in 50% of cases and this was the target that was set when IAPT was set up (National Institute for Health and Clinical Excellence, 2006; Layard, 2010). I would say that it works because the patients who can use it already have an idea of being able to accept this sort of help and have a belief that it is possible to be the authors of their own lives. The therapist engages the patient in a process of taking cognitive control over behaviour or beliefs that have caused suffering. It is a different process altogether when the therapist is engaging the patient in an investigation of a part of the mind that he does not have direct access to, the unconscious. In this approach, the main subject of the process is the relationship between the patient and the therapist. The therapist is trying to work out what sort of a person the patient believes he is relating to, in the belief that this will reveal ideas that the patient holds about the world and people in the world. If the therapist can pick this up in vivo, as it is experienced in the immediacy of the therapeutic relationship, then this offers the possibility of changing these core beliefs that are manifest in the individuals' relationships with others in their world. This is a very different approach from the invitation to set aside maladaptive cognitions that the CBT approach entails.

When Balfour refers to couple psychotherapy and particularly when he talks about the effectiveness of working with a couple for improving parenting and family health, I think that he is writing about a similar role for the therapist in that he is advocating an approach that recognises the impact of unconscious beliefs on couple and parenting practices. The psychoanalytic study of the mind has shown us that we are continually explaining to ourselves what is happening to us and these explanations appear to be represented in the deepest part of our minds in the form of pictures of ourselves in relationship to others. In healthy development these images change in the light of experience. However all of us will have some images that have not changed in spite of experience. Britton (1998) calls these "unconscious beliefs" and they have a tendency to superimpose themselves on top of whatever is going on in the external world at the moment. Thus the child who has grown up with a violent father may develop an unconscious belief that men are dangerous; this belief will colour that person's image of any men who come into his life. In this way unconscious beliefs become self-fulfilling. Patients whose unconscious beliefs lead them to feel anxious or depressed will not be able to alter their emotional state simply because a friendly professional points out that the thought patterns that maintain these emotional states are mistaken. The only thing that will help them to change will be the discovery that something which they have taken to be a fact of life is only a belief that can be questioned and given up. You do not help somebody to become aware of their own unconscious beliefs by taking up the role that is equivalent to being a friend. You do this by modelling a capacity which, at least in this area of their functioning, has been temporarily lost. This capacity can be described as curiosity and interest; it is often referred to as the third position, the meta-position, a place from which one can take a more dispassionate view of oneself and one's actions. It is this capacity that enables us to learn from experience.

Balfour has referred to the research of the Cowans showing how important work with the couple is for better parenting. In my view a healthy couple relationship depends upon each of the two partners being able to think and feel themselves to be part of a couple, and this image of themselves as a couple can become the third position from which each can find a vantage point to think self-reflectively about their relationship; to both be in it and involved, but also able to move to a position that allows them to look at and think about what they are doing and feeling, and how they and their partner are behaving in the relationship with one another. This may seem obvious, but is actually an important developmental achievement and a difficult state of mind for any of us to maintain. Couples can lose contact with this capacity, particularly in the face of the massive intrusion of children. If you lose the capacity to think about how you are functioning, particularly in the context of looking after children, you are liable to re-enact something that belongs to your own early experience. Although it will be possible to provide some parents who have lost the capacity to couple with models for how to provide parenting of their children, this will not stop the projection of those internal objects onto their children and onto their partner. On the other hand, understanding those unconscious beliefs that have become expressed in the relationship with one's partner can enable the individuals in a couple to re-create a third position from which they can contemplate the impact each is having on the other, and the impact that the child is having on them as a couple. This can make the couple, the relationship, a place where there can be a more thoughtful approach to the business of parenting.

If we apply some of the thoughts that Balfour has raised to the question of politics, we can see that we must first of all understand that politicians and those involved in social engineering are very often, if not always, expressing an unconscious belief. It follows that, if we are to have any impact on policy for families and children, we must begin by naming the beliefs and demonstrating that they are false. Parenting or "child rearing" over the last 100 years provides evidence of the dangers inherent in prescriptive advice. Although it may be true that the best way to deal with a temper tantrum is to ignore it, adopting this as a rule is more likely to lead to further damage if the parents have not had a chance to understand their own unconscious beliefs about being ignored or being watched. Just as with the business of providing help to those charged with child protection, rules will not do the job. Parents who are struggling to bring up their children need help to understand the complex matrix of unconscious processes that push them into a state of mind in which they feel they need certainty (like the certainty of rules), so that they can develop, instead of certainty, a trust in a process of genuine communication between themselves as a couple which will enable a capacity for a real engagement with their children.

References

Britton, R. (1998). *Belief and Imagination*. London: Routledge.

Layard, R. (2010). A campaign for psychological therapies: the case. London: MIND. Available at http://www.mind.org.uk/assets/0000/7445/lord_layard_document_new.pdf

NICE (2006). *Computerised Cognitive Behaviour Therapy for Depression and Anxiety*. Review of Technology Appraisal 51. London: National Institute for Health and Clinical Excellence, www.nice.org.uk

CHAPTER NINE

Her Majesty's department of love?
The state and support for couple
and family relationships

Honor Rhodes

Miniluv was one of the four most powerful and the most secretive super ministries governing the state of Oceania. It was housed in a building with no windows, heavy steel doors, barbed wire fences and strategically positioned snipers. Its bright lights were never turned off; it was a place "where there is no darkness". Its function was not to support its citizens in loving one another better but to instil in them an abiding love for Big Brother. It achieved this end through fear, the antithesis of love, through the work of the Thought Police and the known existence of Room 101, "the worst thing in the world", where each unfortunate occupant would face their worst fear and be broken by it. (George Orwell, *Nineteen Eighty-Four*, 1949)

Introduction

Is the idea that the government could create a Department of Love, to implement its policy for the improvement of human relationships, entirely fanciful? Or is the very idea of this an Orwellian step too far? In this chapter I will examine some of the social policies of recent decades that have sought to promote, either directly or indirectly, improved family and couple relationships. Inevitably the state's intervention

251

in family life raises important legal and ethical questions about the respective rights and responsibilities of the citizen to live life as a free person and of the state to intervene when the exercise of this freedom adversely affects the lives of others.

Orwell's Miniluv captures an image of an extreme totalitarian system, the purpose of which was to control thinking and to subvert individual autonomy in the service of asserting state control. Perhaps this nightmare image of what a state's involvement in the intimate lives of its citizens might become connects to deep anxieties about the intrusion of government into the realm of family life. Given such a pedigree, albeit a fictitious one, is it sensible to entertain, even for a moment, the idea of a Department whose existence would be hugely costly and whose outcomes would, inevitably, be mixed? What would it do? Who would work in it? Would it be a major Department with a Secretary of State of Love (the SoSoL) or, would it be better called the Department for Love with the change of title implying the higher purpose of striving to encourage ideal human relations. However far-fetched it may seem, this picture may be a useful *reductio ad absurdum* to prompt our thinking about the different and, sometimes, conflicting arguments used to justify the involvement of statutory and non-statutory organisations in family life.

To ask such questions is also timely as there is popular debate about how to maximise well-being and happiness on the one hand (Layard et al., 2006) and, on the other hand, how to minimise family breakdown and social disorder. It is important that we ask such questions now, after the announcement of grant funding from the Department for Education (DfE, 2011) for the children, families, and couple relationships charity sector. Of this sum £7.5 m is specifically designated for couple relationship work with a four year commitment of £30 m in total. At a time of extreme financial retrenchment such an investment in an area as complex as couple relationship support looks generous and, perhaps, evidence of making good the promise within the Conservative Party manifesto to support marriage. For recipient organisations such as the Tavistock Centre for Couple Relationships, Relate, and others it is neither more nor less than they have received in the recent past and a reduction compared to earlier marriage support funding (Boucher, 2008).

We need also to retain a sense of proportion. While £7.5 m to support couple relationships is undoubtedly welcome, when set against the annual cost of relationship breakdown, conservatively estimated at

£20 bn (Callan, 2007), it looks and feels like a small sum. It is equivalent to the £7.5 m spent by Stockport Council in one year providing a range of recycling bins for its residents (*Manchester Evening News*, 22 June 2011) or the amount Devon County Council paid for gritting and salting roads during the snows of 2009 (*BBC News* online, 9 September 2010).

In reviewing recent policy initiatives the suggestion is made that specific aspects of family functioning have been targeted which, with few exceptions, have excluded help to parenting couples. The aspects of family functioning that have commanded priority have been those promoting children's early health and well-being or those combating antisocial behaviour. These imperatives will be outlined briefly and the chapter will conclude with an account of new policy developments which are now beginning to focus directly on parenting skills and the couple relationship, given the increasing salience of evidence for their strategic relevance in supporting and maintaining family well-being.

"Every Child Matters"

Plainly the creation of a Department for Love will never happen. As soon as we begin to play with the idea and its possibilities we realise that the proposal subverts and corrupts the meaning of love. We find it hard when a government, of whatever colour and stripe, colonises the words we use and redefines them to suit political ends. A phrase such as "Every Child Matters" has made a short and hectic journey from a commonplace truism to the title of a huge raft of policies. These affected the lives of a whole generation of children's workers who strove to measure everything they did against its desired outcomes. There were five: "Be healthy, stay safe, enjoy and achieve, make a positive contribution, and achieve economic well-being", but these should be written in the past tense as the Every Child Matters website is nearly impossible to find in the old DCSF Archived Web pages section of the website for the renamed Department for Education.

Every Child Matters, or ECM for short, is a good worked example of the state's articulation of government policy and the fact that it is a policy of the previous government is neither here nor there (James, 2009). How is it that the government's intention to provide every child with the necessary environment at home and at places of learning turns into an enormous policy apparatus of national scope? In all children's centres workers must enquire of themselves, and of parents, how work done in a Monday "Messy Play" session helped a child "enjoy and achieve"; a judgement that necessarily involved measuring just how much that child was enjoying and achieving. This complex outcome, however worthy, was not the intention of the policy but the inevitable concomitant of a state intervention that must have within it a data collection regime to evaluate its effectiveness. Measures of outcome are now a necessary policy adjunct, enabling the responsible government department to report success to "stakeholders". This is another colonised word meaning you and me as taxpayers, government and Parliament as policy "owners", interested professional groupings, and other communities of interest, including the private sector for whom the work might represent an opportunity to be tendered for and delivered under contract in the future.

Local authority policy making and service delivery

National imperatives to make every child matter were tailored to local circumstances. For example, in local authorities with high levels of deprivation, the planning and execution of policy was shaped to bring targeted benefit to children from minority ethnic communities or to children with disabilities. With the sole exception of one London borough, Islington, which had received assistance from a consultancy interested and active in the field, no local children and young people's plan included support and guidance on parental couple relationships. Even the much vaunted parenting strategies, created with great labour and excellent intentions, failed to recognise the strategic importance of couple relationships in shaping effective parenting. This was despite the relationships sector's briefings and papers to senior DCSF policy makers pleading that such guidance and research be included within the government circular that set the work in motion and despite some civil servants' best efforts to promote such ideas. It is this "couple blindness" that must interest us and inform how we help policy makers put couple relationship spectacles on and view the world differently.

As this chapter is written (summer 2011) the coalition government is making a huge reduction in public funds for local government, a blow sweetened by an equally large swathe of freedoms to spend monies as is seen fit at local government level. This policy shift, which represents a departure from the Labour government's "top-down" approach, will have important consequences for the types of family programmes given central and local government backing and the ways in which they are reported and evaluated. How this shift in policy and emphasis affects the children's centre worker following a Monday Messy Play session remains to be seen. It may be unlikely that such locally led initiatives will be any more successful in bringing a greater emphasis on the couple relationship to family policy and practice given no central government specific ring-fencing or requirement. Although research has shown the importance of the couple relationship in the mental health of the child and the family (Davies, Harold, Goeke-Morey & Cummings, 2002; Hanington, Heron, Stein & Ramchandani, 2011), a recognition of which has, at times, been evident in government policy aspirations, it has struggled to keep this in its sights, as the recent history of the fate of strategic endeavour in this area testifies.

Supporting families: the adoption of a programme approach

> Children need stability and security. Many lone parents and unmarried couples raise their children every bit as successfully as married parents. But marriage is still the surest foundation for raising children and remains the choice of the majority of people in Britain. We want to strengthen the institution of marriage to help more marriages to succeed. (Home Office, 1998)

This quotation is taken from an ambitious, and contentious, Home Office green paper, *Supporting Families* (1998). Amongst its recommendations was one which identified married couple relationships as an area worthy of investment. Putting to one side important differences of view about the respective merits of married and unmarried partnerships and the steady reduction in the popularity of marriage as measured by the marriage rate, this Home Office document sought to focus attention on the value of couple relationships, a focus which seems to have become fainter and more diffuse over the last thirteen years. There has instead been a steady advance in the connections between parenting and antisocial behaviour. Perhaps the generalist support to couples and families in the early green paper had to give way to a harder edged policy project that focused resource and attention on those families who did not appear to subscribe to a prevailing view of what family life ought to be.

These families, the new "troubled" families, were perceived in the media as under-regulated, over spilling their lives into streets and communities. In the tabloid press these families were dubbed "nuisance families" or the "neighbours from hell" and were seen to threaten the quality of life of those citizens who wanted to lead lives unmolested by shouting youths. The Labour government made a decision to require local action and enable "good" families to have secure homes, to be able to park their cars safely outside their front doors, and not have their children's school experiences and life chances diminished by the need to attend to children from families where education comes a poor second to other interests.

These troubled or problem families became the central focus of the Respect and antisocial behaviour agendas promoted by Tony Blair as prime minister and influenced by the work of Richard Sennett (2002) and others. Their analysis was that deficient parenting lay at the heart of dysfunctional family behaviour and the remedy for this shortfall was to first identify and then enroll target families into highly specialised, manualised programmes designed to reduce children's antisocial behaviours. Parents were to be supported, cajoled, and finally, if all else failed, required to create an environment within the family home where children "mattered" and where they could safely and healthily develop—with an eye to economic productivity in their later working years. These loud, provocative and often frightening families were the ones that the Respect policy was to target. In a symmetry that is hard to ignore, as poor parenting was increasingly identified as the "deficit" needing to be addressed, so programme after programme was imported from the USA and Australia (see Turner, Markie-Dadds & Sanders, 2010; Webster-Stratton, 1992). It was as if the state, as parent, lacked parenting knowledge and had to find it elsewhere. This meant that local initiatives from organisations like Family Action and Barnardo's were overlooked, their learning and thinking unvalued.

If these families lacked skills the state would teach them. Activity cranked up a gear and local family intervention projects (FIPs) were created, taking an idea formulated in Dundee by the charity Action for Children, previously NCH (Pawson et al., 2009), where families were brought into residential accommodation, signed a contract of work to achieve "better behaviour" targets, and submitted, sometimes very gratefully, to the intensive help offered. They returned to "civilian" life when sufficient change was made and sustained and, for those who could not improve sufficiently, the option of care proceedings was considered for the children at most risk. This is a development of the earlier pioneering method used by the NSPCC in Rochdale for "dangerous" families, where work would only be undertaken once the local authority had instituted interim supervision or care proceedings to allow the agency a clear mandate for its muscular family change work (Dale, Davies, Manson & Waters, 1986).

Very few local FIPs adopted the residential model as very few local authorities had spare blocks of flats at some distance from local communities. So, unlike Dundee, a "dispersed" scheme was most often used, working with families in their own homes and communities where the problems were manifest. The model of change could, and did in some cases, include engaging with neighbours and community groups, intended in part to act as a source of reassurance that "something" was finally being done. It was rather like making the change process visible through the windows and doors of the family's world, and was consciously or unconsciously mimicked in the highly visible Respect campaign of the time that included large posters on hoardings and on the sides of buses showing the faces of individuals successfully prosecuted under the new raft of legislation.

An analysis of these policies in action illustrates the gap between policy intention and policy achievement. Some family policy levers were shown to be unsuccessful. Moreover, good work was thwarted by both the fearful law of unintended consequences and people's capacity for industrial scale unconscious sabotage. For example, much effort was made by housing associations and local authority housing officers, carrying out their new antisocial behaviour responsibilities, to involve social workers from the newly formed Children's Services departments. Housing officers became frustrated and despairing as social workers, delighted at this new resource, drew their own thresholds for intervention tighter and higher.

How did we get here?

If policy work is the machinery that delivers a government's prospectus, we now need to contemplate how we have arrived at this particular point, and to consider whether the nation state's family policy is a story of neglect followed by endeavour, a smooth glide from Poor Law to Every Child Matters, or perhaps, a game of continuous catch-up between policy makers, the public, researchers, and the government of the day. If we are clever and thoughtful we might also divine what particular place marriage and couple relationships occupy in any of the policy development thinking observable in the past and present.

A question we need to ask is why the state decided, with a moral majority, to identify and target problematic families in such a way. Carl Whitaker's perturbing family therapy questions, "Why now? What for? Why worry?" might help us also to consider how relationship policy became increasingly coercive, and involve a complicated dance with the preoccupation of the "red top" national newspapers with hellish neighbours and strident demands for government action (Nichols & Schwartz, 1998).

In 2008 we had arrived at a point where families identified as antisocial were to be better regulated by the use of interventions related to housing tenure. This bricks and mortar approach, used to modulate human behaviour, is a morally complex area and marks a change of scope and scale from the original Dundee project to a new programme implemented in every English local authority. Action for Children had worked with Dundee Council to create a place where families came, having agreed to relinquish any tenancy rights they might have had, and on the further understanding that future occupation of local authority or any social housing stock was, by agreement, a tenancy with conditions. This approach accepts as its basic premise the human need and the human right to shelter; but it adds the often poorly articulated concomitant, that such rights entail responsibilities which in these cases require tenants to act reasonably and in ways that do not cause undue nuisance to others. This reasonable condition of tenure addresses the social "rules" by which people engage with their neighbours but does not, of itself, address the underlying causes of undesirable behaviours. Tenants imperilled their security of tenure through antisocial behaviour that could include making loud and annoying noise, having uncontrolled pets, and being careless with rubbish, and by aggressive or threatening behaviour of family members and their guests in the neighbourhood and beyond.

The original model used highly committed unqualified staff as the family key workers; they were well supervised by qualified social workers and other professionals. The small evidence base they generated for the project was, nonetheless, impressive and, at the time, one of the few places where change for deeply troubled families, on the scale required by the government response to the Respect agenda, could be found. It is little wonder that the model was seized upon as an example of "what works" and gathered considerable support from the Home Office and later the Department for Children, Schools and Families which took the work on.

At this time the Home Office undertook a review of work up and down the country with recalcitrant families. One of the consistent characteristics of much successful practice was the presence of imaginative and innovative schemes staffed by practitioners who had in common a capacity to tolerate the hostility they encountered in the family members with whom they worked. These schemes were often based in voluntary sector organisations or at the very edges of local authority work where practitioners felt free to innovate and to develop their work unfettered by bureaucracy, including systems and measures for thorough evaluation. These small scale projects, often depending for their success on the presence of charismatic and determined leadership, fitted uncomfortably into programmes of intervention that demand a manualised and, therefore, standardised approach. One unresolved question appears to remain—whether it is possible to create policy initiatives that allow a creative tension between the need for systematic rigour on the one hand, and the need to allow personal creativity among front line practitioners on the other. It will be interesting to see whether the recent "contracting out" of project work with families beset by unemployment to a private sector company will achieve this creative balance, and if so how a "family champion", with no therapeutic training will fare (Prime Minister's Office, 2010).

Family change machinery

The presence of staff unqualified and untrained in the skills necessary to help clients change their behaviour meant that family intervention projects required evidence based tools that could be lifted and applied in situ. This resulted in the huge financial investment in the National Academy for Parenting Practitioners, launched in 2007and the purchase of licences and training for the parenting programmes imported from abroad.

What is interesting about these programmes, nearly all developed by clinical psychologists, is their theoretical base: a blend of adult learning theory, skills acquisition, and rehearsal together with a very clear focus on the parent–child relationship. They have all been rigorously road-tested and have a weight of evidence in their ability to enable parents to make positive changes, measured by clinical tools. They appear to be an ideal "off the shelf" solution, provided that the practitioners are trained in the use of the programme manual, select an appropriate cohort of parents, apply the manual's instructions faithfully, and are well supervised themselves. If these requirements are in place then "purchasers" can be confident they get the results advertised.

In terms of family policy and its development, it is worth pausing to consider how it came about that family policy, at this point, became a conversation about very deeply troubled families whom it was thought would benefit from behavioural interventions instead of more psychodynamic approaches. What is it about an understanding of human relationships that generates a profound mistrust or even ridicule on the part of policy makers, acting on the wishes of government? It is worth remembering that politicians and therefore policy makers are working to very short timetables for delivery on election promises; subtlety, nuance, ambiguity, and downright uncertainty are not qualities that can be considered positive. Change if promised must be seen to be delivered whilst interventions that work slowly, undoing years of hurt and harm, that can tolerate worsening before improvement, and need skilful, highly trained practitioners are not likely to be central to the answer, whatever the question.

In the long historical sweep of what could be called loosely "family" policy making, developments accelerated in the last century and have become breathlessly fast in our current one. In this trajectory there have been periods when the state has actively concerned itself with questions about the quality and nature of couple relationships. Concern has often been expressed in the form of enquiry about the durability of the very institution of marriage and sometimes about the "curability" of those couples whose relationships are troubled.

The years of family policy making have been well rehearsed elsewhere and less idiosyncratically than here (Kamerman & Kahn, 1998), and show the slow emergence of state sanctioned "romantic" love, based on degrees of partner choice as opposed to medieval and early modern requirements for dynastic settlements. Family policy concerned itself in the past with dowries, child brides, and wardships, designed far less to protect vulnerable wives and children than to protect vested financial and property interests of husbands and fathers (Waller, 2009). Marriage, and its legal form, was the critical and overarching preoccupation in these earlier centuries, offering assurances as to the purity of the blood-line, the rights of inheritance, and the settlement of political alliances.

It is only much more recently, by and large during and after the two world wars, that the state both created for itself, and accepted responsi-bility for, the moral and other improvement of the monarch's subjects. It is the post Second World War settlement that brings family policy to the foreground and its interpretation by successive Labour and Con-servative governments.

The state at work, the "contested ground", and moral panics

Social policy generally and family policy in particular can be under-stood to reflect, in part, prevailing political values of parties in power concerning the responsibilities of the state and the individual. The political philosopher, George Lakoff (2002) has identified the contested ground most clearly. He argues that the Conservatives on the politi-cal right hold a "strict father" in mind, one who instils in his children firm discipline and a capacity for independence which allows them to prosper in adulthood without recourse to the services of the state. While this fits neatly with the Neo-Con and Tea Party libertarian right in American politics it has a less good fit with English "high church" Tory and Whig historical traditions of laissez-faire paternalism, but the resemblance is clear.

By contrast he argues that the Labour and Liberal Democrat par-ties on the political left give greater prominence to the importance of a "nurturing mother" figure in domestic life who protects her children from harm and by doing so provides greater legitimacy to continuing aspects of dependency than those on the right of the political divide would support. When these "family values" are tested in the political arena it becomes clear that those on the right wing of the political spec-trum are always going to argue for a less prominent role for the state in family life than those in the centre and on the left.

The contest is familiar as politicians, the media, and the public gen-erally adopt these metaphors from parenting and construct arguments using them. For a right wing politician the "nanny state" which tells us all to eat five pieces of fruit a day is just that, a fussy over-particular mother or mother substitute. For the politician from the left to know that fruit improves human health and happiness and not tell people would be remiss and represent neglectful mothering. The fracture is painful as Lakoff observes, with both sides finding each other's views incomprehensible and, to a great extent, immoral so that any political exchange is experienced as an attack on deeply held beliefs about personal morality and one's lived experience of family life.

While we do engage in contest it is reasonable to say that, unlike our European neighbours, Britain has a fairly pragmatic view of policy making. It accompanies our empiricist-rational scientific tradition which is unlike that of the more philosophically driven science of France and Germany, where politics itself remains as a pure science, critiqued and considered within a grand tradition of political thinkers such as Hegel and Adorno (Buckle, 1999).

Adopting a practical approach to policy has advantages. It means that the machinery of government must be light on its feet to welcome any new political administration and able to articulate the manifesto commitments that it brings; this has required the state to fund a large and complex civil service, impartial and expert. The disadvantages are plain also, in that investment in previous policy programmes is lost as they are swept away. It is rare to find a policy area that remains unchanged after a general election which brings a new party to power.

Equally, in the life of a government the policies which Lakoff would identify as most closely aligned with his strict or nurturing parent positions are those that generate the most heat, if not the most light. One striking example of policy formation that disobeyed this rule was the cross-party support for the Children Act 1989, the fundamental reshaping of decades of increasingly creaking child care law. Its passing was a triumph and indeed the statute was immeasurably improved by its committee stages where critical issues were discussed and resolved in a remarkably non-party political fashion.

Child care law, whilst a key part of family policy, is by no means the whole, and it is the other areas - marriage and relationships, family taxation, housing, immigration, and welfare benefits to name but a few—where such a consensus is scarcely ever reached. These areas are highly charged and are the battlegrounds on which politics, as we know it, is fought, with policy following in the battle's wake.

Another issue in pragmatic policy making is the regular perturbation caused by "moral panics". The idea takes hold that "the government should do something", whether that is the public discourse driven by the eugenics debates of the Boer War and First World War on finding that a high percentage of British men were unfit for military service, or the modern anxieties about the drunken rampaging of "feral youth" in city centres on Friday and Saturday nights, and the failure of British parents to raise their children properly leading to such antisocial behaviour. For all political parties, to differing degrees and articulated differently, much of the problem at the heart of society's ills is the breakdown and break-up of family life, with its consequences for the welfare of children in particular.

It is here, in the heart of the panic about family life that the idea of couple relationships has secured a small foothold. One visible manifestation was the commitment made by Gordon Brown, early in his office as Chancellor of the Exchequer, to the creation of a fund that would support parents in particular difficulties. The Parenting Fund started its work in 2004, funding voluntary sector organisations in areas of acute deprivation, and was offered as three different grant programmes of eighteen months to two years, concluding in March 2010. While family relationships were always at the heart of the fund, the last round, Parenting Fund Three, starting in April 2009, has as its first criterion: "Strengthen existing parental couple relationships, whether parents live together or apart, and assist separated/divorced parents who are in conflict to better work together in order to minimize the impact of the poor parental relationship on their child or children, and so improve outcomes for those children" (Parenting Fund Guidance).

This prominence was largely to do with the determination of the couple relationship sector, matched by a commitment from civil servants, to ensure that the opportunity for new projects in communities of high need could take shape and be tested as prospective solutions to family breakdown.

Many of the couple relationship organisations were successful in Round Two and Three: Relate and One plus One together with the Tavistock Centre for Couple Relationships (TCCR) all ran projects. TCCR used the funds granted to it to develop parental couple relationship counselling in children's centres, together with some group work activity for parents living with postnatal depression. It became abundantly clear that the offer was viewed as helpful and accessible by communities who had not previously been seen as a "market" for counselling approaches. Whether the communities were Turkish, black African, or Vietnamese, outcome measures indicating improvement for both the parents' couple relationship and the children's well-being were positive (Clulow & Donaghy, 2010). What was equally interesting was the cultural shift made by the workers in the centres. Reluctant to refer at the beginning of the project's life, they became increasingly clear that this focus was the missing link in the range of services on offer to parents. Politicians and policy advisers made visits and heard first-hand how sensitive, evidence based approaches can and do tackle the "wicked" problems that lead to family breakdown, child poverty, and poor physical and mental health.

Changing families and fragile families

Governments must have answers, or something that looks like the beginning of part of the answer, to these public outcries of concern, wherever they come from. Most governments find themselves spending valuable time and public resources on issues that relate to family life without having an over-arching and fully worked ideological position from which to start. That is not to say the successive Conservative and Labour governments have no position on the centrality of family life and how it might be sustained and supported, and indeed both have concerned themselves with it. It is just that we, as a nation, are deeply sceptical and, indeed, resistant to the idea that the state has much of a part to play in the ordering of our domestic relationships. It is not an issue that we go out to vote on or one that is easy to campaign on. Indeed, many politicians prefer to keep their own personal lives out of public view, concerned for the welfare of children or because they are fearful what judgement the public would make of their living arrangements, and this makes talking about the family lives of others a good deal harder. It is misconduct in the areas of money and sex that brings most politicians down. We only need to see the faux horror that attended Jacqui Smith's expenses claim (revealed in the *Daily Mail*) that appeared to include the cost of renting pornography to see how potent the two can be when combined.

Sceptical or not, some people accept the state's sanctioning of our couple relationships but increasing numbers do not. In 2006 one in six couples in the UK were cohabiting (2.3 million couples) and more than a third (36%) of the public in England and Wales had been in a cohabiting relationship at some time (Office for National Statistics, 2008).

By opting out of state recognised unions, cohabiting couples place themselves, by and large, outside the provisions of the law to end marriages and civil partnerships, with the consequence that the care of children and the division of property and financial assets may be less equitably distributed than for divorcing peers. For many new Conservatives the nature of the family in Britain is fragile, an argument set out in detail in the 2006 *The State of the Nation Report: Fractured Families* report (Callan, 2006). This contains a list of endeavours that any Conservative government would be urged to deliver, the answers ranging far and wide, from preferable taxation status in marriage to something called "Building relationship competence". The welcome emphasis on preventing breakdown is amplified by the analysis of the consequences for children, communities, and the state of families that are not able to sustain themselves, intact and employed.

The consequences are indeed grave for children raised in families living in poverty, and the ideological battle lines are drawn on whether poverty is a contingent ill of single parenthood and family breakdown or vice versa. However, in fact, neither party adopts such a purist approach in their policy making, and both in times of power and opposition have offered thoughtful policy outlines. One of the clearest of these was the development, in Labour's years of opposition and policy renewal, of the Sure Start programme, however imperfectly implemented whilst in government. The imperfection is critical. How can it be that a government holding all the policy levers and able to direct huge resources can find its best ideas—and ones for which there is, by and large, general if grudging support—distorted and occasionally perverted as they land on the ground? It seems that as a populace we continue to resist being told what to do and call such attempts the "nanny state", whilst increasingly and ceaselessly searching for help in being better parents. The evidence is plain to see: a plethora of television programmes urging us to tackle our tiny tearaways with "naughty steps" and time-out sessions, and "infotainment" in the form of badly parented adolescents being required to camp out in inhospitable terrains so that they can be returned to their despairing, and usually culpable, parents as reformed characters.

Public aversion to state interference, private distress, and remedies

We remain fast in our belief that the state has only very little to do with how and whom we love, for how long we love them, and what provision we might turn to when things go wrong. We look to lawyers to extricate us from failed relationships as a matter of course; as a nation we rarely seek counselling or therapeutic help to save a relationship or help one end well. Of all the therapies, couple counselling and therapy is the one that is, largely, only available as a private purchase, and few can bear the financial cost. The price we pay for keeping our private lives private is high indeed and yet, while lamenting family breakdown, the state has done very little to make the idea of seeking early help acceptable and accessible, even though the evidence is there that it works.

Something hidden is at work in this lack of capacity in the state and its citizens to hold in mind the nature of love and to build the emotional support "architecture" in which it can flourish. We are unable, as we know, to bear much reality, as T. S. Eliot (2001) suggested, while carrying a longing for deep and abiding intimacy. The push and pull of public policy exemplifies this ambivalence and our human frailty.

It is no wonder that a Department for Love is a long way off. Even if we wished to see some of its positive features introduced, we would need a secretary of state who was not so in thrall to performance measures as to overlook the important and the immeasurable. The deeply complex nature of the human heart would be accepted without a five point programme to deal with it; as if by magic the Department's work would be to sweep away the small and large cruelties and indignities that afflict and diminish our capacity to love, from hospitals, schools, and prisons as well as our family lives. We would be better educated in the hard graft of loving one another and know that there were places to go with people to see when we found ourselves in emotional distress. Couple counsellors and therapists would be found in accessible locations on the high street.

As a result our children reared with "good enough" (Winnicott, 1973) love would have an enhanced capacity to attend to others, including the old and the vulnerable. Ideally, of course, we would achieve some of this without the help of an Orwellian government. Children's and adults' services, some statutory and some voluntary, operating within the welfare state as we know it, can help us to live together and love better but to do this more effectively requires that they communicate better about what they do and, by so doing, challenge the idea of the exclusively private family and privatised couple relationship.

Bravery is required to argue for expert help when a "Big Society volunteer helper" is offered as an answer to the need for a massive reduction in public spending. By choosing to work as couple therapists and counsellors though, in preference to other areas, the resources we have to hand in the people who work in the arena of love—and hate—are already the bravest of the brave. So, to Emily Dickenson (1973) the last word on the matter,

That love is all there is, is all we know of love.

References

BBC News (2010, 9 September). http://www.bbc.co.uk/news/uk-england-devon-11246670

Boucher, D. (2008). Marriage Support Services Review. London: CARE, http://www.care.org.uk/wp-content/uploads/2010/10/Marriage_Support_Services.pdf

Buckle, S. (1999). British sceptical realism. A fresh look at the British tradition. *European Journal of Philosophy*, 7: 1–2.

Callan, S. (2006). *The State of the Nation Report: Fractured Families*. London: Centre for Social Justice.

Clulow, C. & Donaghy, M. (2010). Developing the couple perspective in parenting support: evaluation of a service initiative for vulnerable families. *Journal of Family Therapy*, 32: 142–168.

Daily Mail (2009). Blue movies on expenses: Jacqui Smith's husband apologises for watching porn … paid for by the taxpayer, 29 March. http://www.dailymail.co.uk/news/article-1165611/Blue-movies-expenses-Jacqui-Smiths-husband-apologises-watching-porn-paid-taxpayer.html#ixzz1 WWn2eXMv

Dale, P., Davies, M., Manson, T. & Waters, J. (1986). *Dangerous Families: Assessment and Treatment of Child Abuse*. London: Tavistock.

Davies, P. T., Harold, G. T., Goeke-Morey, M. C. & Cummings, E. M. (2002). Child emotional security and interparental conflict. *Monographs of the Society for Research in Child Development*, 67, i–v, vii–viii: 1–115.

Department for Education (2011). Voluntary and community organisations awarded £60 million grant (press release). http://www.education.gov.uk/inthenews/inthenews/a0074906/voluntary-and-community- organisations-awarded-60-million-grant

Dickenson, E. (1973). *Poem 1765. Complete Poems of Emily Dickinson*. London: Faber and Faber.

Eliot, T. S. (2001). *Four Quartets*. London: Faber and Faber.

Hanington, L., Heron, J., Stein, A. & Ramchandani, P. (2011). Parental depression and child outcomes—is marital conflict the missing link? In: *Child: Care, Health and Development*. doi: 10.1111/j.1365–2214.2011.01270.x Blackwell online.

Home Office (1998). *Supporting Families*. Now only available as an electronic archive at http://www.nationalarchives.gov.uk/ERORecords/HO/421/2/acu/sfpages.pdf

James, C. (2009). Ten years of family policy: 1999–2009. London: FPI. Available from http://www.familyandparenting.org/Filestore/Documents/publications/10_Years_of_Family_ Policy_WEB_FINAL.pdf

Kamerman, S. & Kahn, A. J. (Eds.) (1998). *Family Change and Family Policies in Great Britain, Canada, New Zealand, and the United States (Family Change and Family Policy in the West)*. London: Clarendon.

Lakoff, G. (2002). *Moral Politics: How Liberals and Conservatives Think*. Chicago: The University of Chicago Press.

Layard, R., Clark, D., Bell, S., Knapp, M., Meacher, B., Priebe, S., Turnberg, L., Thornicroft, G. & Wright, B. (2006). The depression report; a new deal for depression and anxiety disorders. London: The Centre for Economic Performance's Mental Health Policy Group, London School of Economics. http://cep.lse.ac.uk/textonly/research/mentalhealth/DEPRESSION_REPORT_LAYARD2.pdf

Manchester Evening News (2011). "The colour of money: New bins cost Stockport Council £7.5 m", 22 June. http://menmedia.co.uk/manchestereveningnews/news/s/1424375_stockport-council-gets-60000-phone-calls-over-new-75 m-bin-scheme

National Academy for Parenting Practitioners (2007). (http://www.familyandparenting.org/page/264)

Nichols, M. & Schwartz, R. (1998). *Family Therapy: Concepts and Methods (8th edn.)*. London: Pearson.

Office for National Statistics (2008). *Focus on Families, 2007*. London: ONS.

Orwell, G. (1949). *Nineteen Eighty-Four*. London: Penguin, 1998.

Pawson, H., Davidson, E., Sosenko, F., Flint, J., Nixon, J., Casey, R. & Sanderson, D. (2009). Evaluation of the establishment, operations and impact of 5 projects focused on families at risk of eviction for antisocial behaviour. Scotland: Scottish Government Research.

Prime Minister's Office (2010). (Press release, 10 December.) Government launches drive to support families http://www.number10.gov.uk/news/government-launches-drive-to-support-families/

Sennett, R. (2002). *Respect: the Formation of Character in a World of Inequality*. London: W. W. Norton.

Turner, K. M. T., Markie-Dadds, C. & Sanders, M. R. (2010). *Facilitator's Manual for Group Triple P (3rd edition)*. Brisbane, Australia: Triple P International, http://www1.triplep.net/

Waller, M. (2009). *The English Marriage*. London: John Murray.

Webster-Stratton, C. (1992). *Incredible Years: Trouble-Shooting Guide for Parents of Children Aged 3–8*. Toronto, Canada: Umbrella Press.

Winnicott, D. W. (1973). *The Child, the Family, and the Outside World* (pp. 17–44). London: Penguin.

COMMENTARY ON CHAPTER NINE

Janet Walker

The state's role in promoting strong relationships

The central question in this chapter relates to the extent to which the state should intervene in family life and seek to promote strong couple relationships. Should governments encourage particular kinds of families or support particular kinds of adult relationships, and how far should they go in promoting their expectations of how families should behave? The right to privacy in family life would seem to suggest that governments should leave well alone, except to prevent, as far as is possible, the perpetuation of domestic abuse and the potentially detrimental consequences of parental separation and family breakdown. The challenge, therefore, is to define an appropriate role for governments and determine policies which can concurrently safeguard privacy and vulnerable family members, particularly children. A single department devoted to this would be unable to achieve this balance and a joined-up approach to family policy is essential: a Department of Love is certainly not the answer. What, then, can be done to promote strong families, regarded by most as the cornerstone of a strong society?

A two-way relationship?

It is the protection and well-being of children which has drawn the most public attention over the last half-century. In 2004, a commission on families and the well-being of children was established to advise on the crucial question of what should be the pattern of relationships between the state and families in the upbringing of children. It envisaged a two-way relationship between families and the state, each with responsibilities and each needing support (Rutter, 2005). It also acknowledged the difficult balance between the care and the control functions of the state, and advocated that the state should actively promote an ethic of care and enhance trust between it and families. Achieving this is not straightforward, however: families are complex, family life is infinitely variable, and family structures are not static and will continue to change. Nevertheless, evidence (Barrett, 2004; Williams & Roseneil, 2004) shows that, despite social flux, there are strong emotional and caring bonds within today's families which offer a positive dynamic upon which governments can build to support families and children.

Fragile families

In her chapter, Honor Rhodes draws attention to the changing and fragile nature of family life and the ways in which the "breakdown" of parental relationships has engendered a moral panic. Such panics often result in policy making which fails to address the underlying causes of family breakdown and which unwittingly stigmatises or labels whole families or specific family members. Concerns about "deadbeat dads" failing to take their parental responsibilities seriously, for example, led to measures which focused on reinforcing maintenance and contact orders, while an understanding of the enormous challenges associated with non-resident parenting and the emotional complexities of recasting and sharing parental responsibilities when parents live apart might have resulted in more appropriate interventions which support parents and children (Ahrons, 2004; Walker, McCarthy, Stark & Laing, 2004). The potentially detrimental consequences of family break-up are not avoided by making separation and divorce "harder" or by promulgating policy initiatives which set out to promote marriage as the best kind of adult couple relationship.

The evidence is unequivocal that what matters most to children is the *quality* of the relationships they have with their parents and wider kin, irrespective of the family structures within which they live (Walker, 2008). We know that children thrive best in families characterised by predictable and consistent care, and such care is associated with stable and harmonious relationships between parents: having parents who are able to maintain sound adult partnerships and negotiate flexibly is beneficial for children. This evidence provides clear clues about what the state should be doing to support and protect children and to support parents to establish and maintain sound partnerships in all kinds of circumstances, while at the same time promoting a sense of order and continuity and respecting change and individual human rights.

Supporting parents

Modern partnerships demand a high degree of personal maturity and good communication and negotiation skills. Moreover, the increased freedoms inherent within conjugal relationships in Western societies often conflict with the constraints and challenges inherent in parenthood. We know that the transition to parenthood marks a particularly vulnerable time for couples. However equal and shared roles appear to be prior to starting a family, traditional parenting roles tend to change the dynamic, with responsibilities for child care in most democratic societies falling primarily on mothers, even though most mothers are employed outside the home, while fathers take a smaller share of the parenting tasks. It is perhaps not surprising, therefore, that successive governments in Britain have sought ways to support families at key transition points.

Recently the coalition government committed funding for relationship support services between 2011 and 2015 with a view to encouraging couples to seek help before relationships deteriorate to the point of no return. Seeking help for the most intimate of relationships is not something that adults in Western cultures find easy (Chang & Barrett, 2009). As Rhodes has commented, the price paid for keeping family life private is high. But how far should the state go in encouraging attendance at marriage/relationship preparation courses, relationship enrichment courses, and couple counselling? Should the services be free and/or mandatory?

Couples have indicated that what they do not need is patronising, morally driven, paternalistic interference but straightforward advice and information on which informed choices can be made (Walker, McCarthy, Stark & Laing, 2004). The call is for services that focus on improving the quality of family relationships and supporting parents to execute their responsibilities, irrespective of how they manage their day-to-day lives. Many governments have struggled to find appropriate ways to achieve these goals, and debates continue as to whether separating parents, for example, should be required to attend a parenting education programme. While these programmes are widely appreciated and regarded as supportive in countries such as the US and Canada, worries rumble on in Britain about whether they constitute an invasion of privacy or reflect an over-protective nanny state. Given the evidence, however, it is difficult to see how such support via targeted interventions can be regarded as anything other than an indication of responsible government. But to be effective, these kinds of services need to be readily accessible and non-stigmatising.

Balancing care with control

A problem emerges when family interventions are designed to offer support and, at the same time, punish family members for non-compliance. Rhodes has illustrated this tension in the last Labour government's attempts to deal with antisocial behaviour and deficient parenting through family intervention projects (FIPs). Dedicated practitioners found it difficult to impose sanctions while building intensive relationships with some of the most vulnerable and chaotic families. The apparent balance between "tough love" support and sanctions appealed to politicians and to an electorate that is highly influenced by a media which promulgates scare stories about "families from hell" and out-of-control teenagers. Critics pointed out that so-called "tough love" was used to justify forcing very vulnerable families into interventions under the threat of eviction from their home, loss of welfare benefits, and the removal of their children into care (Gregg, 2010).

Evaluators of the programme expressed serious concerns about the positive claims made by stakeholders for the success of the intervention (Nixon, Parr & Hunter, 2008; Sheffield Hallam University, 2006; White, Warrener, Reeves & La Valle, 2008). In a review of the evidence Gregg (2010) commented that while the government of the day chose to present the programme as a solution to antisocial, "chaotic families" who "bring misery" to their neighbourhoods, the families targeted were socially inadequate, often with serious mental and physical health difficulties and learning disabilities. These families did not receive appropriate medical support because the programme focused on antisocial behaviour. Gregg described FIPs as an interesting experiment in social engineering "which had the potential to help poor, very vulnerable families who failed to fit into their communities". Instead, the families were demonised, and the intervention demonstrates "the nightmare place to which populist political rhetoric and 'policy-based evidence' can deliver us" (Gregg, 2010, p. 16).

This example reminds us that balance and proportionality are key principles that should underpin all attempts to support families and strengthen couple relationships. Social interdependence and a two-way relationship between families and the state requires governments to manage separate interests within the complex rules of personal, family relations, and to uphold children's rights and those of all family members. In so doing, the challenges facing families and democratic societies can be recast as opportunities for individuals to maximise their potential, within a framework of connectedness and mutual support (Walker, 2006). This approach encourages social justice, respect for diversity, and enhancement of social capital. Within the spirit of the coalition government's "Big Society", it underlines effective partnerships within families and communities, between the professionals whose remit is to offer support, advice, and guidance, and between families and the state.

Rights and responsibilities

If support is to be provided from a combination of the family, the community, and the state, then it is essential to understand the realities facing families, the roles family members play, and the contexts in which they operate and make choices. Under advanced liberalism, the state expects families to take responsibility for the "risks" which permeate family life. This is clearly demonstrated in economic policies which are generally encouraging greater financial autonomy, wider participation in the workforce, saving for the future, specifically for old age, and decreased reliance on the welfare state. The welfare of families is a legitimate interest for all governments which rely on families to meet their daily material needs, care for and raise children, care for dependent, elderly, or frail adults and satisfy the intimacy needs of partners; and support needs to be targeted towards those who need it most, when they need it.

So how can the state support couple relationships? It can begin by acknowledging that all families face difficulties and challenges at one time or another and that a focus on couple relationships adds value in terms of promoting the healthy development and well-being of children and their parents (Cowan, Cowan, Pruett & Pruett, 2007). A recent study (Walker, Barrett, Wilson & Chang, 2010) asked over 1,000 people about the problems they had experienced, the help they sought and/or received, and the interventions which might have supported them at different times in their relationship. It demonstrated clearly that the fairytale vision of falling in love and living happily ever after does not reflect the reality for the vast majority of people who form committed couple relationships. Instead, people talked about the importance of working at relationships and about the stressors which can so easily destabilise the strongest of partnerships. Although the expectations of intimate relationships have shifted and roles and responsibilities have changed, men continue to feel under pressure to provide for their family, while women feel under pressure to care for family members, particularly children. Tensions can fester as these traditional expectations are challenged and tested.

What governments can do

There are considerable barriers to acknowledging and seeking help with problems that impinge on relationships. Yet research indicates (Walker, Barrett, Wilson & Chang, 2010) that most people would welcome support to strengthen interpersonal relationships, and very few actually take the view that family relationships should be purely private and personal. Suggestions about what governments could do fall into two categories: first, they can offer appropriate information, advice, and support at times of stress and during key transition points in family life; and second, they can do more to promote cultural changes in society. The specific steps that can be taken include the following:

1. Enhancing the understanding of stresses and strains and relationship problems more generally.
2. Providing better training for practitioners who work with families to enable them to spot relationship problems and signpost them to specific support services.
3. Making support services more accessible and available.

4. Extending the range of services to provide support and information via new technologies and innovative channels to offer greater choice.

The biggest challenge, however, is promoting cultural change to reduce stigmatisation and normalise help-seeking behaviour. This would include debunking overly romantic conceptions of couple relationships and family life and challenging the taboos which prevent people from talking freely about personal problems. Perhaps the most effective way to promote change is to ensure that children and young people learn about and prepare for relationships as early in their lives as possible. There is a widespread consensus that it is never too early to teach children how to form and maintain healthy relationships. Relationship education in schools provides a vehicle through which values can be transmitted and embedded in all aspects of daily interaction. In this regard, it is a matter which falls within the remit of a Department of Education—it does not need a separate Department of Love!

In her chapter, Rhodes also calls for better education in "the hard graft of loving one another" and knowing that there are places to go to receive help with troubled relationships. Struening (2002) has argued that the voluntary nature of modern partnerships, for the most part freely entered into, has rendered them both strong and fragile: strong because freely chosen relationships carry with them an integrity and dignity which those embedded in economic dependence or coercion do not; and fragile because feelings are changeable and intimacy is not always satisfied. Building on these strengths and reducing the risks that fragility will cause relationships to crumble remains a legitimate task for all governments.

References

Ahrons, C. (2004). *We're Still Family: What Grown Children Have to Say about Their Parents' Divorce.* New York: Harper Collins.

Barrett, H. (2004). *UK Family Trends 1994–2004.* London: National Family and Parenting Institute.

Chang, Y.-S. & Barrett, H. (2009). *Couple Relationships: A Review of the Nature and Effectiveness of Support Services.* London: Family and Parenting Institute (formerly NFPI).

Cowan, K. P., Cowan, P. A., Pruett, M. K. & Pruett, K. (2007). An approach to preventing coparenting conflict and divorce in low income families:

strengthening couple relationships and fostering fathers' involvement. *Family Process*, 46(1): 109–121.

Gregg, D. (2010). *Family Intervention Projects: A Classic Case of Policy-based Evidence*. London: Centre for Crime and Justice Studies.

Nixon, J., Parr, S. & Hunter, C. (2008). *The Longer Term Outcomes Associated with Families Who Had Worked with Intensive Family Support Projects*. London: Department for Communities and Local Government, HMSO.

Rutter, M. (Ed.) (2005). *Families and the State: Two Way Support and Responsibilities*. Bristol, UK: The Polity Press.

Sheffield Hallam University (2006). *Antisocial Behaviour Intensive Family Support Projects: an Evaluation of Six Pioneering Projects*. London: Department for Communities and Local Government.

Struening, K. (2002). *New Family Values: Liberty, Equality and Diversity*. Lanham, MD: Rowman and Littlefield.

Walker, J. (2006). *Supporting Families in Democratic Societies: Public Concerns and Private Realities*. Lyons, France: ICCFR.

Walker, J. (2008). Family life in the 21st century: the implications for parenting policy in the UK. *Journal of Children's Services*, 3(4): 17–29.

Walker, J., Barrett, H., Wilson, G. & Chang, Y.-S. (2010). *Understanding the Needs of Adults (Particularly Parents) Regarding Relationship Support*, DCSF Research Report, DCSF-RR233. London: Department for Children Schools and Families.

Walker, J., McCarthy, P., Stark, C. & Laing, K. (2004). *Picking up the Pieces: Marriage and Divorce Two Years after Information Provision*. London: Department for Constitutional Affairs.

White, C., Warrener, M., Reeves, A. & La Valle, I. (2008). *Family Interventions Projects: An Evaluation of Their Design, Set-up and Early Outcomes*, DCSF Research Report, DCSF-RBW-047. London: Department for Children Schools and Families.

Williams, F. & Roseneil, S. (2004). Public values of parenting and partnership: voluntary organisations and welfare politics in New Labour's Britain. *Social Politics*, 11(2): 181–216.

CHAPTER TEN

Supervision: the interdependence of professional experience and organisational accountability

Lynette Hughes and Felicia Olney

Who might read a chapter on supervision in a book by a couples' agency? Counsellors, psychotherapists, social workers, health workers? Would they be working in statutory or voluntary agencies, or private practice? The very fact that we ask this question highlights the way that the worlds of health and social care on the one hand, and counselling and psychotherapy on the other, have moved away from each other over the decades since the Family Discussion Bureau (now the Tavistock Centre for Couple Relationships) was founded by analysts and social workers, who originally came together to establish a service that straddled the inner and outer worlds of their clients.

On reflection, we realise how much of what we have learnt about supervision is based on our experience of having been both social workers and couple psychotherapists, working in contexts where the interaction of conscious and unconscious factors, of the external and internal, is taken as read. In surveying the literature on supervision, we have been struck by how little cross-referencing there is between professions, and how each profession tends to address its own supervisory issues as though they are specific to itself (e.g., Brown & Bourne, 1996; Shipton, 1997; Wiener, Mizen & Duckham, 2003). There is a sense of the wheel being constantly rediscovered in different decades by different professions and work settings. Our teaching on supervision, to a broad range of professions and agencies, has convinced us that the underlying issues in supervision are similar regardless of context, profession, or theoretical approach, though their relative importance will be more context-specific. With this in mind, we think of our reader as any supervisor or supervisee, whatever her/his profession or setting.

The contextual changes in the political, financial, organisational, and professional climate of service delivery have been well documented elsewhere (e.g., Cooper & Lousada, 2005; Hughes & Pengelly, 1997). Within this context of "remorseless uncertainty" (Cooper & Dartington, 2004), health and social care have become increasingly specialised, the psychoanalytic and social work worlds have moved further apart, and disciplines and therapeutic approaches make omnipotent, competitive claims for effectiveness as they bid for scarce resources. The struggle for survival, rather than cooperative work, dominates the scene.

One effect of this within many public sector agencies has been a major reduction in a dynamic understanding of supervision (Cooper & Lousada, 2005). Their worlds, controlled by an ethos of risk-aversion and simplistic performance measurements, have become more prescriptive to the detriment of professional confidence. Meanwhile, within the counselling and psychotherapy worlds to which many front line workers have fled to escape agency prescriptiveness, the confidential twosome of supervisor and supervisee has been increasingly challenged by new organisational and registration requirements. The need for an approach to supervision that attends to client, practitioner, and agency has never been more relevant in all the caring professions.

In this chapter we shall look at ways in which the Tavistock Centre for Couple Relationships' contribution to thinking about supervision addresses some of today's supervisory dilemmas. Because of the limitations of space there are many areas of supervision that we will not be including. Most significantly, we are taking the fact of the importance of supervision as read and refer readers to other texts for more general discussion of supervision (e.g., Brown & Bourne, 1996; Hawkins & Shohet, 1989; Hughes & Pengelly, 1997; Martindale, Morner, Roderiguez & Vidit, 1997; Wheeler & King, 2001). We shall focus instead on two ideas that are particularly linked to couple work—the reflection process and the supervisory triangle, ideas first introduced by Janet

Mattinson (1975) and subsequently developed in TCCR's continuing teaching and writing about supervision.

For ease of reading we shall refer to patients/service users/clients as clients and to members of the caring professions as supervisors, supervisees, or practitioners. The examples we use are based on our own clinical and supervisory practice.

The reflection process/mirroring

In *The Reflection Process in Casework Supervision* (1975) Mattinson highlighted two key themes in supervision: first, the need for practitioner and supervisor to engage with the complex feelings involved in the work, and second, the reflection process—the phenomenon whereby unprocessed feelings can become enacted in supervision. Mattinson emphasised the need for professionals in all settings to be sufficiently undefended to be affected by the emotional impact of the work, and to be able to think of these feelings as potential information, rather than experience them as something shameful and unprofessional, to be managed and got rid of.

The term "mirroring" is used these days to distinguish the reflection process from the broader term "reflective practice". The ambiguity of the term "reflection process" may partly explain why Mattinson's (1975) text (the first, we believe, to introduce into the UK the idea of mirroring in supervision) seems to be unknown to many who are very familiar with the concept—though the fact that it was written mainly for a social work audience may also be relevant. It is also referred to as "parallel process"—a term that seems to us particularly inappropriate for a process whose essence is a blurring of the boundary between two distinct areas. The dynamic in fact keeps being rediscovered and renamed (e.g., Vollmer et al., 2007). So, what is mirroring? Put simply, mirroring is a phenomenon where something is enacted in supervision that belongs to the client-worker relationship where it cannot be fully experienced or acknowledged. Thus, by the unconscious process of projection, it is displaced into another part of the system as if it belongs there. Mattinson touches briefly on how mirroring can take place in the opposite direction, from the supervisory to the practitioner/client relationship, though this needs to be distinguished from conscious or semiconscious modelling by the practitioner of the supervisor's behaviour (Hughes & Pengelly, 1997).

The following example illustrates both this dynamic and the importance of understanding the underlying communication.

> An enthusiastic young social worker in a social services department had a client with a very deprived background who suffered from a severe eating disorder. The client was unable to set any limits on her food intake and was consequently obese. Her handling of her children showed similar aspects as she stuffed them full of food rather than being able to attend to their needs, including their need to have limits set. Overweight and beyond control, they were displaying severe problems in school, and there was considerable pressure to apply to court to have them removed from home. In the supervision, an enactment had taken place over time where a vast amount of the department's cash budget was poured unthinkingly into the family in the face of their desperate need. The supervisor was also doing more than usual for the worker in relation to this case (offering to write reports, attending inappropriate meetings, extending supervision sessions at the expense of other workers). It was only when supervisor and supervisee were eventually able to see that their behaviour mirrored both the client's shovelling down of undigested food, and her avoidance of setting limits in the face of her children's demands, that it was possible to confront the awful feelings that this client consciously denied by consuming unnecessary food that, far from nourishing her, actually made things worse.

Mattinson makes the important point that in assessing what behaviour is actually an enactment, it is essential to have some idea of how the supervisor and supervisee usually conduct themselves. If, unlike the example above, the worker was always emptying the budget, then clearly this would not be mirroring. But if, as in this example, the worker is normally able to think about appropriate boundaries of financial intervention, then it might be the case that some mirroring is occurring. In the above example, once there was an understanding of what the enactment meant, some appropriate limits were set on the financial help, and it became more possible to confront the desperate feelings involved and to begin to help the mother to set limits with her own family.

There is, of course, a danger that a supervisor might too readily interpret the supervisee's presentation and behaviour as evidence of mirroring, thus avoiding real problems in the supervisee's functioning. All this requires that the supervisor, and ideally the supervisee, know themselves and their usual responses, so that it is the departure from these that invites the enquiry about mirroring. This is more easily said than done. Inevitably practitioners and supervisors bring their own issues to work and we all have a predisposition to get caught up in particular areas. Mattinson usefully delineates, however, that as long as it is clear that some of the behaviour in question is an enactment, it can be worked with as such, even if the issue also relates to a similar aspect in the supervisee—and that the latter may indirectly be helped too (as Skynner, 1964, also stresses). Indeed an acknowledgement by both supervisee and supervisor that they have personal "hooks" may be liberating and lead to greater personal insight. Of course if the supervisee's "hook" is too pervasive, to the detriment of the work, the supervisor has to decide what "managerial" type action is required.

If all this suggests a struggle, then we have conveyed something of the difficulty of working with mirroring. Often the evidence occurs over time and is only recognisable through painful examination of the experience. In the social services example it took some months and a lot of the department's money before it was understood.

So where does this leave us in relation to contemporary practice in the various professions? Most of what we have been saying about the use of feelings is clearly the bread-and-butter of the psychotherapy world, and understood in terms of the use of countertransference, where the feelings experienced by the practitioner or supervisor are understood to be evidence of a depth of feeling that the client is unable to know about or put into words. Meanwhile, many practitioners work in settings, or have undergone training, that overtly or covertly discourage the exploration of painful feeling (Cooper & Lousada, 2005; Evans, 2006). However, practitioners in all fields and of all theoretical persuasions are more than familiar with clients who get under their skin or up their nose, make them feel uneasy, or fill them with dread, but they may lack the language to help them process and make sense of this. We share with many others the experience that practitioners who are not dynamically trained can readily grasp the idea that something going on in the here-and-now, within the supervision relationship, might be related to the client-practitioner relationship, and that by trying to understand this there could be some transferable learning to their work with clients. Those who engage with this often find themselves up against an organisational culture which wishes to turn a blind eye to such painful complexity (Steiner, 1985). More surprisingly, in our experience, supervisors in the psychotherapy/counselling field have been inclined to concentrate on the practitioner-client relationship (be that client an individual, couple, or family), without reference to the possible impact of this on the practitioner-supervisor interaction, despite frequent references to this in the literature. We wonder whether this in part arises from the preoccupation in much of the psychotherapy literature on supervision with defining the appropriate boundary between supervision and therapy (Wiener, Mizen & Duckham, 2003), which may unnecessarily inhibit an exploration of the relationship between supervisor and supervisee.

While Mattinson's examples of mirroring make only brief reference to the intrusive impact of the organisational context, the intrusive impact of recent environmental and organisational changes has meant that members of all disciplines are increasingly likely to behave in a manner that enacts core organisational dynamics. Armstrong (2004) carefully delineates how a supervisee's behaviour in supervision increasingly needs to be understood as information about how the agency context affects the work, rather than as a sign of the supervisee's pathology. This leads us into thinking of the relationship between professional and organisational accountability.

Supervisory triangles

In today's organisational climate, we would argue that while the idea of "supervisory triangles" is now familiar to many, there are probably few supervisors or supervisees who know that this concept grew out of Mattinson's work on the reflection process. In her slim pamphlet *The Deadly Equal Triangle* (1981) she described her observations that, when a case is discussed in supervision, there are, dynamically, not two but three "participants" in the room and that keeping this fact in mind often proves difficult.

In Figure 1, the triangle of participants, the supervisor corner includes any organisational or professional authority and accountability, the supervisee corner covers the direct work and related professional needs, while the client corner represents the needs, strengths, demands, and rights of individuals, couples, and families. This original triangle gave rise to thinking of the functions of supervision in a triangular way, as illustrated in Figure 2. The three functions are linked

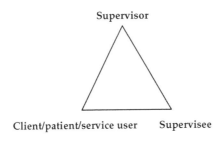

Figure 1. Triangle of participants.

Figure 2. Triangle of supervisory functions.

(Hughes & Pengelly, 1997. Reprinted with permission.)

in some ways to the participants in Figure 1, but never exactly corner-to-corner. Clearly the attention required by each corner will vary greatly and be dependent on a range of factors—the profession of supervisor and supervisee, agency employment versus private practice, trainee or experienced supervisee, supervisor who is also the manager versus external supervisor, etc. We shall argue, however, that all three corners are relevant irrespective of these variations.

While many other functions of supervision are presented in the literature in a range of diagrammatic forms (e.g., Brown & Bourne, 1996; Ekstein & Wallerstein, 1958; Martinez del Pozo, 1997), a valuable aspect of the triangular configuration is that it is small and familiar enough a shape to allow a focus on the dynamic relationship between the functions. The key points in Mattinson's (1981) thinking have proved highly adaptable to current supervisory challenges across disciplines and agencies. We shall describe briefly the thinking behind the triangles and then expand on their use in today's context.

Three underpinning principles of the supervisory triangles

1. *The interdependence of the three corners of the triangles*

   The following questions/examples, focused on the "triangle of functions", implicitly illustrate the dynamic and practical interdependence of the corners:-

   a. How far is it possible to make safe decisions about what action to take in risky situations ("management" corner) without investigating fully the dynamics of the client/practitioner interaction ("exploring work" corner)?

      In their critique of the Victoria Climbie Inquiry Report (Laming, 2003), Cooper and Lousada (2005) present an impassioned argument for the impossibility of doing so.

   b. How can the best standard of service delivery be provided ("management" corner) if no consideration is given to the impact of the work on the practitioner in terms of the information it may convey about the countertransferences ("exploring work corner")? This information may also indicate some training needs of the practitioner ("professional development corner").

   c. To evaluate supervisees' performance, supervisors need to explore not only their capacity to think about their client work but also their capacity to work under pressure, keep an eye on a full caseload, and manage the inevitable tension between thoughtful practice and organisational requirements.

2. *Two's company, three's a crowd: the inevitable difficulty of bearing all three corners in mind*

   There is a danger that the above questions with their implicit answers may suggest that the interdependence of the triangles' corners is a straightforward matter. This is far from the truth. There will at times, especially in today's climate, be a persistent tension between the different functions—for example between the organisation's need for rapid client turnover and the therapeutic needs of the client, or between a trainee's level of professional skill and the agency requirement that the most disturbed clients are taken first off the waiting list. Supervisor and supervisee may at times have good reason to feel the task is impossible. Yet at other times "It is just this tension between different necessities that gives institutional supervision its imaginative edge and acts as a spur to creativity" (Crowther, 2003).

But in addition to these external challenges to bearing all three functions in mind, there are dynamic pressures. Mattinson (1981) stressed how the impact of the dynamics of face-to-face work could easily skew a supervisory interaction. For example, a supervisor attending to a supervisee who was distressed and fearful after an interview with an aggressive client might find it difficult to leave the supervisee corner and return to the "third position" (Britton, 1989) of the supervisor corner, to be able to stand back and use the information from the supervisee to think what was needed in the client's corner.

Organisational dynamics, demands, and requirements are at least as powerful and intrusive in supervision as those from the client work, resulting in an over-preoccupation with the managerial corner at the expense of consulting to practice issues. While Mattinson saw the corner that was avoided as that to which most anxiety was attached, in our experience supervisors often find themselves paralysed and unable to move out of the anxiety-inducing corner.

Good clinicians do not automatically make good supervisors or good supervisees. Though Mattinson made this point in 1975, it has been slow to be grasped, and in the UK the idea of supervisor training is a recent development in many professions. Supervisor and supervisee need to be able to value and understand the significance of the "third position" that the supervisor corner represents, a position that allows the possibility of a different viewpoint to emerge (Britton, 1989), when a supervisor can both listen and hold on to her/his own thoughts (Evans, 2006). A new supervisor may well be drawn into responding as though she/he were the professional working with the client and fail to explore the supervisee's experience and opinions, while a supervisee who is a highly experienced practitioner may behave as though the supervisor's corner has little to offer.

It is not surprising that thinking about supervision in terms of triangles developed in an agency committed to the study of couple dynamics. However well-trained a supervisor and supervisee may be, the significance of their internal maturity in relation to the Oedipal configuration cannot be overestimated in considering their capacity to tolerate excluding and being excluded, to be interested in rather than threatened by difference, and to cope flexibly with moving between two- and three-person relationships—and so between the corners of the supervisory triangles. Crowther (2003) makes the point that supervision in institutions can exaggerate any parent/ child dynamics and so may pose a greater challenge to professionals' capacities to behave in a mature way. Perhaps it is not too far-fetched to suggest that, especially where supervisor and supervisee are free to choose to work together, their choice may at least, in part, be based on an unconscious "fit" in the dynamics of their internal couple, a fit that, as with partner choice, has the potential for both growth and retreat. But neither should we underestimate the powerful longing for agreement and the comfort of sameness that is in most of us and which will inevitably exert its influence on even the most mature professionals amid the discomfort and disagreement in their clients and organisations.

3. *"The deadly equal triangle"*

Mattinson (1981) demonstrates how a preoccupation with attending to all three corners of the triangle can run the risk of a mechanistic approach, of not risking being drawn into any corner sufficiently to explore what is really going on, resulting in a sterile, ineffective supervision. The key question is whether the concept of the triangles proves a useful tool for checking whether any aspect of supervision is regularly neglected or overemphasised. Supervisors and supervisees have sometimes found it helpful to use the triangles to share their experiences of how attention is given to the different corners.

The triangles in supervision in today's caring professions

As the idea of the supervisory triangles was developed in relation to social work supervision in agencies where supervisors were also managers, we have heard it said that it is of limited relevance to other professions and agencies. We argue, however, that recent changes in the caring professions and health and social care organisations make the triangles more relevant than ever across the board. The interdependence of the corners of the triangle does not necessarily require that the manager be the supervisor, but only that the lines of communication are clear between those responsible for the different functions.

While the struggle between professional and organisational accountability is long-standing, the history of social work's dual loyalty to profession and agency, care and control, has certainly given it a head-start over other disciplines in its experience of grappling with this "marriage" in supervision (Kadushin, 1976; Westheimer, 1977). It is in fact to an old social work text that we regularly turn for the best summary of the place of supervision amid professional and organisational demands— "the supervisor/worker relationship is *the key* encounter where the influences of organizational authority and professional identity collide, collude or connect" (Middleman & Rhodes, 1980). This history has recently been drawn on in the production of national occupational standards on supervision in social work and social care (Skills For Care, 2006) which now provide a template for supervision available for use by other professions. Despite this, there is no doubt that social work in today's world needs to reconsider the meaning of the triangles; we shall return to this shortly. Other disciplines within the caring professions have a history of either independent practitioner status (for example, psychology and psychotherapy) where supervision, if it existed at all, took the form of clinical consultation, while others, such as nurses, have until recently had a history of mainly managerial supervision. Counsellors have long been advised by their professional body to try to avoid being supervised by their managers.

Under the recent external and organisational pressures, many professions have, for the first time, begun to face supervision as the meeting place of professional requirements and organisational accountability. This was forcibly brought home to us about ten years ago when we were involved in a Tavistock Centre for Couple Relationships conference entitled "Management and Supervision: Can there Be a Creative Partnership?" It prompted us to look afresh at the relevance of the Oedipal configuration to supervision, applying Klein's work (1946) on how the defences of splitting and fusion may be employed to protect ourselves against either the internal struggle between two conflicting feelings or against confronting the reality of the difference another person may represent. The core tasks of professions and agencies may directly influence the defence they habitually employ to ward off the impact of the core anxiety in the work (Menzies, 1959; Woodhouse & Pengelly, 1991). The way splitting and fusion are employed in supervisory arrangements may highlight this. In professions involving one-to-one therapeutic work, the danger is for professional and organisational responsibilities to be split off from each other, with supervision embodying the image of a cosy, totally confidential two-some that has to be defended against the feared contamination of any external intrusion. Splitting may of course also take place when a managerial supervision is all that happens, with a more reflective space denounced as a luxury. Meanwhile, we believe that within social work the defence of fusion increasingly predominates, as the corners of the triangles merge, embodying the myth of there being no tension between reflective practice and organisational demands. Managers then supervise as though they are doing all that is necessary, denying the fact that their preoccupation with meeting organisational demands has obliterated the space to explore the work. It may also block out any acknowledgement of their not having the skills to engage with the dynamics of the face-to-face work, thus preventing the possibility of the "exploring work" corner being undertaken by someone else.

Application of the triangles to current supervisory scenarios

The concept of the triangles lends itself to looking, not only at what happens within a supervisory session or relationship, but at the place of supervision within its professional and organisational context. The following examples, which we consider to be fairly typical, are based on situations we have encountered recently. They all highlight the need for a clearly defined connection between the three corners of the triangle and some of the ways in which this can fail to happen. While not in agreement with Langs's (1994) dogmatic and limited view of supervision, we echo his concern that professionals who attend meticulously to the boundaries of their clinical work may be much more casual about ensuring that the framework of supervision is firmly in place, and that this undermines the capacity of supervision to be a safe, accountable thinking space. While examples such as these are discussed in the literature, our purpose is to highlight the usefulness of the triangle in addressing the problems they raise.

Internal specialist supervision

Within a multidisciplinary mental health team, a highly experienced psychologist provided supervision to a young nurse on his cognitive behavioural work (attending to the "professional development" and the "exploring work" corners of the triangle of functions). The supervisor became concerned when the nurse, in treating a worrying patient, acted against her supervisory advice but in accordance with that of his nurse line manager.

This incident highlights the confusion that can occur when no arrangement is in place to link the "managerial" and the "exploring work" corners of the triangle of functions. It is probably helpful for the term consultation to be used for the supervision provided here (and in the next example) to ensure there is no confusion about the responsibilities involved. Though this lack of clarity in the use of internal consultants is regularly discussed in literature (e.g., Huffington & Brunning, 1994; Rushton & Nathan, 1996), it remains a common concern. It is often during crises in the most difficult cases that the nature of the differing assumptions about accountability and responsibility is thrown into sharp relief.

External supervision

A psychotherapist provided clinical supervision to counsellors in a student counselling service, with the clear understanding that any concern about unsafe or unethical practice would be reported to the head of the service, but that otherwise information from the sessions would remain confidential. As the budget for training and supervision tightened and the college introduced more structures for auditing and accountability, the crisis was seized on as an opportunity to take a fresh look at the supervisory arrangements. It was decided that a brief report from the supervisor on each staff member would be included for consideration in her/his annual personal development review with senior managers. This not only drew attention to the considerable skills of the counsellors but also ensured a more accurate assessment of their training needs. By linking all three corners of the functions triangle, the new arrangement also helped to educate the senior managers, who had no clinical background, about the value of supervision. As the benefits emerged, the initial disquiet of some of the counsellors abated.

An invitation to be an external supervisor of work undertaken in an organisation usually requires a proactive "consultative" response (Copeland, 2001). Certainly job descriptions and person specifications are rarely thought about even in the most efficient and boundary-conscious organisation. For the supervisor to be effective, the organisational meaning of the request needs to be explored, and the work to be supervised understood in the context of the policies and primary task of the agency. Such requests may turn out to be a covert attempt by staff and/or managers to avoid confronting a perceived management problem (Obholzer & Zagier Roberts, 1994), while sometimes the request, in its longing for a comfortable "outside" liaison apart from everyday organisational accountability, has something of the flavour of an affair. Exploration may reveal the unsuitability of any contact between supervisor and organisation but may alternatively merely highlight the ignorance of managers about supervision and provide, as in this example, an opportunity for development. If an agreement to work is to be made, then a minimum requirement would be the clarification of the extent and limits of confidentiality and of the respective responsibilities of supervisor and manager.

Placement of trainee counsellor

> A counsellor in a primary care team was concerned about the poor time-keeping and abrupt manner with colleagues of a student counsellor undertaking a placement in the team. She had spoken to the student about her behaviour to no effect. The college course expectation was that clinical supervision should be undertaken by a supervisor outside the placement setting and there was no mechanism in place for more "managerial" concerns to be relayed to the supervisor or college. The counsellor had to make a lonely professional decision to pass on her information to the college and supervisor, thus ensuring that the three corners of the functions triangle were in communication.

That such a scenario is not uncommon in counselling is confirmed by the two thoughtful chapters that address the problems in Wheeler and King's (2001) valuable book on issues of responsibility in supervising counsellors, and by the reference in the new code of ethics of the British Association for Counselling and Psychotherapy (2010) to the need for communication between supervisor and manager.

Psychotherapist and counsellor registration and accreditation

> In the current state of therapist and counsellor registration, even therapists in private practice are more clearly confronted with their organisational accountability. Professional organisations increasingly require evidence of supervision as part of continuing professional development, with supervisors and/or supervisees having to write brief reports about the supervision that has taken place—a real linking of the three corners of the functions triangle.

Some organisational responsibility that could broadly be called "managing service delivery" has, however, always been present even in private practice. Supervisors have always needed to check, in a range of practical ways, that their supervisees operate acceptably, such as having suitable consulting rooms, confidential storage of records, and have made professional wills. They have also always carried responsibility for taking action if for any reason a supervisee became unable to function competently. While this is clearly very different from the managerial responsibilities of a supervisor with the authority to make case decisions about a supervisee's work, the principle of the need for clear lines of communication between the functions applies to both situations.

Contracts

These four examples illustrate both the way in which the triangles provide a potential basis for a supervisory contract and the necessity for such a contract if supervision is to be professionally and organisationally accountable. A contract can reduce unfounded assumptions about respective authority and responsibilities and define the boundaries of confidentiality (Hughes & Pengelly, 1997)—providing a model for face-to-face work. At worst, if gaining no serious response from a manager, a supervisor might need to resort to sending the manager a summary of her/his understanding of the parameters of the supervisor's role, including a statement that no response will be construed as agreement. Clarification is particularly important as different professions attach different meanings to the terms "supervision" and "consultation". While our understanding of the term supervision includes all three corners of the functions triangle and consultation refers only to the "exploring work" corner, this is by no means universal. What is important, however, is not the terminology used but that the nature of the contract is clear to everyone involved, that all three corners are attended to, and that the lines of communication between them are clear.

Conclusion

While supervision contracts and policies provide a first step towards ensuring that supervision takes place, they are not panaceas, and their presence may even be used by senior managers as a defence against hearing about the pain and anxiety of the work. Effective supervision ultimately depends on how the dynamic interactions are understood and managed.

In many public sector agencies, prescriptive supervision is constantly found wanting. Inquiries into child deaths have over decades spoken of the need for attention in supervision to the feelings engendered by the work (e.g., Department of Health, 1991; Laming, 2003). Unfortunately, Cooper and Lousada's (2005, p. 155) criticisms of Laming's Report would apply to most other inquiry reports, namely that they end up making "the same kind of lifeless, abstract series of recommendations that has flowed from every other similar exercise", avoiding the serious question of how staff may be enabled to develop and sustain "the capacity to both endure the intensity of emotional and intellectual pain and turmoil, and exercise measured thought, analysis and judgement". In so many such areas of work, with their embedded attacks on linking (Bion, 1959), Mattinson's (1975) plea for the importance of risking feeling in the service of true thought is more relevant than ever.

Even in agencies and professions where there are excellent supervision guidelines that clearly define the value of dynamic consultation and its relation to organisational accountability (e.g., Rhodes, 2008), the reflection process and the supervisory triangles offer ways of thinking about the nitty-gritty of what actually goes on between people. Meanwhile, the interdependence of the corners of the triangles is freshly relevant where there has been little thought about the accountability of the "confidential" supervision session. A robust, containing supervision that is able to experience and think about the huge impact of face-to-face work requires supervisors and supervisees who are firmly grounded in their professional and organisational accountability. This may prove to be of even greater importance in the near future. As we face the prospect of severe cuts in services, time for supervision, always seen as the soft option when professional diaries are under pressure, may need its defenders to be firmly positioned.

In this chapter, we have argued that concepts relevant to supervision are relevant across the board of profession and agency—a belief perhaps not dissimilar to that of the analysts and social workers who brought together different approaches in founding the Tavistock Centre for Couple Relationships. Important to us all, though, is Mattinson's reminder that, however sophisticated our understanding of threesome relationships and however obvious its relevance to the supervisory encounter, "What is not so obvious is the intensity of feeling that threesome situations, or the pairings within them, can arouse, or, if these are defended against, the massiveness of the defence that is used" (1981, p. 12).

References

Armstrong, D. (2004). Emotions in organisations: disturbance or intelligence? In: C. Huffington, D. Armstrong, W. Halton, L. Hoyle & J. Pooley (Eds.), *Working Below the Surface: the Emotional Life of Contemporary Organizations* (pp. 11–27). London: Karnac.

Bion, W. R. (1959). Attacks on linking. In: *Second Thoughts* (pp. 93–109). London: Karnac.

British Association for Counselling and Psychotherapy (2010). *The Ethical Framework for Good Practice in Counselling and Psychotherapy*. Rugby, UK: BACP.

Britton, R. (1989). The missing link: parental sexuality in the Oedipus complex. In: R. Britton, M. Feldman & E. O'Shaughnessy (Eds.), *The Oedipus Complex Today* (pp. 83–101). London: Karnac.

Brown, A. & Bourne, I. (1996). *The Social Work Supervisor*. Buckingham, UK: Open University Press.

Cooper, A. & Dartington, T. (2004). The vanishing organisation: organisational containment in a networked world. In: C. Huffington, D. Armstrong, W. Halton, L. Hoyle & J. Pooley (Eds.), *Working Below the Surface: the Emotional Life of Contemporary Organizations*. London: Karnac.

Cooper, A. & Lousada, J. (2005). Surface and depth in the Victoria Climbie inquiry report. In: *Borderline Welfare: Feeling and Fear of Feeling in Modern Welfare* (pp. 145–169). London: Karnac.

Copeland, S. (2001). Supervisor responsibility within organisational contexts. In: S. Wheeler & D. King (Eds.), *Supervising Counsellors: Issues of Responsibility* (pp. 59–74). London: Sage.

Crowther, C. (2003). Supervising in institutions. In: J. Wiener, R. Mizen & J. Duckham, (Eds.), *Supervising and Being Supervised: a Practice in Search of a Theory* (pp. 100–117). Basingstoke: Palgrave Macmillan.

Department of Health (1991). *Child Abuse: a Study of Inquiry Reports 1980–1989*. London: HMSO.

Ekstein, R. & Wallerstein, R. (1958). *The Teaching and Learning of Psychotherapy*. New York: Basic.

Evans, M. (2006). Making room for madness in mental health: the importance of analytically- informed supervision of nurses and other mental health professionals. *Psychoanalytic Psychotherapy, 20*: 16–29.

Hawkins, P. & Shohet, R. (1989). *Supervision in the Helping Professions*. Milton Keynes, UK: Open University Press.

Huffington, C. & Brunning, H. (Eds.) (1994). *Internal Consultancy in the Public Sector*. London: Karnac.

Hughes, L. & Pengelly, P. (1997). *Staff Supervision in a Turbulent Environment: Managing Process and Task in Front-line Services*. London: Jessica Kingsley.

Kadushin, A. (1976). *Supervision in Social Work*. New York: Columbia University Press.

Klein, M. (1946). Notes on some schizoid mechanisms. In: *The Writings of Melanie Klein, Volume 3: Envy and Gratitude and Other Works 1946–1963*. London: Hogarth, 1975.

Laming, H. (2003). The Victoria Climbie Inquiry: *Report of an Inquiry by Lord Laming*. London: The Stationery Office.

Langs, R. (1994). *Doing Supervision and Being Supervised*. London: Karnac.

Martindale, B., Morner, M., Rodriguez, M. E. C. & Vidit, J.-P. (Eds.) (1997). *Supervision and its Vicissitudes*. London: Karnac.

Martinez del Pozo, M. (1997). On the process of supervision in psychoanalytic psychotherapy. In: B. Martindale, M. Morner, M. E. C. Rodriguez & J.-P. Vidit (Eds.), *Supervision and its Vicissitudes*. London: Karnac.

Mattinson, J. (1975). *The Reflection Process in Casework Supervision*. London: Tavistock Marital Studies Institute (reprinted London: Tavistock Institute of Medical Psychology, 1992).

Mattinson, J. (1981). *The Deadly Equal Triangle*. London: Tavistock Marital Studies Institute (reprinted 1997).

Menzies, I. (1959). The functioning of social systems as a defence against anxiety. In: I. Menzies-Lyth, *Containing Anxiety in Institutions. Selected Essays, Volume 1*. London: Free Association, 1988.

Middleman, R. & Rhodes, G. (1980).Teaching the practice of supervision. *Journal of Education for Social Work, 16*: 51–59.

Obholzer, A. & Zagier Roberts, V. (1994). *The Unconscious at Work: Individual and Organizational Stress in the Human Services*. London: Routledge.

Rhodes, H. (2008). *Supervising Family and Parenting Workers: a Short Guide*. London: Family and Parenting Institute.

Rushton, A. & Nathan, J. (1996). Internal consultation and child protection work. *Journal of Social Work Practice, 10*: 41–50.

Shipton, G. (Ed.) (1997). *Supervision of Psychotherapy and Counselling: Making a Place to Think* Buckingham, UK: Open University Press.

Skills For Care (2006). *Health & Social Care National Occupational Standards: Leadership & Management For Care Services*. London: Skills For Care.

Skynner, R. (1964). Group analytic themes in training and case-discussion groups. In: *Institutes and How to Survive Them*. London: Methuen, 1989.

Steiner, J. (1985). Turning a blind eye: the cover-up for Oedipus. *International Review of Psycho-Analysis, 12*: 161–172.

Vollmer Filho, G., Pires, A. C. J., Berlim, G. I., Hartke, R. & Lewkowicz, S. (2007). The supervisory field and projective identification. *International Journal of Psychoanalysis, 88*: 681–689.

Westheimer, I. (1977). *The Practice of Supervision in Social Work*. London: Ward Lock Educational.

Wheeler, S. & King, D. (Eds.) (2001). *Supervising Counsellors: Issues of Responsibility*. London: Sage.

Wiener, J., Mizen, R. & Duckham, J. (Eds.) (2003). *Supervising and Being Supervised: a Practice in Search of a Theory*. Basingstoke, UK: Palgrave Macmillan.

Woodhouse, D. & Pengelly, P. (1991). *Anxiety and the Dynamics of Collaboration*. Aberdeen: AberdeenUniversity Press.

COMMENTARY ON CHAPTER TEN

David Lawlor

Introduction

This chapter is a timely reminder of the usefulness of two ideas, the reflection process and the supervisory triangle, ideas first introduced by Mattinson (1975) and subsequently developed in TCCR's continuing teaching and writing about supervision. Hughes and Olney clearly lay out the concepts and their application to supervisory practice. At the same time they draw our attention to the current organisational context of health and welfare agencies.

In this commentary I will pay attention to the application of these ideas in contemporary child care social work. My own view and experience of teaching and supervising social work managers and supervisors is that the overall territory has changed so significantly that the application of the reflection process and supervisory triangle is extremely hard to sustain. Simmonds (2010) quotes a UNISON survey (2009) of 369 social work members, asking them to compare their experiences in 2008 with those of 2003. He reports that although 20% said that their access to professional supervision had improved, 52% thought that it had remained the same and 28% thought that it had got worse. He also then goes on to quote Hunter (2009) that in a survey of

422 social care professionals 29% reported they received no supervision and 28% that what they did receive was inadequate. These surveys give a bleak picture of the social care domain and its professional culture. Yet at the same time numerous inquiries into child protection disasters point out the necessity for regular supervision.

The contemporary field of child care social work

So what might be happening to create conditions that make it so difficult to provide what should be a basic requirement for professional practice? Hughes and Olney in their chapter point out that there is a process of "the wheel being constantly rediscovered in different decades". There is some evidence to support this. The example they give is the national occupational standards on supervision in social work and social care (Skills For Care, 2006) which now provide a template for supervision. This document carefully spells out the skills and requirements for supervisors. The latest initiative is one by the Children's Workforce Development Council (2011) who are providing training to support 1,200 front line social work supervisors and managers. Employers are being encouraged to register for the places designed for aspiring, new in post, and experienced front line managers of social workers. The training is designed to equip participants with the right skills and confidence to carry out their role. This programme will focus on developing core supervision skills. It is a three-day training programme delivered in a two-day block with the final day delivered a month later. At the same time there is a "train-the-trainer programme" to equip staff to deliver their own in-house supervision training and has 200 places available. This is a two-day programme designed to equip individuals with the ability to develop and deliver the direct supervision training within their organisation. While all these initiatives are laudable we may wonder about their effectiveness and impact on practice. The recent Munro Review of Child Protection (2011) has made the point that reflective practice and its commitment to supervision has been neglected and needs to be rediscovered. However, we need to recognise that the organisational context has changed so radically that new initiatives are based on a model of service delivery that hardly exists any longer. Without taking this into account no training programme will bring into existence the changes that it espouses. This point is reinforced by Simmonds

(2010) who points out that the current provision of public services has fundamentally altered to one which Power (1996) has described as being underpinned by the ideology of a general audit culture. The audit culture promotes the dominance of the administrative control of performance outcomes and is now the prevailing approach in most social work management and supervision. The need to meet targets set by central government results in a tension between professional cultures. On the one hand social work managers can become very pre-occupied with the need to deliver targets whilst on the other hand their supervisees have to take account of the dynamic interaction with their clients as they seek to achieve performance targets. These tensions make for very uneasy bedfellows.

The change in professional culture

How do we account for the painful reality that professionally it has been so hard to combat the worst aspects of the performance and audit culture? While some aspects of the audit and performance culture have been helpful in obliging agencies to sharpen up their thinking about how to allocate scarce resources, this has been at the expense of strengthening the professional identity and skills of their front line staff. In my view the difficulties have arisen as a result of greater emphasis being given to the control aspects of the social work task. Social work has always had to balance the competing tasks of encouraging the autonomy and independence of its clients and controlling their anti-social behaviour. This balance has been influenced by public concern following a succession of child abuse inquiries and the failures of psychiatric services to safeguard members of the public who have been injured by mentally ill patients in the community. This public concern has created an understandable sense of uncertainty and fear in the professional community which has led to an ever- increasing reliance on the audit culture and control dimensions of practice. Staff are guided by the maxim: "If we can assure ourselves that we followed all the correct procedures then we can rest easy." But this shift in emphasis denies the complexity of people's lives and the need for sophisticated thinking if we are to be able to offer realistic help. More worryingly, it can work against establishing relationships with clients on the basis of which some of their worst anxieties and their most deviant behaviours can be acknowledged and worked with.

The reflection process and the supervisory triangles provide a conceptual framework for understanding the dynamic processes within the supervisory relationship *and* the organisational context of the work. Together they address the management of service delivery (which accounts for a review of performance outcomes), the facilitation of professional development, and the exploration of the supervisee's work. This is a comprehensive framework providing opportunities to think about the complexity of front line social work practice where clients' experience and problems intersect with organisational agendas. So why is it that these ideas are not commonplace in supervision? I believe that the answer lies in a combination of factors all coming to bear in recent years. The pervasive sense of fear and uncertainty has infected the professional community and made it hard to hold on to old and well known practices. The blaming and scapegoating culture has led to more primitive and destructive processes within the workplace. The public vilification of leaders such as Sharon Shoesmith, sacked after the death of Baby Peter, has reinforced the paranoid-schizoid culture that already was part and parcel of the performance and audit culture. Klein (1946) suggested that in the paranoid-schizoid position an individual deals with conflicting emotions by splitting them into good and bad. In this state of mind other people are also seen as either good or bad rather than a more reality based mixture of good and bad aspects. The application of the paranoid-schizoid concept to organisational work transposes an individual model of development to institutional and group processes. Institutions where staff have to manage anxieties associated with some of the most basic human tragedies, such as those generated by death, mutilation, and abuse of all kinds, will have to construct defensive systems not usually required by the "man in the street". My experience is that groups of staff working under such stressful conditions where the fear of failure and professional annihilation is ever present find complexity and uncertainty hard to bear. It becomes extremely difficult to tolerate contradictory or opposing emotions and to achieve an unbiased appraisal of reality.

The supervisory triangles, by seeking to balance the competing pressures of care and control, offer the possibility that both supervisor and supervisee can occupy a depressive position state of mind in their working relationship; or, at least, move in and out of it. In the absence of this capacity they will be pushed into paranoid-schizoid thinking and look for easy and oversimplistic solutions to relieve them of overwhelming anxiety. Sustaining the tension between competing pressures implies that the supervisor is able to contain in a psychological sense these different frames of reference. Although Hughes and Olney do not mention the importance of containment I know from working with them that both would see this as essential to create the safe space for good supervision. However, supervisors who are able to offer a containing space for their supervisees and to identify with their face to face work will be subject to the same clinical dilemmas and anxieties as their staff. This is not a comfortable position to hold and may explain the statistics that Simmonds (2010) quotes on the experience of supervision. Some of the dissatisfaction with supervision may result from supervisors refusing to get alongside their supervisees so that the latter are abandoned to manage work-generated anxiety through a paranoid-schizoid state of mind. Hughes and Olney quote Mattinson as emphasising the need for professionals in all settings to be sufficiently undefended to be affected by the emotional impact of the work and use this experience as data. But this does require the emotional resilience associated with contained depressive position functioning.

As I have argued, the current organisational context does not support reflective thinking. The lack of stability of organisational boundaries, the impact of cuts on the workforce, the use of locums and freelance social workers, the vacancy rate of 12% to 15% in social work, all mitigate against the provision of thoughtful practice. Hughes and Olney draw our attention to these processes when they say "In today's organisational climate, we would argue that the impact of organisational dynamics, demands, and requirements are at least as powerful and intrusive in supervision as those from the client work, resulting in an over-preoccupation with the managerial corner at the expense of consulting to practice issues." I would argue that the organisational dynamics are now more powerful and intrusive than that of the client work. For some it is a relief to see a client and have an experience of being helpful in contrast to the demoralising nature of organisational life when so many staff feel they are unheard and not listened to.

The turbulent field

Cooper (2010) has pointed out that targets and the audit culture are not "accidental features of modern organisational landscapes, but integral parts of the new welfare settlement". The turbulence and uncertainty that organisations and individuals currently face cry out for the concepts covered in Hughes and Olney's chapter. There are signs of a revival of interest in reflective practice. The Munro Review (2011) and the Social Work Reform Board (2011) are both working hard to raise standards of practice and the quality of supervision that social workers receive. But the performance and audit culture have had a profound effect on the socio-technical system in which social work operates. Emery (1993) and Trist (1993) both proposed that "socio-technical/open systems" theory conceives of an organisation in terms of the separate dynamics and requirements in the "technical sub-system" and its "social sub-system". The theoretical basis for joint optimisation and "socio-technical/open systems" was introduced at the Tavistock Institute of Human Relations in the early 1950s and has achieved status as an established strategic intervention for organisational change (Cummings & Worley, 2001). Socio-technical theory focuses on the interface of the worker and the technology of the work. In its simplest form, it states that joint optimisation of the social and technical aspects of the organisation will produce better results than if either is separately optimised. There is synergy available in the collaborative and cooperative process. Appelbaum (1997) further explains that:

> Because the social and technical elements must work together to accomplish tasks, work systems produce both physical products and social/psychological outcomes. The key issue is to design work so that the two parts yield positive outcomes; this is called joint optimization. (p. 453)

The audit and performance culture—the impact on social work practice

The audit and performance culture has had a dramatic impact on the technical system by which social work is now practised. In former times, the technical system was largely the staff member carrying out face to face work but his or her functioning is now heavily influenced by the performance management system plus the IT system. Much of social workers' time is spent in front of a computer in-putting data to meet performance objectives. Waterhouse and McGhee (2009) point out that:

> The increasingly prescriptive procedures and protocols of child protection systems act as service controls and are an alternative claim on practitioners' time, deflecting attention away from direct

face to face work with families. Alongside new electronic systems, they come to represent first-order importance in attempting to protect children. This arguably forms a "grand collusion" unconsciously made, that the act of professionals meeting together to animate the regulatory systems is of itself protection for the child. Herein, contact with the family becomes relegated to secondary importance.

But to some extent the social system or professional culture has attempted to continue as if the technical system has not been subjected to profound and deep structural change. The demands of the data system to record activity now mean that a large proportion of supervision takes place in front of the computer where the primary activity of the supervisor and the supervisee is to in-put data, not to consider relationship based work. Relationship based practice is often of a second order and usually tied to making a procedural decision. The determining factor is the requirement to gather data and tick a checklist as opposed to consider what might be happening in the relationship between worker and clients.

How to go forward?

Some have argued that a rule-bound approach to the formalisation of organisational procedures and the IT system to support them has led to a situation in which there is the possibility that more, not fewer errors are likely to occur in decision making around child care cases (see Broadhurst et al., 2009). These authors make the pertinent point that effective systems need to be based on the needs of the professional and on a thorough understanding of their working practice. In this analysis there may be a reluctance to acknowledge that there may well be a collusive pull to join with these ineffective IT systems as they do provide a psychological protection from the impact of the work. The decline in reflective supervision has meant that workers have had to use other mechanisms to protect themselves from anxiety.

In order to provide a competent and confident workforce there needs to be a planned and thoughtful approach to changes in both the technical system and the socio-professional culture. We are not going to be able to go back to the so-called "good old days" but we do need to urgently address how to integrate good professional practice in supervision as outlined by Hughes and Olney in today's performance and customer focused culture.

References

Appelbaum, S. H. (1997). Socio-technical systems theory: an intervention strategy for organizational development. *Management Decision*, 35(6): 452–363.

Broadhurst, K., Wastell, D., White, S., Hall, C., Peckover, S., Thompson, K., Pithouse, A. & Davey, D. (2009). Performing "initial assessment": identifying the latent conditions for error at the front-door of local authority children's services. *British Journal of Social Work*, 40: 352–370.

Children's Workforce Development Council (2011). http://www.cwdcouncil.org.uk

Cooper, A. (2010). What future? Organizational forms, relationship-based social work practice and the changing world order. In: G. Ruch, D. Turney & A. Ward (Eds.), *Relationship Based Social Work*. London: Jessica Kingsley.

Cummings, T. G. & Worley, C. G. (2001). *Organization Development and Change (7th edn.).* Cincinnati, OH: Southwestern College Publishing.

Emery, F. (1993). *Characteristics of Socio-Technical Systems, Introduction to the Concept of Socio-Technical Systems*. In: E. L. Trist & H. Murray (Eds.), *The Social Engagement of Social Science: A Tavistock Anthology, Volume 2. The Socio-Technical Perspective*. Philadelphia, PA: University of Pennsylvania Books.

Hunter, M. (2009). Whatever happened to supervision? *Community Care, http://www.communitycare.co.uk/Articles/22/04/2009/111327/ Poor-supervision-continues-to-hinder-child-protection.htm*

Klein, M. (1946). Notes on some schizoid mechanisms. In: *The Writings of Melanie Klein, Volume 3: Envy and Gratitude and Other Works 1946–1963*. London: Hogarth,1975.

Mattinson, J. (1975). *The Reflection Process in Casework Supervision*. London: Tavistock Marital Studies Institute (reprinted London: Tavistock Institute of Medical Psychology, 1992).

The Munro Review of Child Protection: Final Report (2011). *A Child-centred System*. London: The Stationery Office.

Power, M. (1996). *The Audit Explosion*. London: Demos.

Simmonds, J. (2010). Relating and relationships in supervision: supportive and companionable or dominant and submissive? In: G. Ruch, D. Turney & A. Ward (Eds.), *Relationship Based Social Work*. London: Jessica Kingsley.

Skills for Care (2006). National Occupational Standards on supervision in social work and social care http://www.skillsforcare.org.uk/

Social Work Reform Board (2011). http://www.education.gov.uk/swrb/

Trist, E. L. (1993). *A Socio-Technical Critique of Scientific Management.* In: E. L. Trist & H. Murray (Eds.), *The Social Engagement of Social Science: A Tavistock Anthology, Volume 2. The Socio-Technical Perspective.* Philadelphia, PA: University of Pennsylvania Books.

Trist, E. L. & Murray, H. (Eds.) (1993). *The Social Engagement of Social Science: A Tavistock Anthology, Volume 2. The Socio-Technical Perspective.* Philadelphia, PA: University of Pennsylvania Books.

Waterhouse, L. & McGhee, J. (2009). Anxiety and child protection—implications for practitioner-parent relations. *Child and Family Social Work, 14*: 481–490.

INDEX